# The Making of Exile Cultures

# The Making of Exile Cultures

## Iranian Television in Los Angeles

### Hamid Naficy

University of Minnesota Press
Minneapolis
London

Portions of Rumi, "Song of the Reed," were reproduced from the Everyman's Library
edition of *Persian Poems: An Anthology of Verse Translation,* edited by A. J. Arberry
(London: J. M. Dent & Sons, 1954), copyright David Campbell Publishers, by permission.

Published by the University of Minnesota Press
2037 University Avenue Southeast, Minneapolis, MN 55455–3092
Printed in the United States of America on acid-free paper

**Library of Congress Cataloging-in-Publication Data**

Naficy, Hamid.
    The making of exile cultures : Iranian television in Los Angeles / Hamid Naficy.
        p.    cm.
    Includes bibliographical references and index.
    ISBN 0-8166-2084-9 (hard : alk. paper). — ISBN 0-8166-2087-3 (pbk. : alk. paper)
    1. Ethnic television broadcasting—California—Los Angeles.    2. Television broadcast-
ing, Iranian—California—Los Angeles.    3. Iranians—California—Los Angeles.    4. Los
Angeles (Calif.)—Ethnic relations.    5. Los Angeles (Calif.)—Social life and customs.
6. Iranians—California—Los Angeles—Social life and customs.    I. Title.
PN1992.8.E84N34      1993
791.45'0899155079494—dc20                                                          93-13428
                                                                                                              CIP

To beloved Kelly, Cam, and Shay
and
to my parents, Batul and Abutorab

# Contents

# Acknowledgments

Many people helped me in different phases of this evolving project. First of all I want to thank the television producers and advertising agents who spoke with me about their programs and procedures: Shohreh Aqdashlu, Beni Atoori, Masu'd Assadollahi, Leili Bakhtiar, Homa Ehsan, Parviz Kardan, Daryush Mirahmadi, Nader Rafi'i, Mansur Sepehrvand, Hamid Shabkhiz, Barbod Taheri, and Hushang Towzi. I want to thank especially producers Parviz Qaribafshar, Iraj Gorgin, Ali Limonadi, and Manuchehr Bibian, who spoke with me several times and shared their insights about producing television in conditions of marginality. Various KSCI-TV officials were generous with their time and information, among them Caren Garces, Marti Quan, and Rosemary Fincher. Jonathan Friedlander and Georges Sabagh of the UCLA Center for Near Eastern Studies supplied funds for transcribing the interviews. Mahmud Naficy helped me complete the list of Iranian periodicals. Jalal Fatemi provided me with some of the music videos I have analyzed. The song-writers and performers Jaklin, Homeira and Homa Mirafshar kindly gave me permission to quote their lyrics. Mehdi Bozorgmehr and Claudia Der-Martirosian generously gave me their time and supplied me with valuable data from their UCLA research project on Iranians in Los Angeles. I appreciate Mehdi's additional review of my analysis of their data. Several people read parts of the book as it evolved and gave me very constructive comments. I thank them all: Nick Browne, Michael M. J. Fischer, Steve Mamber, Ali Mohammadi, Ahmad Okhovat, Donald Preziosi, Kaveh Safa, Nazif Shahrani, and Lynn Spigel. Teshome H. Gabriel read and reread sections of the book and engaged with me in lengthy discussions. I particularly benefitted from his concerns and insights. When I ran into various computer troubles, Mehrdad Amanat and Nader Nafissi were there to help me. My editor at the University of Minnesota Press, Janaki Bakhle, was efficient, forthright, and a friend as she saw the project through to its fruition. Ann Klefstad copyedited the book with verve and sensitivity. I cannot say the degree to which I am indebted to Kelly, Cam, and Shay for their forbearance and good cheer during the years this project took, which sometimes necessitated long physical and mental absences from home. I thank Kelly especially for her love, incisive comments on my work, and her encouragement to listen to my own inner voices.

# Introduction

I begin with a dream and a letter, two motifs of exile narratives. Many of the themes explored in this study are embedded in this single dream and the accompanying letter which I recently wrote to my parents in Iran. By starting with a narrative about myself, a third motif is woven into this discourse, which is autobiography. I include the letter containing my dream here.

"I had a disturbing dream last night, as a result of which I woke up at 4:20 in the morning. No matter how much I tried, I could not make myself go back to sleep. My fractured dream and my more fractured life created a maelstrom that engulfed me, bewildered me, confused me.

"In my dream, I was inside an open elevator rising up the face of an unfinished building. I had pushed the DOWN button, but the elevator had a mind of its own and it was going up. The building was under construction, it was only a skeleton without all the floors and the sides in place. The elevator, too, was of the type used in construction, a skeleton of an elevator, through whose walls, floor, and ceiling the passenger can see out. The more we climbed, the more horrified I became at our increasing distance from the solidity and the comfort of the earth. I was developing vertigo and I averted my eyes. Finally, we reached the top of the building which, like the end of the fabled beanstalk in the "Jack and the Beanstalk" fairy tale, seemed to open onto a city, an ancient unnamed and unrecognizable place with old, dark alleys. There were others who got out of the elevator with me. I don't know who or how many, I only felt their presence.

"A great number of construction workers were at work on the building's roof. I asked one of them what time it was. He replied 2:30 P.M. Or perhaps I asked when the elevator would descend, to which the man answered 2:30 P.M. At any rate, I looked at my own watch and saw that it read 12:30. I asked someone else the time and received the same response as before. I looked at my watch again and read the same time as before. The contradiction between these two time reports, the workers and mine, confused me: Is someone playing with me? Has my watch gone to sleep? Have I gone mad? In exile, synchronicity dissolves, and more than any other affliction one feels out of step and out of sync with the new world.

"Some of the people, among whom I sensed a woman, decided to go for lunch and headed for the alley that led off from the roof of the building. It was like a typical alley that leads into or out of a bazaar on an off day: high mud walls, paved with brick or hardened earth, shop doors boarded up, silent. We headed toward a niche in the wall ahead of us, which seemed like a wide and shallow elevator, perhaps thirty feet wide and two feet deep. As I neared this elevator with these other presences, I suddenly became aware of a number of small but amazing and hideous hybrid creatures: they were frogs with large and powerful crustacean claws like crabs. The largest grabbed my key chain in its claws and would not let go. Other hybrids joined in, I pulled and they pulled; the unresolved struggle went on for a while.

"I awoke drowned in anxiety. Tossed and turned. I could hear the asthmatic snoring of my daughter and the calm and regular breathing of my son and my wife lying next to me. In an effort to calm myself, I placed my hand in her warm hand. No use. It was dark outside and the sound of dogs barking in the distance was the only sound that broke the silence. At times, too, I could hear the crash of the waves of the Pacific ocean against the shore. I got up and looked out of the window at Pacific Avenue. Red, green, yellow. Red, green, yellow. Red, green, yellow. The traffic light was caught in its eternal cycle of repetition. How similar was this light to my life, to life in general! I am reminded of Omar Khayyam's horrific and haunting poetry: you are caught in a useless cycle, so resign yourself to it and enjoy the moment. The cycle of the light also reminded me of the moments of decision and indecision that one faces in exile daily, with each decision enhancing or diminishing attachment to the past or to the present.

"Without wanting to psychologize, I realize now that part of what Freud calls the 'day's residues,' the events that provoke dreams, for me can be located in 'I am a refugee,' a poem written by my brother, Majid, which I had read only a few days earlier in the course of writing one of the chapters. Written in exile, the poem begins with these words: 'In this large elevator I am alone, with the dream of a piece of land in my head'; and it ends with these: 'Is there a piece of land in which I can be at peace?' As a metaphor, this image of ambivalence provokes several questions: Is a person in exile entitled to a piece of land as small as an elevator? Is he condemned to travel up and down in it between two cultural poles, two memories, two lives? Is there a third in-between zone or territory that is safe from both? Is exile merely a claustrophobic space that provides shelter and acts as a prison, or is it a liberatory slipzone of possibilities and potentialities?

"I suddenly recall a cool early morning before dawn, in which I, barely a teenager at the time, had seen my mother off at the bus station. She was going to the city of Shiraz some 300 miles south to visit her sister. I had said good-bye to her and was on my way back home. The streets were deserted except for an occasional passing car. I was walking down Chaharbagh Avenue in Esfahan, a wide boulevard made up of two streets for vehicular traffic with a wide pedestrian walkway bordered by two bikeways in the middle. Between the bikeways and the streets, there were rows of tall sycamore trees, fed by irrigation gutters. As I walked down this middle walkway, in the distance I saw a cloud of dust. As I neared, I made out the figure of a lone street sweeper at work sweeping the ground with his extra-long-handled broom. Left, right. Left, right. Left, right. He was not really sweeping the dust off the dry street but merely transferring the particles from one side to another. Recalling these scenes, my sorrow at separation from my mother combines with my anger at the futility of the sweeper's task, my task, all of our tasks. Life's most profound queries (and answers) are often provoked by the most banal and the smallest of life's daily events. What is reality? What do we know? How do we know the things we think we know? Why do we do the things we do?

"Separation from you is in fact a series of separations, like links in a chain: separation from the earth—that dry, cruel, and yet nurturing earth of the homeland; separation from the fragrance of spices in the bazaars and from the smell of urine on the mud walls outside mosques; separation from the native language and the control one has in using it—a control that is gradually diminishing; separation from childhood and from the places of childhood; separation from mother, the mother and the model of all separations; separation from father, brothers, and sisters—strands that become thinner and more fragile from this position of exile, causing the tapestry of your faces to grow stark, faint, and threadbare. With the news of each natural death in the family, my separation widens: Khanom Jan, Haj Aqa Reza, Kazem Khan, Da'i Mortaza, Da'i Haj Abolqasem,

Sakineh. . . . Those that I knew are dying one by one, and those who remain, I do not know: the children of Nafiseh, Nahid, Nasrin, and Nushin, the children of the children of Nafiseh and Nahid—these I have not seen, I do not know. Even their names, once received in letters, are forgotten. I have not seen the pictures of some of them. Suddenly, I am profoundly struck by the seemingly mundane thought that life does indeed go on in the homeland without me.

"Another of the day's residues, which can help explain some of my dream, can be found in an episode of the *Twilight Zone* series I had watched the night before on KABC-TV. It was entitled *The Mind of Simon Foster*, and showed an unemployed man a dozen years into the future, living in a 1984-type technological and totalitarian society. When he goes to pawn his last possession, the pawnbroker offers to buy something more valuable: Foster's memories. Rich clients place orders with the pawnbroker for specific memories they desire, which he then extracts from the memory banks of his poor donors, leaving behind blank spaces. Foster makes a number of donations, such as his memories of high school graduation and various birthday celebrations. He realizes the extent of the loss only during a job interview, when he fails to recall the date of his graduation, field of study, or his birthday. Having failed the interview and under pressure from his landlord for overdue rent money, Foster visits the pawnshop again, and sells the memory of his first love affair. Immediately, however, he realizes the tragic path he has taken and in an ill-fated effort to retrieve his own memories, he mistakenly inserts those of others into the blank spots of his own memory bank. At the next job interview, he is seen confusedly recalling other people's memories mixed in with his own. His past is mixed up, his present fragmented, and his future uncertain. Is this how loss occurs, first selectively and locally until piece by piece it becomes global and total? Is this how I am losing you one by one to natural death? Khanom Jan, Haj Aqa Reza, Kazem Khan, Da'i Mortaza, Da'i Haj Abolqasem, Sakineh. . . . Is this how my own *self* is being sliced away to be replaced by other slices, other newer selves?

"These natural deaths, of relatives and of the self, gradually distance me in time and place from you and from myself, step by step, slice by slice, drop by drop, corpse by corpse—so gradually that I had not realized what had happened. While writing this letter I suddenly understood the parallels between my own situation and that of Simon Foster. There are other deaths, sudden ones, which result from the operation of the killing machine. These are so unexpected that you pretend not to have heard about them or you prefer to think they did not happen. You disavow or repress the loss until with the same suddenness as the deaths themselves, disavowal is removed and the repression lifted, pouring out the accumulated contents, worthless and valuable alike. My real mourning for my brother Sa'id and his wife Fahimeh, who had a fatal accident with the machine of death [they were executed by the Islamic government], occurred in 1989, five years after the event itself. I was at the funeral of a colleague of mine, a Jewish scholar whose body had been metastasized out of existence by cancer. She was lively and kind and a good scholar with two daughters, roughly the same age as my own children. She was an intellectual, and those gathered to mourn her likewise were men and women of words. They spoke eloquently of their loss, recited poetry, played Kitty's favorite music, and they cried. . . . . Suddenly I realized that I was weeping, too.

"We went to her grave site. They lowered the coffin into the earth. The smell of freshly dug earth in that cloudy, rainy day was poignant and evocative. I bent down, picked up a handful and dropped it on the coffin. I understood right away that it was the earth of Iran that I was pouring on the lost grave of my brother [a grave the government has refused to identify]. I knew then that my mourning and weeping that day stemmed from a tripartite sense of loss: that of Kitty to cancer, of Sa'id to the firing squad, and of my country to exile. Everyone lined up at the graveside—they line up for everything here—to pour dirt over the coffin by hand or with a shovel. Kitty's husband, Steve, was the first in line. Then his elder daughter who, while weeping, threw a shovelful of earth. Next came the six-year-old daughter, who grabbed hold of a grandmother and refused to move. They politely urged her, but she repeatedly moved her head left and right with a dazed look, as though saying NO, I WON'T DO IT. Clearly, she had not finished with her mother, why should she bury her? Like I who was not finished with my brother, until then.

"Soon, I noticed that those who lowered the coffin into the grave with a specially designed instrument—there are instruments for every purpose here—are Mexican-Americans. Through teary eyes I see before me the increasing social inequality in the United States: a class of poor, Third World immigrants carrying out the most menial tasks of a class of affluent European immigrants. In this little but cathartically powerful scene of burial I discover the new, emerging America: a country that is transforming from one populated by European immigrants to one peopled increasingly by Third World emigres, expatriates, asylees, refugees, homeless, evicted, vagrants, exiles. Los Angeles is becoming a "world city," itself composed of a series of interlocking small Third World communities: Taiwanese, Vietnamese, Filipino, Iranian, Korean, Arab, Ethiopian, Chinese, Mexican."

This book is an attempt to make sense of this new, emerging America by focusing on the case of one of these Third World exilic communities. Exile is a special case of transnational and postcolonial discourse. Exiles cannot be viewed only as "ethnics"; they operate within an order of their own. I offer here a model of syncretic cultures, based in transition rites theories, with which to examine exile culture.

Exile is a process of becoming, involving separation from home, a period of liminality and in-betweenness that can be temporary or permanent, and finally incorporation into the dominant host country. Although separation begins with departure from the homeland, the imprint, the influence, of home continues well into the remaining phases and shapes them. Liminality and incorporation involve ambivalences, resistances, slippages, dissimulations, doubling, and even subversions of the cultural codes of *both* the home and host societies. The end result is not unified or stable; it is an evolving syncretic and hybrid exile culture.

In the United States, exile media more than literatures "speak for" exiles. They also do more than that. They are a force in shaping the experience and the discourse of exile. In the popular culture and television programs produced by exiles, and in the institutions that produce and distribute them, can be read the tensions of postcolonial discourse and exilic transformation.

Iranian exiles in Los Angeles will be the focus of this study, meant to investigate how exiles process, through the popular culture and television programs they produce and consume, their own experiences of separation, liminality, and incorporation, as well as their resistance to incorporation and their efforts at differentiation and dissimilation. This process is marked by two overarching, conflicting impulses. On the one hand, Iranian exiles have created via their media and culture a symbolic and fetishized private hermetically sealed electronic communitas infused with home, past, memory, loss, nostalgia, longing for return, and the communal self; on the other hand, they have tried to get on with the process of living by incorporating themselves into the dominant culture of consumer capitalism by means of developing a new sense of the self and what can be called an "exilic economy." This economy is fueled principally by various advertising-driven media, which cross-fertilize each other and hegemonize the consumer lifestyle as ideal.

Mass media typically are thought to be homogenizing agents, resulting in loss of ethnic identity and hastening of assimilation. This study, focusing particularly on liminality, the middle phase, demonstrates the power of the media to enhance and consolidate subcultural identities based on location, ethnicity, race, class, religion, politics, language, and nationality. It also shows that the relationship between the mainstream culture and subcultures is fraught with ambivalence and contestation on the one hand and enrichment and assimilation on the other.

No culture, especially that of the exiles, is homogeneous or totally harmonious. As a result, there are considerable tensions between the resistive communitas and incorporative structuration, which become evident when television is studied intertextually. By studying nodes of tension and disharmony, one can obtain a deeper appreciation of exilic syncretism and television's contribution to it.

The period under study covers the years from 1980 through 1991, during which the largest Iranian emigration into the United States took place, years marked by extreme political polarization and antagonism between the United States and Iran. Since the first regularly scheduled Iranian television program began in the United States in 1981, some 62 regular programs have been aired in Los Angeles, with the current number standing at 26 and lasting over 17 hours per week. Currently, three programs are aired daily and the rest weekly on commercial broadcast and cablecast channels in Los Angeles. A number of them are beamed nationally via satellite, and others are syndicated for rebroadcast in other cities with large Iranian populations, from San Francisco to New York, from Washington, D.C., to Houston. Tapes of some of the shows are available in European cities as well as in Iran. These programs form the corpus of the study.

I have chosen to focus on Iranians in Los Angeles for a number of reasons. First, the Iranian community in the United States is an appropriate subject for this study of exilic liminality because much of it has come together only since the revolution of 1979. The community is sufficiently large, affluent, and diverse to support a thriving advertising-driven exilic popular culture and television. The large size (between 200,000 and 800,000 people) and the heterogeneity of the community also permit us fruitfully to incorporate into the exile discourse the Iranian "local frameworks" of exile, knowledge, psychological orientation, and historical and political perspectives that influence the way Iranians experience exile individually and collectively.

Even though relative newcomers, Iranian exiles have been more active producers of popular culture and television programs than most new emigres in the United States, producing over the years a large corpus of mass media products for study. Their televisual output in the period under study topped, with the exception of Spanish-language programming, all other locally produced ethnic programs in Southern California. With the increasing arrival into the United States of massive new immigrant groups from non-Western societies, there has developed a concomitant rise in the use of mass media, particularly television, by these groups. A critical analysis of the heavy use of a mass medium to meet the needs of a small segment of the population points out a promising new direction in film and television studies, expanding the underappreciated discourse of "narrowcasting." Unlike most studies of "minority" media, which are primarily empirical, economical, or institutional in viewpoint, this study will present a culturalist and interpretive perspective, which will attempt to unpack the complex forces that are at work in liminal states. As a person born in Iran and now living in exile, I have a personal stake in understanding my own culture and my own experience of exile.

This is primarily a work of cultural theory, criticism, and interpretation, informed by contemporary critical discourses. In addition to taping shows, I have interviewed Iranian television producers, distributors, and advertising and sales agents, as well as officials of KSCI-TV, which over the years has aired the majority of Iranian programs in Los Angeles. To provide a context for the study of television in exile, extratextual ethnographic data will be mobilized, including literary works written abroad and letters to editors and reviews of television programs printed in the local Iranian press. One chapter—chapter 2—is given to contextualizing television within the popular culture of exile.

I have attempted to clarify my own stakes and location in the project at hand by providing a short sketch before each chapter, introducing in a personal voice one of the themes of that chapter. Exile generates experiences in many registers that need to be theorized without lapsing into cultural nationalism, ethnic jingoism, or sentimentalism.

# 1
# Exile Discourse

## Crossing Boundaries

*A couple of years ago, my brother and his wife and their daughter,
who live in Germany, came to visit us in Los Angeles. Their daughter
Setareh and ours, Shayda, are almost the same age (then eight years
old). They did not share a common language—Setareh spoke German
and Persian and Shayda English—yet they communicated beautifully
through the songs of Disney's then-current hit film* The Little Mermaid. *That such crosscultural communication by means of movies
should occur was, of course, nothing new. What made it unusual was
that the version Setareh had seen was entirely in German (including
the songs) while the one Shayda had seen was in English. They took
turns singing the songs in German and English, but at times they
sang in two languages simultaneously; their joint performance reso-
nated with the film's story: a young mermaid longing to cross the
boundary of species and become her other, a human. Setareh and
Shayda seemed to use this story to cross the boundaries of their own
cultures. Perhaps such difference made each alluring to the other,
and the family environment permitted safe transgressions of boundaries of culture and selfhood.*

*Four days later our guests left. On the way to the airport, Shayda
decided to learn one of the songs in German and Setareh set out to
teach her. In an amazing feat of mutual instruction, within the span*

1

*of some 45 minutes the mission had been largely accomplished—they sang the German song in unison. At the departure lounge, the two girls hugged each other hard and long. Shayda was very sad, and she wanted to go with Setareh. That night Setareh's mother called to say that Setareh had cried when she left Los Angeles, the first time she had done so upon leaving someone. She then put her on the line to speak with Shayda and I stayed on to translate what at first appeared to be a very mundane conversation. But something remarkable happened: Setareh began singing to Shayda—like a lover serenading—the German song she had taught her earlier that morning. Shayda did not miss a beat: she followed her in halting German, though missing a few words here and there and having to stop and start a few times.*

*The globalization of American pop culture does not automatically translate into globalization of American control. This globalized culture provides a shared discursive space where transnationals such as Setareh and Shayda can localize it, make their own uses of it, domesticate and indigenize it. They may think with American cultural products but they do not think American. As a result, the contents of the culture of transnationals is not only transnational but also personal. The personal may become global. The exile television that Iranians in Los Angeles produce and consume is an instance of creating such personal and local voices amid the cacophony of transnational media in this capital of the postindustrial era.*

## Locations of Cultures

All cultures are located in place and time. Exile culture is located at the intersection and in the interstices of other cultures. Exile discourse must therefore not only deal with the problem of location but also the continuing problematic of multiple locations. The deterritorialization that produces exile is pandemic and endemic in the postmodern era, and has created seemingly permanent "other worlds" of disaffected people who voluntarily or involuntarily are not, or do not want to become, fixed in any identity.[1] By their status as liminal hybrids and syncretic multiples, they form a global class that transcends their original or current social and cultural locations. Such figures tend to have more in common with their exilic counterparts at home and in the West than they do with their fellow citizens—either at home or in the host country. It is a relationship that is not so much based on shared originary facts (birth, nationality, color, race, gender) than on adherence to a common imaginary construction. Discourse thus replaces biology.

The "international proletariat" may have failed to materialize, but the "exiled intellectual" seems, at least for the time being, to fulfill that dream of a universal category, cutting across geographical cultural boundaries.

There is, however, no utopian universality for the global exiles. Exilism is doomed to failure unless it is also rooted in some type of specificity and locality, even essentialism of some strategic sort. This distinguishes exile from other cultural expressions that are based on difference. Without such rootedness, exile discourse, like all other oppositional or alternative discourses, will be co-opted and commodified through defusion and diffusion. In the cultural domain, as in literature and film, specificity, locality, and detail are all.

Location of culture, of course, refers to not only discursive but also sociopolitical and physical locations, and it connotes conditions not only of the sending but also of the receiving countries. Migration into the United States has not been uniform nor has it followed a steady rate or a regular pattern. It has vacillated widely and peaked twice in the present century: once in the 1910s and again in the 1980s. The chief difference between these two waves is one of origin: while the former began predominantly in Europe, the latter is primarily from the Third World and from the so-called newly industrialized nations.[2] Even though the current "development gap" between these "new" nations and the United States is much wider than that which existed between European countries and the United States during the peak of European migration at the turn of the century, the new immigrants are distinguished from earlier European immigrants by higher levels of education, skill, and professionalism.[3] Whether rich or poor, they have helped to revitalize the U.S. economy and the decaying inner cities by creating jobs and innovative industries and by expanding the tax base. Iranian immigrants are part of this rejuvenating new force in America.

Difference in origins entails difference in power relations in exile. The colonial, neocolonial, and imperialistic history that characterizes much of the exchanges between the originating Third World countries and the United States provides a tumultuous context against which cultural, ideological, and religious differences in exile are played out, contested, and negotiated by the new immigrants. Certain metaphors long thought to accurately describe the United States—such as the "melting pot" and the "salad bowl," with their connotations of conformism, homogenization of differences, and benign pluralism—no longer hold. The more recent celebration of "diversity" and "multiculturalism" by businesses, culture industries, and academe is a postmodern reworking of the same melting-pot ideology. The problem with unproblematical championing of these conformist ideologies is that they wrongly imply that there is no hierarchy among the various ethnic and minority groups that form the fabric of American society. In fact, these groups neither contribute equally to nor benefit equally from this liberal doctrine of putative future delights. Differences are there, they matter, and they are necessary if the idea of democracy is to prevail.[4]

Current Third World immigrants live and work predominantly in large urban areas, "world cities."[5] Theoretical work on world cities has since Patrick Geddes coined the term been expanded by urban planning and immigration scholars through "world system" theories.[6] Briefly put, world cities as defined today are strictly a post-World War II phenomenon, when transnational capitalist institutions freed themselves from national constraints and boundaries and began global production and marketing of products.

Los Angeles, the location and the subject of this study, is one such city. Like all world cities, it is attracting to itself the wealth—the capital, the cultures, the creativity—of the world it rules. Polarization is a chief characteristic of these cities; indeed, in Los Angeles "social polarization has increased almost as rapidly as population" (Davis 1990:7). Spatially, this is expressed in the "citadel" and the "ghetto," inhabited by the "transnational elite" and the "underclass," respectively (Friedman and Wolff 1982:2).[7] The differences of these two classes often exceed ethnicity and involve race, skin color, language, religion, and culture. The Third World is no longer "out there," in some far-off land; it is "here" and located within the so-called First World. In fact, every large-scale metropolitan city in America harbors several small Third Worlds whose relations of power within the metropolis appear to duplicate in large measure the previous relations between the Third World and the First World.

The city has responded to the massive injection of Third World lower-class populations and to the crime, violence, and drug traffic many residents associate with their presence in two ways: militarization of city life and co-optation of the threat of the "other" as nonthreatening difference or as style. One is dystopian and the other utopian, but as will become clear, these two responses are characteristic not only of Los Angeles as a postmodern megacity but also of the world of exile itself. A siege mentality has been growing in Los Angeles, transforming the citadel into a fortress, characterized by an ever-increasing presence of stealth, repressive spaces, and surveillance technologies designed to control and keep in place the underclasses. Unlike the majority of non-Western immigrants into California, Iranian immigrants do not live in a single physical ethnic enclave that can provide a measure of ethnic safety for insiders. Instead, they live in small pockets, usually in prosperous neighborhoods across

Southern California, where the siege-and-stealth mentality is elevated to an art form.

If this siege attitude and militarization of space is fueled by fear of the underclasses and the threat posed by the poor immigrants, there is a celebratory response to moneyed non-Western immigrants. If the former mentality is rejectionist, the latter is assimilationist, and both of them are inscribed in the mainstream press accounts that speak of the new immigrant and of Los Angeles itself in such alternately glowing and alarming terms as "The Big Mix"; "New Prosperity, New Power"; "Fear and Reality in the Los Angeles Melting Pot"; "A New Persian Empire"; "L.A., the Ultimate Culture Shock"; "Nation of L.A.: A City at War with Itself."[8] If poor immigrants are perceived as a threat to be shunned, rich immigrants are embraced as revitalizers of culture and economy—although they are often marginalized as junior partners and in the end appropriated as "diversity" by a culture industry that capitalizes on harmless difference.[9]

This hegemonic strategy of corporate culture, however, cannot hide the basic truth of the tremendous diversity of the region. People from nearly 140 countries and many more internal ethnic communities live in Los Angeles County, some of them in substantial numbers:

> Los Angeles is the second-largest Mexican, Armenian, Korean, Filipino, Salvadoran, and Guatemalan city in the world, the third largest Canadian city, and has the largest Japanese, Iranian, Cambodian and Gypsy communities in the United States, as well as more Samoans than American Samoa. (Pearlstone 1990:27)

The Los Angeles School District figures reflect this diversity: some 96 languages are counted as first languages by the student body (1990:33). The ethnic economies and the very active ethnic media in Los Angeles help to maintain the original native languages and cultural systems far beyond the borders of the ethnic enclaves. This is partly due to the transformation from production-driven to marketing-driven capitalism, which has entailed a number of consequences for world cities germane to this study. One of these is a shift in megacities—from being centers of producing, storing, and transporting material goods they have become centers of producing, storing, and transmitting information (Dogan and Kasarda 1988). Sensitive to this structural shift, the new immigrants and exiles entering the megacities have increasingly turned to the production and consumption of information and knowledge as a chief vehicle for creating ethnic solidarity and regulating their own assimilation. This is particularly true in the case of Iranian exiles, who in general arrived with money, education, and transferrable professional skills that allowed many of them to "leapfrog" low-income natives and immigrant minorities in obtaining desirable jobs and housing, and to enter the U.S. economy not as an ethnic underclass but as a sort of transnational elite, requiring minor adjustments but not massive retraining.[10] This explains not only the fact that many Iranian immigrants reside in fortress L.A. instead of ghetto L.A., but also their widespread production and consumption of exilic popular culture, particularly television.[11]

The role of Los Angeles as the "entertainment capital of the world" has meant its cultural and ideological domination far exceed its economic prowess. In fact, in 1990, next to aerospace, American popular culture—movies, music, TV programming, and home video—outstripped all other U.S. exports, accounting for an annual trade surplus of some $8 billion (Huey 1990:50). This has helped Los Angeles to influence ideologically the world cultural agenda, set the standards for taste and fashion, and encourage a transnational video culture. Many of the television programs broadcast by the new ethnic and exile communities in Los Angeles are movies and TV programs imported from the home countries. Copies of these are also available in video stores and ethnic groceries.[12] However, some of what is aired in Los Angeles—in the case of Iranians, almost all of it produced in exile—is in turn pirated and exported to the homeland. These cultural exchanges to and from Los Angeles have helped to globalize the Los Angeles culture to an unprecedented degree, in terms of both exporting culture from it and importing culture into it—with the profits naturally favoring the metropolis.

## The Paradigm and Paradox of Exile

Traditionally, exile is taken to mean banishment by governments for a particular crime, for a limited time or for life. Exile can be internal or external. This work is concerned with physical relocation to another country. While most definitions of exile consider it to be a dystopic and dysphoric experience stemming from deprivation, exile must also be defined by its utopian and euphoric possibilities, driven by wanderlust and a desire for liberation and freedom. Indeed, these seemingly contradictory attributes of otherness and alterity can be formulated into a paradigm of exile, containing three modes (see table below). Modes A and B are expressed by a variety of attributes and tropes whose connotations are never as discrete, stable, or distinct from one another as the table implies. They operate as interplays of signifiers that simultaneously conceal and expose one another. What results is the liminal state (mode C), which is not located firmly between modes A and B but oscillates between them. To traverse these modes of exchange is to open up new spaces for becoming, spaces of liminality.

Topographical Reading of Exilic Liminality

| | Mode A | Mode C: Exilic Liminality | Mode B |
|---|---|---|---|
| DISCOURSE | | | |
| | Diachrony | HISTORIES | Synchrony |
| | Identity | AMBIVALENCE | Difference |
| | Deterritorial | LOCATIONALITY | Reterritorial |
| | Determinacy | INDETERMINACY | Uncertainty |
| | History | HISTORIOGRAPHY | Autobiography |
| IDENTITY | | | |
| | Identification | MIMICRY | Imitation |
| | Whole | MULTIPLE | Fragmented |
| | Exclusion | OTHERNESS | Inclusion |
| | Stable | OSCILLATION | Unstable |
| | Subjectivity | POSITIONALITY | Collectivity |
| | Visibility | REPRESENTATION | Invisibility |
| PLACE | | | |
| | Sacred | RUIN | Secular |
| | Recollection | MEMORY | Forgetting |
| | Root | RHIZOME | Surface |
| | Nostalgia | LONGING | Wanderlust |
| POLITICS | | | |
| | Order | CHAOS | Disorder |
| | Radical | EXTREMISM | Conservative |
| | Paranoia | CONSPIRACY | Schizophrenia |
| | National | TRANSNATIONAL | International |
| TEXT | | | |
| | Tragedy | IRONY | Parody |
| | Story | PASTISCH | Discourse |
| | Temporality | CHRONOTOP | Spatiality |
| | Genre | INTERTEXTUALITY | Text |
| ICONOGRAPHY | | | |
| | Objects | SIGN | Icons |
| | Immensity | SPATIALITY | Claustrophobia |
| | Singularity | REPETITION | Complexity |
| | Fetishization | SYNCRETISM | Hybridity |

This table is a "discursive snapshot," meant only to be suggestive. Many more nuances of exilic liminality are explored throughout the book than are noted in the table. The dynamic exchange between the two modes involved is appositional: the opposites do not refuse, they re-fuse. The most important point is this: to be in exile is to belong to neither of the two modes A and B; rather, it is to be traveling in the "slipzone" of fusion and admixture.[13] What results is an agonistic liminality of selfhood and location oscillating between the two extremes of interpellation. Oscillation does not imply total weightlessness, nor does interpellation connote irreversible or absolute "hailing." What they do imply, however, is the capability and potential of the exiles to continually negotiate or "haggle" for new positions.[14]

The object of this study is to locate, albeit provisionally, and to theorize as a dynamic social and cultural force, the liminality of the exile universe and the syncretic space it inhabits. This is a late-twentieth-century phenomenon characteristic of postcolonial scatterings, with its own processes of meaning production and identity formation. Liminal spaces were perhaps best formulated by Arnold Van Gennep (1908) in his work on the rites of passage that accompany every change of state or social position. He posited three phases for these rites: separation from the community, the threshold or liminal state, and reaggregation into the original community (1960:11). Territorial passage from one country to another is another transition to which Van Gennep's formulation can be applied. In this move one not only crosses a territorial line (with its ceremonies of obtaining passports and visas, the interview at the border, obtaining or being denied permission to cross, or the illegal crossing of the border) but also undergoes a profound symbolic and ideological transformation: "A man at home, in his tribe, lives in the secular realm; he moves into the realm of the sacred when he goes on a journey and finds himself a foreigner near a camp of strangers" (12). Van Gennep notes that in classical antiquity national and tribal territories were not contiguous; rather, they were separated by neutral zones that assumed the status of sacred: "Whoever passes from one [territory] to the other finds himself physically and magico-religiously in a special situation for a certain length of time: he wavers between two worlds" (18). It is this spatial and symbolic zone of neutrality, sacredness, liminality, and ambivalence that is the object of this study.

In our overcrowded world, territories everywhere are contiguous and the neutral zones between them have not only shrunk but also become war zones, where military clashes and cultural conflicts are continually waged. To be sure, liminal border towns will continue to emerge in which syncretic cultures thrive. But since population movements today are not restricted to crossing contiguous borders, liminal zones are no longer only physical. Indeed, increasingly they are symbolic constructs, condensed in the aesthetics of the portal and the border and the creation of "virtual worlds." Located in such a zone, the "liminar," in the words of Victor Turner, becomes "ambiguous, neither here nor there, betwixt and between all fixed points of classification; he passes through a symbolic domain that has few or none of the attributes of his past or coming state" (1974:232).

Clearly, transnational immigration constitutes a passage of profound individual and social significance whose phases parallel those of rites of passage. As such, exile is a process of perpetual becoming, involving separation from home, a period of liminality and in-betweenness that can be temporary or permanent, and incorporation into the dominant host society that can be partial or complete. It must be emphasized that the three phases of exile are not just consecutive but also simultaneous—so that a unified or stable culture seldom results.

The push-pull drama of becoming chiefly grows out of the conflict between "descent" and "consent" (Sollors 1986). Descent relations are ancestral and hereditary, emphasizing bloodline and ethnicity; consent relations are contractual and self-made, involving law, marriage, and nationality. Exiles attempt to hold on to their descent relations while becoming part of the consensus that forms the new host culture. These impulses fuse to create an uncanny, liminal state and a cultural threshold in which the liminars live in a continual state of otherness and exile from former and new attachments. Freed from both, they are "deterritorialized." Under normal conditions, society's established structures consciously differentiate and regulate roles and the status of their citizens—but in liminality old structures dissolve and in their place communitas emerges. The exiles, who live in two competing, even antagonistic societies, tend to become cosmopolitan (Park 1950:376). An important component of exilic cosmopolitanism is fundamental doubt about the self, reality, home, traditions—in short, doubt about absolutes, ideologies, and taken-for-granted values of one's home or host societies. In speaking of Gunther Grass and his writings, Salman Rushdie sums these up well:

> This is what the . . . disruption of reality teaches migrants: that
> reality is an artifact, that it does not exist until it is made, and
> that, like any other artifact, it can be made well or badly, and
> that it can also, of course, be unmade.

Located in this slipzone of doubt, the liminars are between the structural force fields of both home and host social systems, and as a result they are in a position not only to question, even subvert, much of their previous authenticities, authorities, identities, and cultural practices but also to forge new ones in their place. It is this slippery doubt that changes interpellation and hailing into negotiation and haggling.

Exilic haggling stems from holding two essentially incompatible attitudes simultaneously involving the disavowal and recognition of difference. The exiles know they are different but simultaneously they deny it; they know they are separated from home but simultaneously they disavow it. Such an ambivalence injects slippage and creates a "dislocatory presence" between the self and the other, between the exile and the home culture. Thus the exilic liminars cannot be easily hailed because they are not really there. They are always already (dis)located by doubt and ambivalence.

Liminality, therefore, is a period of vast potential, capable of eradicating one set of codes and replacing them with different sets of syncretic inscriptions. As Victor Turner notes, "it is the analysis of culture into factors and their free recombination in any and every possible pattern, however weird, that is most characteristic of liminality" (1974:255). Because liminal states are so potentially powerful, all societies attempt to control or at least guide them through the authority of the state, communal elders, and traditions. In exile past and present authorities come under severe questioning and "analysis" (in the sense of separation into constituent parts). Exilic liminality is neither a free nor an empty state, however, and neither is it free from its social context. The host society provides a context that exerts not only direct "control" through enforcement of its laws but also indirect "guidance" via its popular culture, which attempts to transform the liminars into productive subjects (citizens) and the exile group into a stable ethnic community.

## Iranian Exilic Liminality

The impulses to doubt, analyze, and transcend one's own culture and society are some of the privileges that exile produces.[15] But with a few exceptions, established Iranian intellectuals abroad appear to have failed to use this privilege in their works. If anything, they seem to have become more deeply attached to their culture and descent relations than to universal issues affecting humankind. An exception is Fereidun M. Esfandiary, who in the 1960s, from exile in America, wrote novels about the horrors of Iranian life under the Shah. Over the years, he turned to futurism and in the late 1980s changed his name to FM-2030 and developed the notion of transhumanism, a concept that breaks all links with descent, continuity, homeland, religion, language, nationality, ethnicity, race, and gender and instead foregrounds discontinuity, fluidity, provisionality, optimism, globalism, and cosmic sensibilities. To be transhuman, he says, is to be a universal species, a new "evolutionary being" (FM-2030 1989:205). FM-2030 is not nostalgic for the past so much as he is for the future.

Not all exiles reach for Esfandiary's utopian self-fashioning or achieve the Sufis' detachment from worldly attachments. For those who assimilate successfully and unproblematically into the host culture and society, liminality remains only a memory and its effects are limited. But any cultural space that structurally encourages analysis and reconfiguration of deep values is capable of breeding radicalism and extremism of all kinds.

Deterritorialization and liminality engender conflicting emotions and attitudes. On one hand, they produce profound dystopia—epistemic and ontological ambivalence—as evidenced from this passage from Gholam hosain Sa'edi, a celebrated Iranian writer and psychiatrist who died in 1985 in exile in Paris:

> It is now nearly two years since I have become a refugee in this place, spending every few nights in a friend's house. I feel uprooted. Nothing seems real. Paris buildings all seem like theatrical set pieces. I imagine I am living inside a postal card. I fear two things: one is sleeping, the other is waking. (1986:4)

Significantly, Sa'edi and many other exiles use a term that in its various connotations highlights all these dystopic and dysphoric senses of deterritorialization. He calls exile *avaregi*, which can be translated as "forced homelessness and vagrancy." In this state one is condemned to a purgatory (*barzakh*), suspended between life and death, between home and exile, but freed from neither (1983).[16] The exile poet Esma'il Kho'i sums up in the following passage the internal dynamics of deterritorialization and uprooting spawned by liminal states:

> The refugee is, and will remain HOMELESS in this sense. For him or her, everything is, and is to remain, unsettled. This is his/her predicament. The time is ALWAYS the time being, and HOME a dreamland in the far far away. Un-wanting to be in the host society and un-able to go back home. Un-welcome here, and unwanted there—except, of course, for imprisonment and/or torturing and/or shooting. An outsider here, an outcast there. Physically here, mentally there. Not a split personality, but a split person. The refugee is, and is to remain, the typical example of what I call "People In Between." (original emphases, 1987:13)

From these passages, and from many others in the popular press, it becomes clear that the conditions of living in exile under the flux of liminality have created for many Iranians a paralyzing crisis, not a liberating euphoria. That for much of the period under study (1980–92) Iranian "high culture" has been far more frozen than freed by exile is evident.[17] Mahshid Amirshahi, in her introduction to her novel *Dar Hazar* (At Home), also portrays exile in this way:

> Sometimes, I do not venture outside for days; sometimes, I do not return home for nights. Sometimes, all states seem figurative; sometimes, all things appear real. Sometimes, I sulk at the world; sometimes, I fight it. Sometimes, I cannot tolerate myself; sometimes, I cannot stand other people. Sometimes, I feel lonely in the midst of others; sometimes, while alone I imagine a crowd.

Fig. 1. Dysphoria: Neusha Farrahi's self-immolation, from Barbod Taheri's video.

Sometimes, I want to forget everything; sometimes, I want nothing to escape my memory.

Paralysis can be deadening; the effort to throw it off can spark new life. A dramatic and tragic case in point is provided by Neusha Farrahi, a young film critic and bookseller in Los Angeles. On September 20, 1987, in front of scores of astonished Iranians protesting the imminent visit of President Khameneh'i to the United Nations, he doused himself with gasoline, set himself on fire, and died a few days later in a hospital. No matter how one characterizes his action, his last letters and testaments indicate that for him self-immolation constituted an attempt dramatically both to acknowledge and to break out of the personal and the collective paralysis that had beset Iranians in exile since the revolution (especially those on the left).[18]

Farrahi's action shows, albeit tragically and ironically, that the response of Iranian intellectuals to the fact of exile has not been uniformly celibate or characterized solely by paralysis. In modern Iranian history, many intellectuals unable to freely speak, write, make films, or participate in the political life of the country have chosen exile, from which they mounted active reformist campaigns. What is being suggested here (and explored further below) is that the mode of discourse of Iranian high culture in exile is such that more often than not the celebrant is repressed in favor of the celibate.

Deterritorialization and liminality, on the other hand, are capable of generating also the type of euphoria and ecstasy that come with freedom from long-held constraining conventions and belief systems. The same liminality that generates dystopia and dysphoria for much of the intellectuals produces for other sectors, particularly the popular culture, its opposites: the potential for utopian imagining and euphoric experiences. In the Iranian popular culture in Los Angeles, one is exposed to many instances of liminal ecstasy, in the elaborate weddings, funerals, concerts, and various religious and national holiday celebrations; in frequent political demonstrations, popular poetry reading nights; and in the profusion of musical performances, nightclubs, and discos. Iranian television programs and music videos produced in Los Angeles both reflect and shape the exile experience in the two modalities of celibacy and celebration.

Music and music videos, particularly the pop variety, imported from Iran formed a major portion of exile television's early programming. This imported source of material was buttressed by the presence in Los Angeles of the largest contingent in the world (outside of Iran) of Iranian entertainers, comics, actors, singers of classical songs, pop singers, and musicians. The presence in Southern California of the largest population of Iranians outside of Iran created a natural audience. Although part of exile TV's programming is in the celibate mode, much of it is celebratory, consisting of dance music, pop songs, and comic skits. A lion's share of each exile TV program is regularly given to music and entertainment material, but on festive occasions such material entirely dominates the screens. To celebrate the onset of Noruz (the Iranian new year) in March 1992, *Jam-e Jam* television broadcast six consecutive hours (from 12:30 to 6:30 A.M.) of pop music, interviews with pop singers, and ads for their products. All other programs in the days leading to and even after the event were filled with such programming and advertisements.

The reason for the suppression of celebratory discourse in the elite culture and its foregrounding in the popular culture is partly to be found in the audience that each culture envisions for itself. Popular culture producers, particularly of television, address an audience that is concerned in all material, affective, and spiritual dimensions with the daily routines of living in a foreign land. As a result, they are focused more on the *here and now* than on *there and then*, in contrast to the producers of elite culture, whose work in the first decade of exile has been characterized by a mood of retrospection. There are a number of reasons for this mood. By and large, exile writers consider the postrevolutionary Islamist turn in

Fig. 2. Euphoria: Celebrating the 1992 Iranian New Year on *Jam-e Jam*.

Iran to be a defeat for them and for their modernist ideological project. This sense of defeat and the distance of exile have encouraged introspection and reevaluation. Exile writers have an intimate and symbiotic relationship with their home culture, language, and society as sources of inspiration:

> The inspiration of landscape, of daily patterns of life, of the minimal gestures and figures of speech which define a culture, the subtle system of cues which connect us to our fellow citizens, can reassure us of our identity: they are for many writers the soil out of which their craft can grow. (Beard and Javadi 1986:257)

In exile this direct, complex, and nuanced relationship is severed, and it must be reconstructed and accounted for through memory and nostalgia. The writers' "loss" of a revolution and a vital source of inspiration is compounded by an additional loss: that of their key audience at home, whom the writers address but cannot easily reach. With this loss comes diminished political influence and moral stature—something that Third World writers and intellectuals enjoy much more than their Western counterparts. It is this triple sense of loss that informs the moods of melancholia, retrospection, and celibacy among the producers of high culture in exile.

These moods are expressed through a local framework of grief and tragedy. In Iranian psychology sadness and grief are associated with depth, thoughtfulness, sincerity, and religious devotion and their public expression is not only authorized but encouraged, especially during rituals of mourning. As psychologists Good et al. note:

> Whereas in some societies, the expression of anger is central to the assertion of selfhood and self-worth, in Iranian society the experience and competent communication of sadness and grief is essential to establish personal depth. (1985:391)

For writers in exile, cut off from homeland and roots and alienated from the host society, public expression of grief is expected, even required, as proof of their deep, sincere emotions. The manner in which grief is expressed by Iranians is deeply informed by that archetype of unjust usurpation of power in Shi'i cosmology that Michael Fischer has called the "Karbala paradigm": the martyrdom of imam Hosain in the plains of Karbala by the Ummayid Caliphate (1980:21). The "work" of the paradigm is psychologically and artistically significant principally because it provides a framework for living and for thinking about how to live; it channels grief, rage, and anger at loss or injustice into "stoicism and quiet determination"; it embodies a vision of the tragic and of grief as a religiously motivated emotion; and it invokes a paradigmatic cluster of emotions: guilt, repentance, and total fusion and identification with the martyrs.[19]

Many exile writers, almost all of whom are secular, use this cluster of painful emotions in their writings, and a few in their muted style of dying (Sadeq Hedayat's suicide, Gholamhosain Sa'edi's gradual death, and Farrahi's self-immolation).[20] Although the cluster of Karbala emotions is invoked by both elite and popular cultures to express the painful experience of exile, in exile the paradigm itself does not appear to be operative (at least openly). The chief reason for the temporary abandonment in exile of this paradigm might be found in the shifting political landscape that brought the clerics into power. By assuming the seat of worldly power, the clerics have lost their role as representatives of the ideal of justice over repressive secular regimes. Most exiles (including internal exiles) see the clerics not as champions of the oppressed but as themselves agents of oppression. The result is a deep ambivalence and a widespread cynicism about religion and its paradigms, which may have been instrumental in the exiles' decision to forsake the traditional methods of expressing the self, deep emotions, and opposition to injustice (Good et al. 1985:388).

This inability to channel emotional expressions in culturally sanctioned ways appears to have created profound psychological disturbances.[21]

Popular and elite cultures are also opposed in the shifts they have made in their "politics of location" in ways that echo Lévi-Strauss's story of Asdiwal (1976:146–97). While in Iran elites often looked to the West for inspiration and modeling (while it also critiqued the West); now in exile, however, they have tended to idealize a largely secular Iranian past and have constructed an arrested and tragic representation of its present. On the other hand, popular culture in Iran before the 1979 revolution often drew inspiration from the Iranian past and its folk tradition; now, in the West, it seems to be reversing itself in the direction of incorporation into the Western host culture. As expected, the ecstasy of liminal exile reflected in various forms of popular culture, especially television and pop music, has come under heavy attack by Iranian journalists and intellectuals who dismiss it as frivolous and morally corrupting, especially during periodic deadly flareups in the war with Iraq during much of the 1980s. This discourse on high and popular cultures in exile is useful because it illuminates the polysemic way in which cultures process the condition of exile and the politics of their location.

## Taxonomy of Exile

To conclude and sharpen the exploration of the exile paradigm, certain distinctions must now be made between exile and various allied concepts. External exile, of course, does involve emigration. But this does not entail an unproblematical or unidirectional assimilation or incorporation into a stable niche of ethnicity. The exiles as defined here are not "native" to either their home or to the host society. They are no longer legally "foreigners," neither are they bona-fide "citizens." They are neither openly, nor secretly, nor dually "marginal." They are not merely "strangers" or simply cultural "tourists," and they cannot strictly speaking be considered members of an established "ethnic group." Finally, they cannot be entirely characterized as "sojourners," "refugees," or "homeless." Exiles, for the purposes of this work, are none of the above entirely but all of them partially.[22]

The term "exile" in this study refers to individuals or groups who voluntarily or involuntarily have relocated outside their original habitus. On the one hand, they refuse to become totally assimilated into the host society; on the other hand, they do not return to their homeland—while they continue to keep aflame a burning desire for return. In the meantime, they construct an imaginary nation both of the homeland and of their own presence in exile. The difference that sets the exiles apart from "people in diaspora" is that the exiles' primary relationship is not so much with various compatriot communities outside the homeland as with the homeland itself. If they do return, it is often only a temporary visit—not what Nabokov has called the "grand homecoming," of which exiles constantly dream (1966:97). Indeed, as Salman Rushdie has cogently noted, "Exile is a dream of glorious return" that must remain unrealized. What turns an emigre, expatriate, refugee, immigrant, or a person in diaspora into an exile is this double relationship to location: physically located in one place while dreaming of an unrealizable return to another. The style of dreaming of the homeland and of staging of a return to it is both dystopian and utopian, with the result that exile becomes, in Rushdie's words, "an endless paradox" characterized by

> looking forward by always looking back. The exile is a ball hurled high into the air. He hangs there, frozen in time, translated into a photograph; denied motion, suspended impossibly above his native earth, he awaits the inevitable moment at which the photograph must begin to move, and the earth reclaim its own. (1988:205)

The exiles create hybrid identities and syncretic cultures that symbolically and materially borrow from both the indigenous society and the new one to which they have relocated. Such a hybrid identity and composite culture is characterized by contradictions and instabilities of all sorts which drive the culture and keep it "honest" in the sense of preventing nationalism, chauvinism, sexism, ethnocentrism, xenophobia, puritanism, solipsism, or absolutism of any kind from hardening it into some putative and dangerous cohesiveness. Overreliance on liminality and on haggling for individual positioning, however, frustrates group solidarity, political agency, and social representation—all of which are necessary if the exiles, in Stuart Hall's terms, are to come into political representation (1988:27). Coiling back on the self by forming hermetic, if successful, ethnic communities does not automatically translate into political representation in the host society. On the other hand, if acculturation occurs and exile turns into ethnicity, then exile is likely to become a steady absence, an alluring memory, a romanticized notion. For those who are still in liminality, it is the threat of absence that drives exilic consciousness toward perpetual nostalgia.

## Exilic Syncretism

Liminality's other face is syncretism: a process following on traumatic cultural contact that results in mutual borrowing, sometimes resurrecting

Fig. 3. Syncretic characters: The blackface character Haji Firuz, from a 1992 television skit.

atavistic forms, but impregnating them with new meanings appropriate to their new context.[23]

As a mode of social and cultural homeostasis, syncretism helps those under duress to survive, and to preserve important aspects of their original culture by adopting the outer forms of the new culture while retaining for a long time much of the original inner meanings and value systems.[24] It represents both a resistance to and an appreciation of the new, foreign culture. The nature of duress and the circumstances of the contact that initiate the syncretic movements vary. Whether these include external factors, internal contradictions, ecological and environmental calamities, migration, or exile, the contact situation itself is rarely symmetrical. In the context of exile in particular, the host society is more powerful and tends to want to assimilate the exiles, while the latter may choose to accept, deny, or defy that domination.[25] When cultures are forced upon each other, conditions become ripe for borrowing.

For syncretic absorption and borrowing to take place, however, there must exist parallels in the two cultures; otherwise syncretism will not oc-

Fig. 4. Syncretic characters: Haji Firuz (*left*) and Uncle New Year, from Giti's 1992 music video *New Year's Gift*.

cur, and the newly introduced culture is likely to remain an unabsorbable foreign body. Two performance figures—Haji Firuz and Amu Noruz (Uncle New Year)—traditionally associated with the Persian New Year (Noruz), can illustrate the dynamics of the parallels. Haji Firuz is an ancient minstrel who, a few days before each new year's arrival on March 20 or 21, appears in the streets in blackface, cracking jokes, singing, and dancing.[26] Immediately after the revolution, Iranian exiles attempted to equate Haji Firuz with Santa Claus, but the equivalence did not last long, chiefly because its new American context, with its own uneasy and racist history of the blackface mode, exposed the hitherto inoffensive subtext of the Iranian blackface character.[27] While correspondences could be set up in the structural and cultural domains between Haji Firuz and Santa Claus, the sociological contradictions undermined it. As a result, the widespread adaptation of Haji Firuz beyond the annual New Year celebration failed to take root in exile.

The situation was different in the case of Uncle New Year, who on the Iranian New Year's Day brings presents and money to family members.

This character seems to have become more prominent in exile because there are no disturbances associated with it that could undermine its syncretic adaptation as the Iranian equivalent of Santa Claus. Many other traditional occasions and rituals inoffensive to the American culture have been transplanted with minor adjustments (such as *haftsin* and *sizdahbedar*).[28] Some others with recognizable parallels in the host society have not only been transplanted successfully but enlarged in the process. For example, Jashn-e Mehregan, which was a minor celebration in Iran of the coming of autumn, has gradually assumed a more prominent role in Southern California, partly due to its proximity to the American Thanksgiving.

There is a correspondence between the ideology that drives the syncretic movements and the discrepancies between expectations and actualities that produce a feeling of deprivation (Aberle 1965). Deprivation of possessions, for example, often causes movements that valorize material things. Syncretism as a response to traumatic transnational contact involves certain universal processes that are independent of individual cultures, but the nature of the contact and the types of deprivations and utopian imaginings for change that it stirs, and the history of previous culture-specific patterns of syncretism, are significant factors in how each culture processes its own syncretism. In this discussion, therefore, I will explore the concept of an Iranian-style syncretism called rearchaization.

## Iranian "Local" Syncretism

Iranian cultural patterns have included syncretism since archaic times. Located at the crossroads that linked China and the Indian subcontinent to Mesopotamia and to what became known as Europe, the country has influenced and been influenced by many other societies, both culturally and politically. In an insightful article Alessandro Bausani notes that from early on there was a particular direction to this process:

> If, conventionally, we call the cultural centers of the Mesopotamian scribe culture "western," and the centers of Central Asian/Indo-Aryan culture "eastern," we may distinguish a slow process of westernization during the entire course of Iranian cultural history. (1975:44)

This Western trajectory, however, has not been linear or rapid. It has been punctuated by syncretic reprocessing, which means that each period of Western impact has been followed by a period of syncretic "rearchaization" or "syncretic westernization" (46). Bausani argues that Zoroastrian reformation, Mesopotamian influences, Hellenization after Alexander's conquest of Iran, Islamization of Iran in the seventh century A.D., and finally Western-style modernization in the nineteenth century, are all instances of cultural contact between Iran and its Western neighbors that engendered syncretic Westernization.

In Shi'i Islam, which is practiced in Iran, syncretism (*elteqat*) is condemned as a practice that contaminates the purity of the Islamic doctrine by implying that it is humanly fabricated and not divinely revealed, and by implicating the Muslims in undesirable practices. It is also denigrated for hindering Islamization of others. However, Bausani shows that syncretism has always been part of the Iranization of Islam and of Islamization of Iran. According to him, "Islam assumed its familiar aspect" only after it was mixed with Iranian elements and that Iranian culture itself also was nourished by Islam, as a result of which neither remained "pure" or retained its preinvasion or pre-Islamic character.[29]

The resulting Islam is a "universal culture" capable of producing such works as the Iranian national epic of the tenth century, the *Shahnameh* (The Book of Kings) by Abolqasem Ferdowsi, which contains both archaic Persian and Islamic mythologies and symbolism. Although much of the book's mythic and epic narratives take place in historical times that far preceded Islam, Islam is inscribed syncretically in them.[30]

In recent years, two types of rearchaization movements have surfaced in Iran: one denies the importance of Islam to Iranian culture while the other denies that Islam could survive without Iranian contribution—both of which are essentialist and illusory. It is a characteristic of syncretic rearchaization to attempt to invoke the period in one's history before "contamination" by the other, a period of putative purity, authenticity, and antiquity. Three major instances of such syncretic rearchaization have occurred in the last two decades in Iran prior to the biggest wave of Iranian exodus to the United States.

The heightened speed of European- and North American-style modernization of Iran in the 1960s and 1970s created discrepancies in the way Iranians viewed their status in relation not only to the past and the future but also to the West. It also created a sense of deprivation of, and utopian longing for, enhanced possessions, status, ethical behavior, and worth. Finally, it fulfilled the criteria put forward earlier for syncretism—Westernization brought about acute and rapid culture contact, unequal power relations, cultural exchange and borrowing, a composite (*montazh*) culture, and the retention of aspects of autochthonous culture. For a Third World society, the unequal power relations embedded in Westernization represent a grave threat not only to traditional economic and political structures but also to the way indigenous people produce and consume meaning. This set the stage for new rearchaization movements.

## Official Culture of Spectacle

Syncretism is usually set into motion at the popular culture level, from the bottom up, but occasionally it can occur also as a result of a state policy, from top down, such as the official culture of spectacle nurtured by the regime of Shah Mohammad Reza Pahlavi. Syncretism's spectacles, rituals, and performances can be both affiliative and disaffiliative—that is, they can defy the foreign element at the same time that they inscribe it. In the 1970s the Shah's government, sensing a threat from indigenous Shi'i religion and from the dislocation caused by Westernization, intensified its attempt to construct and administer a state-sanctioned official rearchaization which depended on revitalizing a partly fabricated monarchic, chauvinistic ideology and history that predated Islam. This revivalism took the form of a series of state-sponsored grandiose national spectacles and rituals such as the Shah's own coronation staged in 1967,[31] and the celebrations and pageantry held in 1971 to honor the 2,500th anniversary of the Persian Empire, which cost some three hundred million dollars (Mottahedeh 1985:327).[32] The year-long festivities in 1975 to celebrate the fiftieth anniversary of Pahlavi rule prompted an unprecedented flurry of film and television productions by all agencies of the vast Iranian bureaucracy throughout the year (Naficy 1979:459), and the Shiraz Festival of Art and Culture became the showpiece for government's revitalization project. In this festival were placed in syncretic tension the most modern world-class theatrical productions (of Growtowski and Peter Brook, for example) and European ballet (of Maurice Bejart) side by side with the most ancient indigenous productions (the *ta'ziyeh* passion play, *siahbazi* performances, *ruhowzi* traditional theater, and classical Persian music)—all performed at Persepolis, in other ancient sites, and in the streets of Shiraz.

Spectacle was clearly part of the Shah's ideological and developmental project, whose overarching label changed over the years from "The Shah-People Revolution" to "The White Revolution" to "The Great Civilization." The core of the project was for the Shah to push Iran into the pantheon of industrial superpowers within less than a decade while simultaneously revitalizing a symbolic construction of a glorious monarchy in the past to which he claimed a direct lineage, which was in fact ersatz. The Shah now called himself *Shahanshah Aryamehr* (King of Kings, the Light of the Aryans). Some scholars viewed this culture of spectacle produced by a combination of bogus industrialization and fabricated ideology and history, as a conflict between an "official culture" and a "traditional culture" (Mowlana 1979). To many Iranians critical of the Shah's policies and politics, this was an official culture assembled from parts that did not fit, a culture without roots, a pastiche culture. No culture is ever uniform or homogeneous. Homogeneity and purity of cultures is a fascist dream. But such an administered simulacrum, such a created scene, clashed with the seen, because it derived its own syncretic fabrications. To many Iranians living in Los Angeles who continue to support the monarchy and who themselves might have been involved as participants or spectators, this official culture looms larger and more truly "authentic" from a position in exile. To them it represents a fulfillment of Iranian national aspiration and utopian imagining. Many of the images circulated by exile television are taken from the films commissioned for these various instances of the Pahlavi official culture.

### Messianic Revivalism

This officially sanctioned culture and the popularly generated practices to which it gave rise, however, were not sufficient to compensate for the relative deprivations—of possession, status, behavior, and worth—that a majority of Iranians seemed to be feeling. Discrepancies between expectation and actuality were felt deeply. What made these deprivations and discrepancies unresolvable was the Shah's firm control of all forms of public expression and participation in the political life of the country, which limited serious political discussion and curtailed genuinely free political parties, trade unions, elections, and mass media. In these circumstances, ordinary individual actions seemed inadequate and futile, thus ushering in the cataclysmic emergence of an antimonarchy revolution, which, with the rise of the Ayatollah Ruhollah Khomeini, became a messianic, charismatic movement with a utopian component. The goals of this movement were to return to a former era of glory and happiness, to restore an egalitarian time, and to revive a preexisting moral order—all of which were construed to have existed in the Islamic society ruled by prophet Mohammad and his disciples some 1,400 years earlier. A royalist revival based on a pre-Islamic construction was replaced with a religious one derived from a post-Islamic fabrication.

Accordingly, in April 1979, in a referendum, Iranians voted to dissolve the Pahlavi monarchy and install in its place an Islamic republic, with the Ayatollah Khomeini, whose title was elevated to "imam," as the *velayat-e faqih* (supreme jurisprudent). Once again a shift occurred: a Light of the Aryans was replaced with a Light of God (Ayatollah), and with that a paradigmatic shift took place, one with a strong moral component. As Afsaneh Najmabadi has argued, while the all-consuming preoccupation from the mid-nineteenth century onward was the "material transformation of a backward society," the Islamist revolution ushered in concern with "moral purification of a corrupt society" (1987:203).[33]

At any rate, this development provided the engines that propelled not only the revolution but also the displacement of Iranians to hostile foreign lands. This goes a long way to explain the virulent antagonism of exile television against the Islamic Republic.

## Popular Montazh Culture

Rearchaization, revivalism, and messianism are often violent moments in history. Cultural contacts leading to such intense responses also engender more leisurely and diffused reactions: manufacturers, businesses, common people, and cultural producers alike borrow certain aspects of foreign culture and impregnate them with autochthonous elements. In the process, they domesticate the other, transform the indigenous, and in the final analysis produce a syncretic culture different from both of the original cultures. In Iran, this was accomplished through development of an economy and a mentality best described at the time as *farhang-e montazhi*, or *montazh* culture, from the French word *montage*. This assembled culture and the economic system undergirding it were based on a kind of market capitalism and comprador industrialization introduced into Iran in the 1960s—under the Shah-People Revolution—which largely entailed assembling in Iran cars, trucks, buses, TV sets, and electronic and household utilities from parts prefabricated in the West.

Government agricultural policies and land reform programs displaced many farmers who flocked to cities in search of day labor, as a result of which the nation could no longer feed itself and had to import many staple food items. The *montazh* culture moved in to compensate for the loss. There is a story told of a visit by then-premier Amir Abbas Hoveyda to a southern region of the country, where he was served the national dish, chelo kabob (grilled filet mignon, rice, raw onions, and garnish). Hoveyda congratulated his host on the deliciousness of the meal, whereupon the unsophisticated provincial cook responded by saying, "Mr. Prime Minister, our national meal is also assembled, since the meat for it comes from Australia, the rice from the U.S., and the onions from Pakistan" (Faruqi 1979:71).

But syncretism was not limited to manufacturing of goods alone; rather, it extended to the realm of ideas, ideology, and the way people produced meaning. The historian Roy Mottahedeh explains:

> In joking, Tehranis called all sorts of jerry-built Iranian versions of foreign ideas true examples of Iranian *montazh*. In fact, even the social life of Tehran itself often seemed a huge unfinished

*montazh*. Almost everybody came from somewhere else, and they all seemed out to prove that by wealth, piety, worldliness, and above all cleverness they had somehow welded themselves onto the never quite finished *montazh* of Tehran. . . . Yet for all its prefab, newfangled, ill-digested character it was an exciting place. If ideas as well as goods were unloaded at the bus stations, railroad depots, and airports of Tehran, they were far less predictable in nature than goods, and every Tehrani seemed to create a special *montazh* of these ideas peculiarly his own. (1985:270–71)

This *montazh* mentality has helped Iranian exiles to rearchaize by repressing the current Islamist Iran, and by revitalizing through their popular and televisual cultures either the pre-Islamic time (before the seventh century) or the prerevolution period (before 1979). By the same means they have also attempted to indigenize and absorb certain features of the dominant American culture, thereby facilitating their own acculturation. All forms of syncretic rearchaization look to the past in order to reconstruct the past, understand (or more often repress) the present, and imagine the future.

## Iranian Exiles and Immigrants: A Demographic Profile

No current reliable statistics about how many Iranians live in the United States or in Southern California exists as yet. Widely circulated press estimates, from the *Los Angeles Times* to *Forbes* to *Time* (which seem to overestimate), give a figure between 200,000 and 800,000 Iranians in Southern California alone, making it the largest community outside Iran.[34] However, the only comprehensive analysis of existing statistics, conducted by sociologists Mehdi Bozorgmehr and Georges Sabagh (which appears to underestimate) shows the number of Iranians in the whole of the United States, and in Los Angeles, not to exceed 341,000 and 74,000, respectively (1988:16). The 1990 census data on Iranian residents released by the United States Bureau of the Census (Ethnic and Hispanic Branch, 1990 Special Tabulation, n.d.) corroborate Bozorgmehr and Sabagh's low figures. The data shows the total number in the whole of the United States of foreign-born Iranians and those who claim Iranian ancestry to be 216,963 and 235,521, respectively. In California the figures for the same population categories are respectively 117,053 and 108,871. It must be borne in mind that the place-of-birth figures ignore those of Iranian ancestry born in this country and the figures concerned with ancestry do not count as Iranian certain Iranian subethnic groups such as Armenians and Assyrians. It is clear, however, that even if these deficiencies are adjusted for, the number of Iranians in the United States and in Los Angeles is much smaller than those circulated by Iranians and the mainline media.

Despite the paucity and unreliability of statistics about the total number of Iranians in the United States, there are clear demographic indications about the composition and socioeconomic impact of the community. Here, only those aspects that pertain to their popular culture in exile will be highlighted. Bozorgmehr and Sabagh's study, for example, demonstrates that, when compared with native Americans or with other high-achieving immigrants, Iranian exiles in general have an unusually high level of income, education, self-employment, and professional skills[35]— all of which are necessary in creating a viable exilic economy, a dynamic advertising-driven popular culture, and eventually political influence. The popular Iranian and U.S. media, too, have picked up on these facts by running features that foreground the high demographic profile of Iranians.[36]

Iranian exiles' surprising heterogeneity and internal ethnic differences are not readily apparent to outsiders. This heterogeneity embraces religion, language, ethnicity, and politics. These major religions are represented among Iranian exiles: Shi'i Islam, Judaism, Baha'ism, Zoroastrianism, and Armenian and Assyrian Christianity. The Muslims form the largest group, followed by Armenians, Jews, and Baha'is, but interestingly, when taken together, Iranian minorities here outnumber Muslims, who form 98 percent of the population in Iran. In exile the Muslim majority finds itself, for the first time, to be a minority. As will become apparent, the higher proportion of internal ethnic representation has a significant effect on the political economy of Iranian popular and televisual cultures in exile.

Another unexpected feature in the domain of religious affiliation is the high level of secularism among all Iranians, particularly the Muslims. A mere 2 percent in Bozorgmehr, Sabagh, and Der-Martirosian's study said they observe religious practice, apparently reflecting their secular background before exile and their current opposition to the Islamic government (1991:14). This finding allows researchers of Iranian demography to conclude that despite the prevalent sociological view, at least in the case of Iranian immigrants, religion does not necessarily reinforce ethnicity (Sabagh and Bozorgmehr 1991:1–2). This overwhelming secularism among the exile population combined with its general opposition to the Islamic government may account for the near complete absence of religion and religious topics in the first decade of Iranian television.

Iranian exiles are also ethnically diverse. Ethnicity and religious affiliation are intertwined in many cases, so that Jews and Armenians, for example, are considered to be both ethnic and religious minorities. Among other ethnic subgroups Kurds, Turks, Gilakis, Turkomans, Bakhtiaris, and

Qashqa'is can be named. There is a relationship between ethnicity and socioeconomic characteristics and achievements which has a determining impact on exile television. Although self-employment is very high among Iranians, 82 percent of Iranian Jews are self-employed, more than any other new immigrant groups in the United States (Bozorgmehr, Sabagh, and Der-Martirosian 1991:12). Self-employment allows Iranians to create not only an exilic and ethnic economy but also what might be called an interethnic or subethnic one.[37] The repercussions of this situation for TV become clear when we consider that with two exceptions (*Sima-ye Azadi* and *Mozhdeh*) all Iranian exile television programs are commercially driven and must rely for their livelihood on Iranian businesses. The high percentage of self-employment among Jews and Armenians means that they have a disproportionate role in sustaining exile television and an extraordinary power to influence Iranian exile discourses. In addition, if we take into account the high representation of Jews, Armenians, and Baha'is in the production and distribution of music and entertainment recordings, the extent of their influence becomes more evident.

Ethnicity is also intertwined with language. The Persian language is considered to be the mother tongue for all ethnic groups, with the exception of Armenians, who primarily use Armenian to communicate with each other and use Persian to speak with other Iranians. Other ethnoreligious subgroups presumably use their own languages at home. As expected, members of the younger generation use a higher proportion of English words and syntax in their communication with other Iranians, especially with other young people, creating an in-between language jokingly called "Penglish." Because of the unifying role that the Persian language has played in Iranian history and continues to play in exile, it is no wonder that the overwhelming majority of all exile television programs have been aired in Persian (although Penglish is creeping in).

In terms of political affiliation, royalists, who desire restoration of some form of constitutional monarchy in Iran, outnumber the other factions. There are, however, significant numbers of leftists as well as middle-of-the-roaders among the exiles. There are also some who support the Islamic government in Iran, and some adherents of the Mojahedin guerrilla group that is fighting the goverment. As I will show in the following chapters, Iranian exiles have undergone a shift from a heavy investment in politics to an increased interest in culture.

The largest influx of Iranians into the United States occurred in two broad phases: the first occurred between 1950 and 1977 and the second between 1979 and 1986. These two waves, one motivated by a rapid, top-down Westernization spearheaded by the Shah and the other by a bottom-up popular social revolution eventually led by the Ayatollah Khomeini, have produced two essentially different types of populations. While the first wave comprised permanent economic immigrants or temporary immigrants, such as a large number of students, much of the second wave is made up of political refugees and exiles (Sabagh and Bozorgmehr 1987:77; Bozorgmehr 1992:130). From this we can deduce that the motivation for leaving the country of origin and the timing of departure can be used as indicators for distinguishing political exiles from immigrants. Using these two factors, Bozorgmehr and Sabagh's study shows that 43 percent of their sample were exiles and 57 percent immigrants. According to them, the exiles are on average older than immigrants, have less education, are forced to accept jobs in exile that are lower in status or pay than what they had in Iran or what they would like to have, and they have less mastery of the host country's language and culture (1991:126–31). These trends show that exile, at least for the first generation, involves drastic shifts in status, often in the form of downward mobility. This partially explains the propensity toward dystopia and dysphoria noted earlier. Significantly, their data also shows that the exile and immigrant categories are not fixed, since the former can become the latter. This evolution is reflected in the contents and forms of exile-produced popular and televisual cultures.

Iranians living in the United States characterize their own status variously. Since the revolution of 1978–79, exilic popular culture and television programs have used the following terms to describe the Iranians living in the United States: exiled (*tab'idi*), immigrant (*mohajer*), refugee (*panahandeh*), political refugee/asylee (*panahandeh-ye siasi*), stranger (*gharibeh*), homeless (*bikhaneman, darbehdar*), vagrant (*avareh*), fugitive (*farari*), self-exiled, and student.[38] Iranians also use distinctions based on place of residence, with homeland as the reference point and geographic borders its defining principle. Those living in Iran are called "Iranians living within Iran's borders" (*Iranian-e dorun marzi*) and those living abroad are called "Iranians living outside Iran's borders" (*Iranian-e borun marzi*).[39] Self-descriptive terms are not static; as Iran itself and the Iranian community abroad changed over the last dozen years, so did this terminology. Immediately after the revolution, Iranian popular press abroad called the community it served "a community in exile" (*jame'e-ye dar tab'id*). As exile gradually evolved into immigration for many, the popular characterization, too, shifted to "an immigrant community" (*jame'e-ye mohajer*). Likewise, characterization of exiles based on reference to the impenetrable Iranian borders is also changing and diminishing. Although most Iranians in the United States have resisted changing their family names, many (some 40 percent in one study) have informally adopted American first names or have Americanized their original first names (Blair 1991:147). With these shifts in self-designation have come a certain loosening and broadening of the definition of what constitutes "Iran" or an "Iranian" identity.[40]

Although not all Iranians living in the United States are in political exile in the traditional sense of the term, I will refer to them as exiles throughout this book because a large percentage, nearly half of the participants in the Bozogmehr and Sabagh study, unable to return to their homeland, considered themselves to be in exile. Their inability to return, their opposition to the Islamic government in Iran, the antagonism of the Islamic government toward them, and their generally hostile reception in the United States have all contributed to placing Iranians in Los Angeles in a liminal state of transcultural otherness, actively in touch, across the borders of nation-states, with the homeland and with Iranians living elsewhere, for example, in New York City, London, Stockholm, and Paris.

As I mentioned earlier, Iranians have not formed a single physical enclave, an "Irantown" in Southern California. Their abundant class resources in terms of financial, occupational, and educational capital and the heterogeneity of the population and the success of major Iranian religious and ethnic subgroups at forming subcommunities and subeconomies have acted against this. There is an ethnic pattern to this physical dispersion, with the largest concentration of internal ethnic Iranians located in the following areas: Baha'is in Santa Monica / West Los Angeles, Muslims in Santa Monica / Palms, Armenians in Glendale, and Jews in the affluent areas of Westwood and Beverly Hills (Bozorgmehr 1992:168–69). There is a high level of identification among these dispersed ethnics with the idea of Iranian identity, nation, and nationalism, however. In fact, the absence of a dominant religion and a single residential concentration as chief markers of ethnicity seems to have heightened the significance of other factors of ethnicity—particularly the shared Persian language, which transcends all internal ethnic boundaries and leads to the production of a popular and televisual culture that is disseminated almost entirely in that language.

These symbolic markers of ethnicity (language and popular culture) have been put in the service of creating in exile an imaginary "national" Iranian identity for all the Iranians, regardless of their religio-ethnolinguistic affiliations. The highly advertising-driven popular culture and broadcast media discursively link the fragmented ethnic subcommunities and subeconomics and produce a "nation in exile," and also make them economically viable. Thus, despite Bozorgmehr, Sabagh, and Der-

Martirosian's contention (1991:18) that "informal and formal social ties in Los Angeles tend to reinforce Armenian, Baha'i, Jewish and Muslim identity rather than an all-encompassing national identity," the popular culture seems to have served the needs of both Iranian internal ethnicity and an overall Iranian nationalism in exile.[41]

# 2
# Iranian Exilic Popular Culture

## A Salon (*dowreh*)

*For several years in the mid-1980s an Iranian intellectual salon was operated by a nucleus of graduate students and professors at UCLA. I was a member and for a year acted as its secretary. The group, which usually numbered a dozen people, met once a month at a member's house for dinner and talk. What is striking about this salon (now defunct) was the diversity of its members in terms of age, fields of interest, professions, ethnicity, religion, class, and nationality. Most were young men and women, graduate students in a variety of fields—from anthropology to cinema studies, from ethnomusicology to literary criticism, from political science to psychology, and from history to Islamic studies. There were professionals among us also: psychiatrists, physicians, university professors, filmmakers, poets, and writers. Armenians and Azeris were among ethnicities represented, as were Muslims, Baha'is, and Jews. The majority of us had been born in Iran and our legal status was that of student. But there were others who were hyphenated Iranian-Americans or Americans and occasionally we had Palestinian, Japanese, Israeli, or French guest scholars.*

*I looked forward to these long evening sessions. If you were not the first to arrive, you could easily spot the apartment in which the salon was being held: the smell of Persian cooking, laughter, and loud con-*

*versations in English, Persian, or their bastard, Penglish. The half-
open door welcomed you to an "ethnic room": a Persian carpet on
the floor, photos of friends and far-away family members on the
shelves, posters of fetishized images of the homeland or of miniature
paintings hanging on the walls, handicrafts and antiques displayed
on the shelves—not to forget rows of books in various languages, a
large bowl of fresh fruit strikingly arranged, and Persian classical
music playing quietly.*

*Shaking hands, hugging, and kissing—or brushing cheeks and kiss-
ing the air—followed. Conversation, perhaps a cup of sweetened tea
or coffee in hand, and the speaker for the night would begin her talk.
The topics—usually related to Iranian current affairs, history, culture, or arts—would be up to the speakers but they would be an-
nounced beforehand. Some sessions were entired devoted to poetry
reading—some written by the members. With the introduction of the
speaker by the secretary, cacophonic synsthesia would give way to an
hour of silent listening and note-taking. Then followed a question
period, more talk—some gossip—and the confirmation of the next
date, place, and speaker.*

*Our salon changed gradually. The same elements that made up the
diversity at times made for discord and tense moments. Clashes of
academic disciplines, research methodologies, political views, and
personalities were not unknown. The income difference between the
professionals and the students eventually forced us to simplify the
proceedings: we limited the refreshments to only cookies and tea and
coffee. The evolving politics of the homeland and our own status as
liminar intellectuals necessitated a more serious attention to issues:
we formalized the presentations, cut down on the entertainment, and
scheduled the sessions a year in advance. As presentations took on
the aspect of an academic duty and as active core members gradu-
ated and moved on to other cities, countries, and stations in life, the
salon dwindled. But some of the strong ties that were then formed
continue to evolve to nourish us—through letter writing, phone calls,
exchange of publications, conference talks, and e-mail.*

## Exilic Popular Culture

Postmodernity and poststructuralism have eroded the "great divide" between high and popular cultures. Structuralist and mass culture critics
have tended to regard popular culture as a "mass culture" imposed by the
"ruthless unity" of the culture industry over an essentially passive and
atomized population (Horkheimer and Adorno 1972:123). This is a view

that until the revolution of 1978–79 was held also by both Iranian secular intellectuals and religious elites, as exemplified by Jalal Al-e Ahmad (1961) and Ayatollah Khomeini (n.d. and 1981), who developed powerful concepts such as *gharbzadegi* (Westernstruckness) and *farhang-e taqut* (culture of idolatry), respectively. The proponents of "pessimistic" mass culture critique urged the study of popular and mass cultures only for the purpose of uncovering the obfuscatory mechanisms of the dominant ideology imbedded in them. Advocates of cultural populism, on the other hand, took up the study of popular culture in order to discover in it an originary authentic essence that putatively expresses the autochthonous culture of "the people." Iranian Marxists conflated mass culture and cultural populist models to criticize the popular *montazh* culture circulated in the Pahlavi era as an "imperialist culture" or a "mummified culture" (Golsorkhi 1980?:5, 1979?). Other intellectuals blamed this culture for alienating or exiling Iranians from their "true" and historic selves; they urged a return to indigenous sources (Shayegan 1977:173–74, and Naraqi 1977:10). In the case of the influential religious thinker Ali Shari'ati, this meant a return to "Islamic culture and Islamic ideology" (1978:13). His syncretic philosophy, forged by combining the deeds of Shi'i saints such as imam Hosain with the thoughts of Third World thinkers such as Frantz Fanon, formed the backbone of the anti-Shah revivalist movement that eventually brought him down. On the other hand, the critics who favored monarchy constructed a different originary source to which Iranian culture could return. Considering the traditional culture of the lower classes, which is heavily imbued with Islam, to be superstitious, backward, and even subversive, they advocated a return to the pre-Islamic glories of the Iranian past. Such an ideology undergirded the Shah's Great Civilization program. In other words, while Marxists and religious populists formulated a spontaneous oppositional culture *of* the people, the Iranian state put into practice an administered culture *for* the people.

The approach to popular culture that most informs this book is derived from the writings of Antonio Gramsci on hegemony. In this formulation, popular culture is not conceived as a static process or a monolithic entity. It is not a deformation or a deception imposed by dominant powers, neither is it a spontaneous opposition bursting forth from the subaltern strata or an unproblematic affirmation of an authentic, originary culture. Rather, popular culture is seen as a terrain in which various groups, cultures, and ideologies interact, struggling to obtain "the moment of hegemony," that is, cultural, moral, and ideological leadership over allied and subordinate groups and over marginalized cultures and ideologies (Gramsci 1988:194). This form of procuring political and cultural ascendency presupposes a dynamic relation of forces within the civil society and is opposed to the static model of direct domination exercised by the political society, namely, the state. Popular culture, therefore, is not so much an instrument of as an access to domination. In consumer capitalism, however, this process structurally favors the dominant.

In the United States the mainstream culture is dominant not because it obliterates all opposition but because it compromises and selectively incorporates the expression of alternative viewpoints into the civil society through the rule of law, education, media, fashion, and consumer capitalism. The incorporation of exilic cultures into the mainstream discourse is no exception. The dominant culture appropriates exilic world views and artifacts in such a way as to soften or neutralize their specificity or their antagonistic content. As a result, whatever exilic opposition or antagonism might have existed is ultimately mapped out as mere difference, as "style," which then feeds the pluralist, multicultural ethnic diversity trends now in vogue in the United States. Having thus *defused* the subcultural and exilic threat ideologically, the remaining unthreatening difference is *diffused* economically to create "new and improved" products with a difference, that is, products with a safe ethnic gloss (Naficy and Gabriel 1993; Hebdige 1980).

Exiles, in turn, employ the host's popular culture and its mediating institutions to create a symbolic communitas and an economy based on descent and consent relations, in which certain fossilized representations of home and the past are repeatedly circulated and reinforced. Individual and cultural identity is thus preserved for the moment, and the exilic subculture is protected temporarily from the seemingly hostile dominant cultures. For Iranian exiles in Los Angeles, this protection is provided by a symbolic and semiotic enclave rather than a physical one.[1] Culture for exiles, therefore, is not just a trivial superstructure—it is life itself.

The resulting syncretic exilic culture tends to procure for the dominant culture what Pierre Bourdieu has called "cultural capital" (1977:187–89). By becoming consummate consumers, the exiles are transformed into an ethnic group. Syncretism via the popular culture is a method for reasserting and symbolically expressing the community's boundary in exile. Outsiders, sometimes even insiders, will have difficulty recognizing these boundaries because of their abstract, simulacral nature and their dispersal across many media. The cultural map thus appears to be indecipherable.

It is the project of this chapter to make decipherable the Iranian exilic cultural map. Exilic popular culture is the proper terrain for this purpose because in it are charted hegemonic haggling over both authenticity and descent and identity and consent. There is considerable vitality within exilic popular culture itself, and tension between the "high" and the "low" ends of the spectrum. The contest over obtaining hegemony exists in exile media as well as between the host and the exilic cultures, and among other internal exilic subgroups. The current culture of the homeland also attempts to enter the exile community. The success of the royalist factions in becoming the dominant voice in Iranian popular culture in Los Angeles does not stem so much from state sponsorship (although they have reportedly received financial assistance from various governments) as from their ability to compete better than their rivals for a "moment of hegemony" within the exile community nested in American civil society.

In this chapter, I will map out an overview that includes a discussion of some of the media (minus television) and cultural events that together form the Iranian popular culture in Los Angeles. As a marginal subculture in the United States, exilic popular culture is in a constant state of flux as it responds to both the host society's economic fluctuations and to the rapid shifts and transformations within its own community. The lifespans of individual exile media and various interethnic social formations are usually not very long. Those that survive are those that can adapt. The analysis that follows, therefore, provides a discursive snapshot that attempts to capture a particular moment in the evolution of Iranian exile culture in Los Angeles; as such, it reflects the relations of forces and the content of the media at the time of the writing. The dynamics of crosscultural encounter guarantee their continued evolution.

## Periodicals

A wide-ranging print culture has evolved in the past dozen years among Iranians abroad. A study in 1983 reported some 316 Iranian periodicals published outside Iran since the 1979 revolution (Moslehi 1984:32). No doubt this figure has increased severalfold since then, with Southern California a key publishing center. Since 1980 nearly 90 periodicals have been published in Los Angeles alone, almost all of them in Persian. (Table 1 provides a comprehensive but perhaps not exhaustive list, indicating their stated ethnic affiliation, political affiliation, and frequency of publication.) A few periodicals have experimented with an English-Persian bilingual format, but the share of English-language text in them is very small. Of the dozen or so Armenian-language periodicals in Los Angeles, only *Kajnazar* is printed in the eastern dialect used by Iranian Armenians.

The frequency of publication varies. There are two daily newspapers (*Sobh-e Iran* and *Asr-e Emruz*) and the rest are published weekly, biweekly, monthly, quarterly, yearly, and some even occasionally. In terms of contents, the majority of the periodicals—past and current—are eclectic, usually containing hard news, news commentary, entertainment news, features, and various departments. The mix of elements depends on the target audience. For example, the weekly magazines, such as *Javanan* and *Tamasha*, highlight entertainment and news about performers in exile. News-oriented periodicals were at first driven primarily by Iranian news, although the proportion of other news is now increasing. *Seda-ye Shahr* was an audiocassette periodical, containing classical Persian music, poetry, short stories, essays, and commentary.

Specialist magazines for women, children, lawyers, and physicians have emerged along with others focusing on such specific interests as earthen architecture, mysticism, literature, sports, astrology, advertising, and real estate. Table 1 makes clear the interethnic diversity of Iranians in Los Angeles and the heavy use that Jewish-Iranians particularly have made of periodicals as a way of marking their interethnic boundary. Ethnicity, however, has a deeper penetration in the Iranian periodicals and ethnic economy than appears in the table. This is because even though some periodicals are not billed as ethnic or published in Iranian ethnic languages, they receive more support from a particular subethnic group because of the ethnicity of its publisher and staff. For example, the weekly *Fogholadeh*, whose publisher and directors of advertising are all Armenian, contains the most ads for Armenian-Iranian and Armenian-American businesses.

Political viewpoints among Iranian exiles are heterogenous, but periodicals also show the dominance of the royalist faction in Los Angeles. While not all the periodicals are political, the overwhelming majority stand firmly against the Islamic government in Iran. Such a surge of oppositional media within an immigrant community must be attributed not only to the turmoil of exile but also to the tumult at home. A number of the periodicals are the official organs of religious minorities or political factions operating against the Islamic Republic. It must be stated, however, that it is very difficult to determine with certainty the precise political affiliation(s) of periodicals and other exile media, because they are kept hidden, and they shift frequently over time. Affiliations noted here, unless they carry the name of an organization, are based on informal data obtained from various sources and they may in part be inaccurate. A few periodicals are affiliated with businesses (*Kabobi, Payk-e Ketab*), with media outlets (*Fogholadeh, Jam-e Jam, Omid, Simorgh, Seda-ye Shahr*), leftist cultural foundations (*Andisheh, Khabarnameh-ye Zanan, Ketab-e Nima*), or ethnic minorities (*Elm va Erfan, Kajnazar, Shofar, Shakhsar*).

These patterns of affiliation have led to a wide-ranging cross-fertilization of contents, discourses, and economies. The political economy of Iranian periodicals takes four basic forms. One group of periodicals receives direct financial support from the political organization of which they are official organs. This turned them into periodicals whose ideology is partisanship not political independence.[2] This form of sponsorship was more prevalent in the early 1980s when the politically exiled groups were most active. In some cases, direct sponsorship was sufficient to distribute the papers to customers at no charge (e.g., *Jebhe-ye Hamgam* and *Jebhe-ye Jam*); sometimes it was not, in which case the paper solicited a small percentage of ads (e.g., *Payam-e Iran*).

A second set of periodicals receives sufficient funds from advertisers to survive without having to charge a fee for newsstand sales in Los Angeles. The two dailies, and until September 1989 some of the mass circulation weeklies (i.e., *Javanan* and *Rayegan*), operated this way. This form of financing resulted in a decade-long ruthless competition among the periodicals attempting to survive on a limited amount of advertising dollars available from Iranian businesses. Political labeling, mudslinging, personal attacks bordering on slander, highly slanted content, and loaded language were the consequences.

Since September 1989, however, the aforementioned weeklies have began to use the third type of mixed financing, which is based on income both from advertisers and from single-issue sales. This seems to have cooled the discourse and toned down the shrillness of these periodicals as they have become less beholden to advertisers and more motivated to attract paying customers. This shift has introduced a move from partisanship toward independence. Yet this emerging political independence entails commercial dependence.[3] The political and financial ramifications of this shift are significant and can be seen in six major developments gradually emerging in the aforementioned Iranian periodicals in exile: depoliticization and less concentration on domestic politics in Iran; reduced emphasis on news as current news is readily available from Iranian and American dailies and broadcasts; commercialization of censorship, resulting in suppression of views that hurt the periodicals financially; development of yellow journalism as a means of attracting paying customers; enhanced emphasis on culture, literature, and the arts with a concomitant reduction of emphasis on partisan politics; and attention to conditions, problems, and processes of living in exile.

A fourth source driving the political economy of Iranian periodicals in exile is the cross-fertilization of horizontally integrated media ownership. When one company owns two or more media, it is able to reach larger and more diverse audiences and so it can theoretically charge steeper advertising fees (or undercut smaller competitors). Horizontal integration also develops an intertextual relationship among the affiliated media, whereby one medium promotes another through advertising and links in content. The radio call-in show *Radio Omid* used to pick up the topic discussed on *Omid TV* earlier that day, or the edited transcripts of the radio programs would appear in the affiliated journal, the quarterly *Omid*. Such links tend to strengthen the readership of the journals and the audiences of the radio programs and also the dominance of the multimedia entrepreneurs.

The tensions and the polysemy of exilic popular culture are evident in the friction between periodicals and television programs, reminiscent of the debate between elite and popular cultures. The popular media, especially television, have come under attack by intellectuals and literary periodicals for being shallow, spurious, partisan, and a threat to morality and Iranian "authenticity." For their part, popular periodicals and television programs have generally either ignored Iranian high culture, ghettoizing it to poetry and literature sections, or they have distorted or politicized the intellectuals' discourses.[4] The intellectuals' own periodicals, most of which are published outside of Los Angeles, tend to have a limited circulation and a somewhat irregular publication schedule.

## Radio Programs

Radio programs have been integral to exile media, not only because of their varied politics and easy availability (in cars, at work, and in homes) but also their long broadcast hours. Table 2 provides a list of all the regularly scheduled radio programs targeted at Iranians and aired in Southern California. *Omid* radio was the first regularly scheduled program, beginning its broadcasts in the early 1980s. During much of the 1980s and early 1990s, *Omid* and *Iran* together accounted for some three hours of programming nightly. *Seda-ye Iran*, which began in the late 1980s, and *Iranian*, which began in 1991, have aired their programs around the clock. With the exception of *Seda-ye Iran* and *Iranian*, all other programs were broadcast by commercial radio stations (chiefly KFOX-FM) on a lease-access basis. Program producers leased their air time from the stations and in turn sold spot advertisements to Iranian businesses. In mid-1991, Korean broadcasters took over much of the prime-time hours of KFOX, forcing Iranian programmers off the air. *Omid* ceased operation altogether and *Iran* was integrated into *Seda-ye Iran*.

*Seda-ye Iran* is transmitted on a sideband frequency that cannot be received by regular radios. Those living in California need a special receiver and all others require an additional satellite receiver.[5] *Iranian* utilizes the same technology, but it requires a different receiver than that used for *Seda-ye Iran*. *Seda-ye Iran*'s coverage, which was at first limited to Los Angeles, has grown to most of California and Washington, D.C., and it is expanding nationally. It generates its revenues from ads and the sale of radio receivers (costing around $100 each).

Most of the shows employ a magazine format incorporating a number of eclectic elements, usually news, commentary, poetry, music, interviews, and ads. The mix of elements varies, as do the elements themselves. Persian music (classical and pop) and advertisements, which frequently interrupt the programs, form two major elements of all radio programs. In using the other elements, however, each radio program has attempted to differentiate itself through specialization. *Omid*, for example, with its mixture of interviews with political, cultural, artistic, and literary figures, its call-in segments devoted to problems of acculturation, and its generally erudite style became the most authoritative and credible source of news and culture in exile. On the other hand, *Iran*, with its strong news orientation, became a reliable source of international and Iranian news. Because of its long broadcasting hours and its targeting of the entire family as its audience, *Seda-ye Iran* is able to carry a wide variety of program formats and genres, including over 10 hours (in a 24-hour period) of live call-in talk shows that appeal to both popular and intellectual tastes. The wide mixture of programming and the familiar manner of its hosts, who engage in elaborate ritual courtesy (*ta'arof*) with guests and callers, have helped facilitate the creation in exile of an entirely Persian environment within the home. *Iranian*, too, in its short life so far seems to be following the same pattern. An anecdotal survey of audiences indicates that older women who stay home during the day form the most ardent listeners of *Seda-ye Iran*, followed by older and retired men.

The marriage of two technologies, radio and telephone, has turned radio call-in programs into potent media for expressing exilic tensions as well as strategies of haggling and resistance to assimilation. *Seda-ye Iran*'s round-the-clock programming means that it can provide a variety of programs and a plurality of voices, and also, and more significantly, it can reproduce the dominant ideology through its schedule, which is pitched to the daily pattern of working within the host culture. Noontime is devoted to women's issues, particularly child rearing, housework, and cooking programs; evening programs are given to talk shows and call-in programs that focus on political and cultural issues; weekends are usually much more entertainment-oriented. Even though the content of the schedule is in Persian and concerns chiefly Iranian exilic matters, the form of the schedule (indirectly and imperceptibly) and the commercials (more directly and obviously) encourage acculturation into the dominant work schedule and into consumer capitalism.

Armenians along with Jews have been the most ethnic of all Iranians in Los Angeles. Armenian-Iranians appear to have used radio more than periodicals, while Jewish-Iranians seem to have used specialist periodicals and the music industry more effectively as markers of their internal ethnicity.

The majority of the radio programs have aired in Persian, although a number of them have been in Eastern Armenian, a dialect used by Armenians from Iran and the former Soviet Union. Throughout the period of this study, program producers and hosts placed particular emphasis on preserving and promoting the correct use of Persian. With the increasing use of talk and call-in formats, however, the vernacular exilic language—Penglish—is being heard more than before. These formats also allow peoples from different regions of Iran and from varied ethnic backgrounds to speak in their own accented Persian. Listeners not only hear different opinions but also a plurality of accents and a mixture of English and Persian, all of which turn exilic radio into a potent instrument of Iranian multiculturalism and interethnic pluralism.

Like television programs, all the current radio programs are secular and against the Islamic government in Iran, with royalists particularly well represented among producers and personalities of *Seda-ye Iran*. Because of the nature of live talk and call-in programs, however, the evolving politics of the exiles themselves, and the exigencies of acculturation itself, radio programmers, including *Seda-ye Iran*, have been forced to broadcast a plurality of viewpoints. There has been more diversity among the radio programs than the television programs, although there are more of the latter; in general, however, these two media have reinforced each other. Over the course of the past dozen years, a number of highly political radio programs, some acting as official voices of various Islamist, anti-Islamist, and leftist factions, have emerged and disappeared. Their failure can be attributed to a variety of causes. In some cases, the sponsoring political factions themselves underwent major ideological shifts or disbanded altogether. Other programs lost their audiences because listeners had become depoliticized or disenchanted with the programs' highly politicized language and slanted contents. These partisan programmers failed to recognize their audience's need for entertainment and for guidance in dealing with the problems of settling down in exile. Like their counterparts in periodicals these programs became ideological dinosaurs, unable to take part in the process of forming exilic identity or aiding acculturation. Those that survived owe their existence to their willingness to continually vary their formats in response to the evolving needs of the community they serve.

*Seda-ye Iran*, aired on a sideband frequency, has become more important since *Omid*, which was an FM program, ceased operation in 1991. But because of the limited number of its special receivers in circulation, it has been able to surpass the wide influence of *Omid* only gradually. This situation demonstrates clearly the significant role that exile-produced popular culture, especially broadcast media, plays in the economic and cultural lives of immigrants, particularly those who, like Iranians, are dispersed over a wide area and must rely on media to create linkages. *Seda-ye Iran* has been picking up new listeners who are driven away from exile TV because of its repetitive programming and overcommercialization.

Finally, there are other programs produced by political exile factions opposing the Islamic government that are transmitted to Iran on shortwave radio from Europe and Iraq. These supplement the Persian broadcasts of the BBC, Voice of America, and Radio Israel, which are popular in Iran now as they have been in years past. The Islamic government, too, transmits a shortwave Persian-language broadcast entitled *Seda-ye Ashena* (Familiar voice) aimed at Iranians in exile, including those in Los Angeles.[6]

Telephonic newscasts are another form of narrowcasting, peculiar to Iranian exile media. What turned the telephone, a two-way medium of communication, into a one-way medium of news and information in exile was the highly volatile political situation at home and intensely politicized factionalism abroad, both of which demanded information, not communication. In the heyday of the revolution and in its immediate aftermath, Iranian exiles hungry for news about Iran flocked to emerging telephone "newscasts" spawned by political organizations. Table 3 lists organizations that have sponsored telephonic news services in Los Angeles and in many other cities in the United States.

All telephonic newscasts have been driven by Iranian national politics. They have not been used by Iranian ethnic subgroups to emphasize their ethnicity. The ebb and flow in the politics and the fortunes of the sponsoring organizations affected the fate of telephonic programs as well. Currently, only two telephone newscasts sponsored by the two strongest adversaries in Iranian politics are in operation.

Telephonic newscasts, typically lasting up to five minutes, are available at all hours of the day and night. The contents consist strictly of news about Iran, usually heavily slanted and rhetorical, either focusing on discord, disasters, and disarray or on positive achievements in Iran, depending on the point of view of the sponsoring organization. The general format of these prerecorded microprograms incorporates music and voice logo identifying the sponsoring agency, greetings, a single voice reading the news, and finally farewell and ending music.

As a communication medium the telephone is anomalous: On one hand, it cannot easily be classified as a mass medium because it does not reach a large audience collectively at one time and in one place; on the other hand, it can reach a large audience addressed individually. As a result, it is an appropriate example of Wilbur Schramm's "little media" typology (1977) because its production and transmission is inexpensive and requires little overhead, capital expenditure, technical personnel, and administrative infrastructure. Its programming, on inexpensive and reusable audiotape, is available 24 hours a day and it costs the user only a local telephone call. As a little medium, telephone has proved to be one of the few viable alternatives for disseminating the points of view of groups that are too small or too marginal to afford the "big" media of periodicals, radio, television, and film, or too clandestine to want to publicize their presence widely. Part of the vitality of exilic popular culture is that it allows for a variety of "niches" from which different, even antagonistic, views can be expressed.

## Film Screening and Production

Over 130 feature fiction films made in Iran before the revolution have been screened in Los Angeles commercial theaters. Khaneh-ye Film (Film House), now defunct, was the major exhibitor of Iranian-made features in Los Angeles, but it suffered from competition with the videocassette industry, chiefly Pars Video, whose latest catalog lists over 200 Iranian films on video available for purchase or rental.[7] In general, the quality of these videos is very poor: the color has faded, the image is blurry, and the contrast is either too high or too low. Despite such poor quality, Khaneh-ye Film was unable to compete with the ready availability of so many films on video at very low prices. The recently displaced Iranian exiles were ravenous for Iranian products, especially films that brought sights and sounds of the homeland to them and rekindled their memories of the "good old days" prior to the revolution. Watching videos from the homeland, at home among friends while sharing Persian meals, added to the synesthetic and nostalgic pleasures of exile. Khaneh-ye Film failed also because of the deterioration of its only copy of the films.

The majority of the prerevolutionary feature films shown would probably be categorized as B movies. Comedies, melodramas, and *jaheli* (tough-guy action) films predominated, but a sprinkling of "new-wave" films and documentaries also were exhibited.[8] The chief reason for the ready availability of B movies might be sought in their sources of finance and ultimate control. While the new-wave films were often cofinanced by the government of Iran and housed in government film archives and vaults, B movies were made by the commercial private sector and copies were under less strict control. Like much of exile television programming, these B movies and videos freeze fetishized images of Iran in the prerevolutionary periods, rekindling viewers' nostalgic memories of their homeland and helping them to *relive* their experience of viewing films in Iran—thus deepening their internal absorption by home. There is an irony here that, if explored, will corroborate a point made earlier about the ways signs shift or reverse their meanings when they cross cultural borders. The B-grade films, which formed the bulk of the films exhibited in exile, were as a rule not popular with the type of highly educated and Westernized Iranians now residing in Los Angeles. That, in exile, this type flocked to see these films shows that, in crossing boundaries of geography and culture, the meanings of the cinematic signs have undergone a shift. The B movies no longer are viewed with categorical disdain, as cheap products put together by charlatan businessmen interested in making a fast buck; rather, they are viewed as souvenirs of an inaccessible homeland, irretrievable memories of childhood, a former prosperous lifestyle, and a centered sense of self. That these films are still being rented on very poor-quality videos further supports these points.

Iranians in the United States have produced a range of specialized videos for home consumption. These include M. R. Ghanoonparvar's *Persian Cuisine* tape, which provides a series of how-to lessons in cooking, and *Persian Nights in L.A.* (1992), a hard-core pornographic tape for Iranians, with a dubbed Persian-language soundtrack.

The anti-Iranian sentiments and policies in the United States and the Iranian government's policies discouraging film export prevented most feature films made under the Islamic Republic from finding their way to this country.[9] Since the mid-1980s and the establishment of the Farabi Cinema Foundation in Iran, Iranian films have appeared at many international film festivals in increasing numbers—where they have been received with generally high acclaim. Because of continued antagonism between successive U.S. administrations and Iranian authorities, however, few entries into U.S.-based festivals had been made and postrevolutionary Iranian cinema had remained largely unknown and unavailable in this country.[10]

The situation drastically changed in the late 1980s thanks to the cease-fire with Iraq, the gradual acculturation and depoliticization of the exiles, the relaxation of the strident political rhetoric of both U.S. and Iranian governments, and the contributions of a major film festival organized at UCLA in 1990. Dubbed "A Decade of Iranian Cinema, 1980–1990," this festival screened for the first time eighteen fictional feature films and a number of shorts to a tumultuous audience response. Since then, many films screened at the festival have been toured to major cities in the United States. The controversy the film festival aroused is dealt with in the last chapter of this book.

Iranian filmmakers in the United States and Europe have produced at least 27 feature narrative films, a majority of them in Los Angeles (Table 4). With few exceptions, Iranian directors are independent filmmakers with no financing from major studios. Not all of the films they have made are about Iran.[11] Los Angeles-produced fictional narrative cinema can be divided into four subgenres of exile narrative cinema—subgenres not entirely distinct from one another. A number of films are informed by the politics and aesthetics of more than one category, although in the examples that follow, I have assigned films *predominantly* to one category or another. In its first subgenre Iranian exile cinema was a cinema of denial; physically located in exile but mentally situated at home, it largely disavowed the fact of exile. Although *The Mission*, for example, focuses on the transformation of a terrorist sent by the Islamic government in Iran on a mission to assassinate an ex-Savak agent[12] in the United States, it centers almost entirely on the politics of the homeland. *Veiled Threat* depicts the problems that an Iranian husband faces when he attempts first to bring his family to the United States and then to track down the representative of the Islamic government who has hired an assassin to blow up his family in their car. The issue in films of this category is Iran, more than Iranians living in exile.

The second subgenre can be called a cinema of transition, focusing on individuals in transit in third countries, trying to get passports, visas, and plane tickets. *Checkpoint*, for example, charts the heated political debate among a group of Iranian and American students who on returning from a field trip to Canada are caught in limbo for 24 hours at a Canadian-American border checkpoint because the U.S. government canceled their visas in retaliation for the taking of Americans hostage in Tehran. *The Guests of Hotel Astoria* portrays the life of a group of Iranians in a hotel in Istanbul and the tragic attempts of a young couple to gain entry to the United States and of an older couple to return to Iran.

The third subgenre may be called liminal cinema, whose diegesis both physically and mentally is located in the host country and whose narrative concentrates on issues of life in exile: the clash of cultures, the consequences of cultural stereotyping, the crisis of identity and epistemology, the potential freedom of exile and the drama of descent and consent. *Cat in a Cage* focuses on the life of a well-to-do Iranian emigre family in the United States that is betrayed by their housekeeper and the driver. *Blueface* is a comic whodunit involving an Iranian family in the United States. *The Nuclear Baby* evokes a surreal and nightmarish vision of the future after the nuclear holocaust, in which past, present, and future are mixed and universal issues of life on earth, exile, and deterritorialization are worked out. *The Suitors* centers on the life of a young recent emigre woman who loses her husband to a police SWAT team in New York City and who must painfully struggle to negotiate a new life and identity in exile, as well as fending off a host of persistent suitors.

A fourth subgenre, transnational cinema, made by hyphenated Iranians, does not necessarily deal with Iranian issues but with universal issues of love and (dis)placement. *Utopia* focuses on the painful lives of a group of prostitutes in Germany while *A Little Stiff* centers on the unceasing efforts of a young man (played by the Iranian-American director himself) pursuing a girlfriend who continually rejects him.

Exile engenders an "exile genre" of cinema that has its own themes, narrative conventions, and iconography. I will confine myself here to three of its dominant themes: claustrophobia, transformation in the status of women, and obsession with chiefly conservative politics.

A sense of claustrophobia pervades the world view, mise-en-scène, shot composition, and plot development of many of the films. These are films of retrenchment in that they portray a community and a mindset under siege, closed off to the host society not only physically but symbolically. Like televisual construction, exilic cinema often foregrounds Iran and effaces or pushes the host society into the background, as Parviz Sayyad, director of *The Mission*, grandiloquently states: "[Milos] Forman wasn't obligated to his culture like I am. I am obsessed. I want to open the windows and show the world what has happened to us in Iran" (*Iran Times*, June 14, 1985, p.15). Home, especially the Islamic government, openly disrupts the diegesis and the narrative in exile films, while the host society beyond Sayyad's window acts as a threat barely held at bay as it continually hovers at both the psychic borders and the cinematic frame edges. In this case, television and cinema in exile resonate with each other, not against each other.

Many of the exile films show characters locked in claustrophobic relationships. Occasionally this results from an intense personal search for companionship (*The Suitors, A Little Stiff*) or from contamination of the personal with the political, whereby an agent hired by the Islamic government in Iran manages to disrupt the loving family relationship in exile (*The Mission, Veiled Threat, Face of the Enemy*). In *The Nuclear Baby* a male "dream terrorist" is hired to invade the dream of a pregnant woman in order to create a nightmare for her. A major portion of the film is devoted to the relationship of this terrorist and his victim. These relationships involve struggles for power, played out in narratives characterized by the trope of the hunt: the lover seeks the loved one with the same insistence and intensity that an assassin or a kidnapper pursues his or her victim. The formulation of relationships as pursuits or hunts might be an expression of the exile condition, which for some of the directors and their native audiences is fed by fear of either persecution by agents sent from Iran or the threatening culture of the host society. This pessimistic vision parallels the point of view of Iranian writers in exile discussed previously. Unable to return and unwilling to assimilate, the filmmakers are haunted and hunted by the homeland and they are threatened and lured by the host society.

Claustrophobia also pervades the mise-en-scène and shot composition in these movies—most of the action in *Checkpoint* occurs in a bus caught in a no-man's-land at the Canadian border; *The Guests of Hotel Astoria* unreels in the closed spaces of the hotel of the title; and much of *Face of the Enemy* consists of flashbacks of the American to his captivity in Iran or of the scenes of the captivity of the Iranian woman in the United States. The action in much of *The Nuclear Baby* takes place not only indoors, in the claustrophobic spaces of a technological society, but inside the head of a pregnant woman. Two characters wear confining face masks in a long sequence of the film. Technical difficulties and a low budget could account for a closed configuration of space and shot composition, but one cannot discount the siege mentality that sets in as an initial reaction to the liminality and indeterminacy of life in exile. Closing up the self is a theme that pervades both the television programs and the films produced in exile.

For Iranian exiles, the cage and the suitcase have become symbols of exile. The caged bird appears in the lyrics of songs, in television programs, and in films. *The Suitors*, for example, draws numerous parallels between a captured sheep being readied for slaughter, a Persian cat confined to an airline carrying cage, and the female protagonist caught in the snare of relentlessly persistent suitors. Being caught in confining spaces and relationships denotes claustrophobia and paralysis but it also augurs the possibility of freedom from them—an impulse that drives much of the narrative of *The Suitors*. The suitcase became an even stronger symbol of exile not only because it may contain souvenirs from the homeland or may denote travel and living a provisional life but also because it connotes a pervasive sense of being closed in, profound deprivation, and diminution of one's possibilities in the world. The suitcase became such a multiplex symbol for Iranians as a result of a tragic and sensational story in the early 1980s involving a young Iranian couple who had recently married. The husband was a permanent U.S. resident but his wife, who was in Europe, was not. Because of the so-called hostage crisis, the U.S. government had tightened the entry of Iranians into the country to the point of harassment. Unsuccessful in obtaining a visa for his wife, the desperate husband attempted to smuggle her into the United States inside a suitcase. Upon arrival in the San Francisco airport, however, he discovered that his wife has been asphyxiated and crushed to death. Unable to break the bad news to her family and devastated by the enormity of the disaster, he committed suicide. This story became a *cause célèbre* in the Iranian popular media for

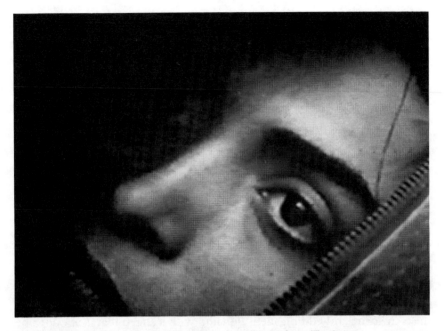

Fig. 5. Claustrophobic space: Maryam inside the suitcase, from *The Suitors*.

some time, and years later it was restaged, albeit with a different ending, in *The Suitors*. Despite the changed ending, the film recreates the sense of claustrophobia effectively. As the suitcase containing the woman (Maryam) is being carried by a conveyor belt in its slow journey toward the aircraft, the screen goes black. We are inside the suitcase and can hear the woman's troubled breathing and her quiet desperation, which builds into a panic. At that point, few exiles would fail to grasp the connotations of constriction and diminution that exile spawns.

That claustrophobic spaces, narratives, and aesthetics are informed by the condition of exile and not by the subject matter is evident when we notice similar claustrophobic tendencies in Iranian films of the transnational variety, which are not about Iranian topics. Shahid Saless's fascinating film *Utopia* takes place in the confining spaces of a house of prostitution in Germany run by a ruthless male whoremaster. Although the life of the female prostitutes inside the house is miserable, demeaning, and violent, they are bound to it, and when one of them dares to leave to experience the outside, she returns disappointed. The order and certainty that confinement represented for her far surpassed the chaos and uncertainty that freedom offered. The dominant spatial and compositional principle of *A Little Stiff* is claustrophobic spaces such as elevators, empty hallways, and closed doors. Claustrophobia both expresses and itself constitutes life in exile.

Another condition of exile is sudden transformation of social position and status. While this often entails a lowering of status in the new environment, it is not always so—particularly for women, as traditional patriarchal family structures are destabilized. *The Mission, The Suitors,* and *The Guests of Hotel Astoria* all feature strong roles and performances by women. In *The Mission*, the sister-in-law of the Savak agent pursued by the Islamist assassin emotionally and intellectually disarms the assassin and undermines his belief in both his mission and in the Islamic regime in Iran. Although the latter two films are centrally focused on women, they posit a dear price for the liberation and prominence of their female characters. In *The Guests of Hotel Astoria*, the female protagonist is determined to do whatever must be done to emigrate to the United States. Despite her obvious strengths, however, she is seen as a victim. Her determination and grace under degrading conditions are written as insufficient— she must perish in order to make possible her husband's emigration.

In *The Suitors* the woman is initially posited as a victim, and in deft mise-en-scène and editing she is equated with a sheep that is about to be slaughtered. Soon, however, the victimized woman surpasses her condition; in fact, exile and the loss of a patriarchal husband empower her, and in a manner reminiscent of Chantal Ackerman's excruciating film, *Jeanne Dielman 23 Quai du commerce, 1080 Bruxelles* (1975), she murders an overzealous and overpersistent suitor. This thrusts her into profound liminality and indeterminacy: not belonging to either Iranian or American societies, she is a free agent, who can potentially be attached to any firm base or to none at all. Politics of the homeland infuses the lives and discourses of recent exiles, and films reflect this theme. Interethnicity is suppressed, national politics foregrounded. Although a number of exile films are made by ethnic Iranians (Jews, Armenians, and Baha'is), none of these emphasize interethnic issues or single out ethnic minorities as protagonists. In general, filmmakers in exile are politically complicit with the dominant view in America, both among Iranians and Americans, which considers the Islamic Republic of Iran to be a "terrorist" state and Iran a wasteland. Such a belief is either encoded at the level of the plot (*The Mission, Veiled Threat, Face of the Enemy*) or in the dialogue and the narration (*Checkpoint, The Guests of Hotel Astoria*). Such highly partisan views tend to suppress differences within Iran itself and comfort the exiles, but they are dangerous because, like televisual fetishization, they blind exiles to the full force of changes that are occurring both in Iran and in exile.

Obsession with home can become a serious drawback to the development of Iranian filmmakers in exile. Intense focus on Iran tends to produce provincial films, limited to their Iranian themes and audiences. The dilemmas for exile filmmakers are these: Who do they speak for? To whom should they speak? To whom should they turn for financing? How should they distribute their films? Where and with whom should their allegiances rest? Until very recently the majority had opted to address chiefly their Iranian audiences by making films in Persian, subtitled in English, which required that the cast and the story be strictly Iranian. Zarindast's films (*Cat in a Cage* and *The Guns and the Fury*) and Shaibani's film (*Revolt*) are exceptions—they are formulaic exploitation films made for export to Third World countries, and they have American casts with a few Iranian actors who speak English.

As liminality is subsiding and the process of acculturation and acceptance of being in exile is consolidating, a shift in film production is taking place, with exile filmmakers producing films in English that feature mixed Iranian-American casts. This inevitably involves physical and mental relocation, from there to here, from politics of Iran to problems of exile. Often this demands a toning down of the political rhetoric of the films, even a depoliticization of sorts. It also means that filmmakers will have to be able to integrate the particular (Iranian) with the general (universal). Such shifts not only break the complicit politics of exiles but also entail other ramifications: New exile films will have to be judged by the same criteria as other films in this country, as technically well-made, money-making entertainment. According to these criteria, most have failed. Iranian filmmakers also run the risk of alienating their compatriots as their films begin to cast a closer, even critical, look on their own culture and the lifestyle of the Iranians abroad. As filmmakers begin to draw on their own experiences in exile, they keep alive their diversity in other terms—rather than explaining themselves and their culture to themselves, exile filmmakers may move to explain themselves and their culture to others. Finally, exile directors may shift their focus from Iranian issues to those unrelated (or not directly related) to Iran. Sohrab Shahid Saless, Marva Nabili, Jalal Fatemi, and Caveh Zahedi are the most successful in this regard.

The case of *The Suitors* demonstrates the complex reactions that moving in new directions might evoke in indigenous audiences. The film shows a group of Islamist Iranian expatriates in New York slaughtering a sheep in the bathtub of their apartment, in a traditional ritual honoring the arrival of a married couple from Iran. The blood from the slaughter, however, seeps into the apartment below, and a SWAT team attacks the premises on the assumption that there are terrorists inside. In the confusion, the newly arrived husband is killed. The rest of the film is the story of his young, attractive wife trying to rid herself of various persistent suitors, all of whom are close friends of her husband. While the film was well received critically in mainline American and European presses and was in commercial release in a number of American cities (unusual for Iranian films), the scenes of the slaughter in particular and of the callous pursuit of the woman in general seem to have touched a raw nerve in many Iranians. One reviewer criticized it for "self-humiliation." His argument can be summarized as follows: Iranians who in the past had humiliated America by taking Americans hostage and by burning the American flag are now humiliating themselves with this film, to appease Americans (Shafa 1989:86). In a letter to a newspaper, a reader accused the film of reinforcing the negative international image that the Islamic Republic's politics has created of Iranians as "barbarian," "cruel," "ignorant," "uneducated," and "uncivilized savages" (*Kayhan* [London] 12/7/1989:9). Such a reading contradicts the director's own aim to depict Iranians not as terrorists but as human beings (Dowlatabadi 1989:31). That the traditional customs of seeking a spouse and slaughtering animals are seen as savage and barbaric practices has more to do with their context than with their portrayal. When these indigenous practices are both produced (by the film) and viewed (by audiences) outside of their natural contexts, they become defamiliarized and devalued, especially if viewers themselves are defensive about those practices. In these and similar criticisms of *The Suitors* one detects also a sense of betrayal at the director's exposure and implied criticism of certain aspects of Iranian culture and moral values to outsiders. In this the director seems to have violated two of the norms of Iranian selfhood: a clear demarcation between self and other, and loyalty to the family and the insider group.

The controversy surrounding this film shows the tremendous burden that exilic and ethnic films must carry. Because they are so few and far between, these films are expected to contain the entire culture, and in the most positive light. As a result, any criticism of indigenous cultural values by the film is likely to be seen as a mark of disloyalty, and as feeding the fires of ethnic and racial intolerance. The dilemma for immigrant filmmakers, therefore, is to balance ethnic loyalty with personal integrity.[13]

## Salons and Associations

Voluntary organizations among Iranian exiles (see Table 5) produce a degree of cohesiveness, fixity, routinization, and security for them, whose lives during the liminal phase are fluid and lack to a large extent the traditional social structures of the homeland. These voluntary gatherings must be seen in the context of the specific demography of Iranian exiles, which, as discussed in chapter 1, enjoys an unusually high degree of professional skills, education, financial resources, rate of self-employment, and ethnoreligious heterogeneity. Each of these factors has provided an opportunity to establish group affiliations. The Iranian salon (*dowreh*) system is an informal method of creating such webs of affiliation. It refers to gatherings of small groups of people, usually not more than 20, who come together for a common purpose and meet regularly, often on a rotating basis in the homes of the members. The common interest that binds the group may be the members' childhood city or their high school or university. It may be based on political, professional, and business affiliations. It also may involve shared religious, ethnic, or subcultural ties. Literary and intellectual interests provide a connection, as do sex and gender politics, which result in mixed-sex or single-sex salons.[14] Finally, familial affiliations are a major source of commonality. Marvin Zonis summarizes the salons' multiple functions among the Iranian elite:

> They [salons] are used to provide fallback positions, to offer the elite a variety of access points through which to approach the formal structure of political power, to multiply the elite's communication patterns, to provide contact with a diversity of individuals within and without the elite, and to establish reciprocal obligations with as many individuals representing as diverse sectors of Iranian life as possible. All such motives, in short, center around the acquisition of a sense of security. (1971:241)

But salons are not solely a feature of urban life, limited to the elite. They operate not only in provinces and in villages in Iran but also in exile, especially in Los Angeles, where the size and diversity of the population foster such formation.

Despite the divergent cultures of Iran and the United States, there is a marked similarity between salons in Iran and those in exile, not only in that they provide psychological security and foster mutual interests, but also in their organization. Salons are usually very festive occasions, offering warm and social language, varieties of food and drink, poetry reading, and musical entertainment. Thus both the body and the brain are nourished. Seen in this light, salons are what Roy Mottahedeh has characterized them as: "the truly Iranian organs of rumination and taste" (1985:271).

For the salons to continue in exile, however, they have had to undergo change. They appear to have increased in number and variety and have become more public, taking place in restaurants as well as in private homes. The restaurants Khayyam and Golestan in Los Angeles have featured weekly poetry reading nights that are similar to salons in that a regular group of friends and like-minded people frequent them to share meals and their favorite classical poetry. The gatherings are not limited to those thus closely affiliated, however; other paying customers, too, can partake of them. Interestingly, these public salons are sometimes organized by a smaller core of members, who hold private salons of their own at a member's house.

Here is an instance of a deterritorialized group adapting and retrofitting an existing social institution from its former homeland so as to reterritorialize itself.

More public and collective venues for reterritorialization are the intellectual and literary societies in exile, some of which are offshoots of salons. Since their rapid and massive emigration into Southern California, Iranian activists have been organizing seminars and conferences about Iran on college and university campuses throughout Southern California. Two factors have coalesced to make the first decade of exile productive culturally. The first is the revolution, which caused the exodus for most Iranians in the first place, and the second is the fact of exile itself. They have spurred an intense curiosity, a passion for knowledge, and a cultural dynamism that achieves great intellectual and artistic zeniths as well as nadirs of pessimism and self-doubt—in which are seen the impulses for celebration and celibacy associated with liminality.

In a number of instances I have shown how elements of exilic popular culture work against or with each other. There is a further tension between the exile mass media and the discourse that intellectuals produce in private salons or in public seminars, lectures, and conferences. In a sense, the conflict is between the mass popular media, with their concern with the concrete and commercial aspects of life, and the more private "republic of scholars," with its pursuit of such a highly general goal as knowledge.

At UCLA most of the exile cultural societies have organized programs designed to reevaluate Iranian art, cinema, literature, language, culture, politics, nationality, feminism, identity, and history. (Table 6 lists the names of these societies and summarizes the types of activities they have sponsored in the 1980s.)

Typically, these lengthy and elaborate functions are celebratory, and they take place over the weekend, starting in the early evening and lasting four or more hours. The general format consists of some of the following elements: prepared Iranian meals; entertainment programs (film screenings, slide-tape presentations, plays, dance and music performances); lectures and poetry readings; and book, audiocassette, and periodicals sales. The atmosphere is congenial rather than combative. As a general rule, the films these associations show are short-subject fiction or documentaries about Iran. Directors are often invited to participate in question-and-answer sessions. Some of the music and dance performances are organized by ethnic Iranians, but often ethnicity is submerged and exists only as a subtext of politics.

In addition to regularly scheduled meetings and celebrations of national holidays such as Noruz, these functions may be held in response to current events in Iran, such as executions and earthquakes, or to commemorate anniversaries of historic developments such as the rise of the guerrilla movements during the Shah's reign. The majority of the sponsoring societies have been student-based and on the left politically, with a few acting as official organs of factions working against the Islamic Republic.

With few exceptions, these societies have been ephemeral. They come into being because of the personal and political needs of their members and the political exigencies of the time, and they undergo major transformations as those needs and exigencies change. An organization may undergo a number of changes in its lifetime (this is particularly true of those that are most radical). The women's organization *Anjoman-e Farhangi-ye Zanan* (Cultural Society of Women), for example, underwent a series of metamorphoses. It began as *Komiteh-ye Defa' az Hoquq-e Demokratik-e Zanan* (Committee for the Defense of the Democratic Rights of Women) affiliated with the *Fada'ian-e Khalq* organization. It soon dropped the affiliation and later split into two groups: *Anjoman-e Defa' az Hoquq-e Demokratik-e Zanan* (Society for the Defense of the Democratic Rights of Women) and *Tashakol-e Mostaqqal-e Zanan dar Jonub-e Kalifornia* (Independent Formation of Women in Southern California). After a while, the former group adopted its current name, *Anjoman-e Farhangi-ye Zanan*. In this series of transformations, the organization's movement away from the political sphere and toward the cultural domain is evident. As this example demonstrates, the evolution of the surviving organizations has not been cosmetic but transformational, involving ideological, political, and theoretical, as well as personal, struggles of the members.

Perhaps the most important goal of these societies is to gain culturally the ground lost politically by the left during and after the revolution. In exile, leftist intellectuals became aware that "culture," even popular culture, is one, or perhaps *the* one, arena for political struggle that must not be vacated to the supporters of the monarchy. This is a radical reorientation among those on the left, from the previous monolithic theories of mass culture critique and cultural populism to the present Gramscian conception of culture as an active arena for struggle over hegemony.[15] Exile and revolution, and the personal soul-searching and political reevaluation they engendered, have taught many on the left that hegemony cannot be imposed by the political society but instead must be won in the civil society. It is to that end that these intellectual and cultural gatherings are organized, and it is in this light, for example, that the shift in focus in the Fada'ian's women's organization from the political to the cultural must be seen. The same is true of the turn of the left and the so-called elite culture toward popular culture, as is evident in the types of events they have sponsored. The predominance of the intellectual left and feminist organizations among exile societies sponsoring intellectual discourse tells us that these are two groups that have been particularly affected by revolution and deterritorialization, requiring fundamental reevaluation and reconceptualization of identity and ideology. A third group undergoing major identity crisis is the rightist supporters of the monarchy, but this group for a long time deluded itself either by acknowledging no crisis in its ideology at all or by engaging in comforting conspiracy theories. Its main domain was the mass media of the exiles, but lately it has begun a more serious intervention in the intellectual sphere.

## Music, Musical Performances, and Music Videos

Music has been an early and favored mode for exilic communication, preservation of cultural heritage, retention of popular memory, and incorporation into the dominant host culture. Immediately after exiles' arrival in the United States, the classical and pop music recorded in Iran prior to the 1979 revolution was duplicated and distributed. As exile wore on, however, first the established artists who had emigrated and later a new crop of emerging talent began recording music here, turning Southern California into "a Persian Motown." Some fifty entertainers and performers and a half-dozen producers and distributors of tapes and cassettes are listed in the 1991 *Iranian Directory Yellow Pages*.[16] There are no accurate or current statistics on sales figures. An early report by a major recording company, Pars Video, claimed that although its production of audiocassettes did not typically go beyond 6,000 copies, its audience worldwide exceeded one million (*Jam-e Jam*, June 1987, pp. 28–29). This latter figure cannot include listeners inside Iran, where pirated copies of exile-produced cassettes are sold by local entrepreneurs.

A number of producers of music and television programs have cited this traffic in their tapes as an indication of their political power. This cannot be corroborated. Indeed, the availability in Iran of music videos, edited versions of television programs, and audiocassettes produced in exile does not constitute a deep penetration into the dominant culture in the Islamic Republic. Some researchers have cast doubt on the relevance of exile media for the politics of the home front (Sreberny-Mohammadi and Mohammadi 1985, 1991b). If politically ineffective across borders, however, the exile media, especially pop music, are culturally influential in Iran, whose own pop music has been practically silenced. Los Angeles-based Iranian pop stars are well known in Iran and they seem to enjoy great popularity with certain segments of the population. As part of the crosscultural war between the United States and Iran, Voice of America radio in its Persian broadcasts not only devotes a good deal of time to playing exile pop music but also at times features live interview call-in shows with exile entertainers. Fans from all over Iran have apparently called to talk with their favorite stars, to the chagrin of the official press in Iran.[17]

The movement of music between the United States and Iran, however, is not a one-way traffic but a two-way flow. If Iranian exiles export pop music to Iran, the Iranian music business exports classical Persian music to the United States. In recent years, this type of music has flourished in Iran and its tapes are highly sought after and readily available in exile. In fact, well-known singers and performers of classical music have been invited to the United States, and they have given several concerts across the country to packed houses. No pop singer in exile has been able to go back home to perform, though, because of the association the Islamic government has established between pop music and moral corruption and undesirable Western influences, and the accusation made against exile entertainers of "collaboration" with the official Pahlavi culture prior to the revolution. The general antigovernment attitude of the exile performers, and their ethnoreligiosity (particularly Baha'is and Jews, who have been persecuted by the Islamic government) also prevent their return.

Iranian pop music in exile is a hybrid, mixing disco, Latin, reggae, and rap backbeat with Persian 6/8 rhythm, percussion, and melodies. The most common arena for the performance of this music in exile is the concert circuit, which allows thousands of Iranian teenagers and adults to bask in the loud, tumultuous, and, by turn, nostalgic and alluring atmosphere pervading the concert halls. The idea in these spaces is to feel the music with the skin instead of hearing it with the ears. Synesthesia and rhythm are more important than words; the texture of the sounds and the buzz of the senses supersede all else. This same interest in the texture and surface of things, a postmodern phenomenon, is present in television ads and music videos (which tend to overuse image processing techniques).

More mainstream stars as well as some pop stars perform in a half-dozen nightclubs that cater to Iranians in Southern California. Some of these are no more than dingy dim-lit restaurants with loud sound systems. Each night's show consists of a series of performances by individual singers backed up often by the nightclub's resident live band. In the larger, more established nightclubs (such as Cabaret Tehran and Baccarat Cabaret), elaborate shows by Iranian and sometimes by Arab, Armenian, Israeli, and

Fig. 6. Television ad for Club Tehran, a nightclub.

other nationalities are presented. Both the concerts and the nightclubs are heavily promoted on Iranian television, radio, and in the popular press. Without the products of the exile music industry and their advertisements, Iranian exile radio, television, and periodicals could not have flourished.

A third venue for pop singers and entertainers is the private party circuit, particularly those that celebrate rites of passage such as weddings, birthdays, bat mitzvahs, and bar mitzvahs. Well-known singers charge a steep fee for their performances in concerts and private parties, demanding up to $10,000 per show (Zinder 1991:7).

One function of popular culture in exile is to provide rituals and events such as concerts, calendrical festivals, nightclub acts, and private parties that mark the boundary between the exiles and the host society. The very fact of staging indigenous rituals and performances within the social context of a foreign country affords the exiles an opportunity to celebrate their difference from the host culture by playing their private, ethnic, and national symbolic forms against those of the host. Moreover, these cultural events not only reduce isolation and loneliness but also promote ethnic solidarity and integration, helping the exiles find new friends and lovers.

Iranian performers, particularly pop music stars, have begun producing and distributing their materials on a variety of media: audiocassettes, laser compact disks, and music videos. Music videos in particular have transformed the celibate, tragic representations of home and the past into much desired and celebratory commodities for the consumers in exile. Indeed, what is responsible for this transformation is not only their entertaining contents and danceable tunes but also the intertextual promotion of the videos and the stars who appear in them. Interconnectedness and intertextuality are characteristics of popular cultures everywhere. In exile, three chief factors account for the creation of an intertextually dense popular culture: economics, internal ethnicity, and politics.

Material-starved exile television is very dependent for nourishment on music in its various forms—a cost-effective time-filler. The videos, usually consisting of a catchy dance number or a nostalgic song, accompanied lately by striking visuals (inspired by MTV), are repeatedly shown. Film clips from musical concerts and music videos, news reports about pop concerts and new albums, interviews with pop singers, and television ads for concerts, new albums, and new videos also form a major part of many of the television shows. Periodicals are filled with such materials and many of them carry full-page pictures of performers on their front cover, week after week. Music videos and their corollary promotional materials account for, perhaps, a good third to half of all exile TV programming. Some programs (*Jong-e Bamdadi*) do not play any music, others (*Jam-e Jam*) exceed this ratio, and still others (*Diyar*) are completely devoted to music and its promotion. On the majority of the shows that do play music, intertextuality is so dense that at times it is difficult to distinguish the music from its promotion.

Internal ethnicity also feeds into the passion for intertextuality. This is because pop music is heavily peopled by Muslim and Armenian performers backed up by Jewish businessmen who produce and distribute the products. In addition, the Jews also are the most active music-buying, concert-going, and party-giving group among Iranians, perhaps partly due to their financial success and their very high self-employment rate. As the director of the Iranian Information Center states:

> Most Moslems seem to just want to forget about their culture and assimilate as quickly as possible. But [many] Jews give lots of parties, weddings and bar mitzvahs, and want to dance to Persian music. (quoted in Zinder 1992:46–47)

The Muslims are not as assimilationist as he claims, but clearly Jewish Iranians use music more than any other subgroup as a vehicle for preserving both their internal ethnicity and Iranian national identity. As major producers, promoters, and consumers, Jewish Iranians are particularly powerful in setting musical trends and in the success or failure of entertainers. This type of control can support a marginal, subcultural music and rescue it from oblivion, but it can also squelch creativity by limiting diversity.

Politically, since entertainers in general and Iranian interethnics in particular are opposed to the Islamic government in Iran and most of them are also royalists, the crossfertilization of music and television is undergirded by internal ethnicity and royalist politics as well. The intertextual relationship between Iranian exile music and television on the one hand and interethnicity and royalist politics on the other looks something like this: one producer, who is Jewish and a royalist, produces and distributes music videos, television programs, audiocassettes, and has a financial stake in the revenues generated from concerts. As a result, such a producer tends to employ music and music videos intertextually on his television shows so that each use of the video (as a program segment, ad, news report or promo about a concert or a new album) promotes one or the other part of the same enterprise in which he has an interest. Such a dense horizontal and vertical interconnection among television, music, and concert producers and promoters accounts for the royalists' (and to some extent Jewish) dominance over important segments of Iranian popular culture in exile.

A chief dilemma facing exilic popular culture is this: if it attempts to remain true to an essentialist view of the culture of the homeland, it will become stagnant and eventually evaporate like spilled water on sand; on the other hand, if it accommodates too much and too rapidly, it will lose all the differences that set it apart, causing it to die from dissolution into the dominant. For Iranian exiles, as for many other marooned people, syncretism has proven to be a viable answer to the dilemma.

Popular culture in the United States is not monolithic; it is a constellation of competing minicultures which are themselves no more monolithic, authentic, or hermetic than the popular culture as a whole. The exiles as a subculture produce in relation to the host society a popular culture that is dense, multifaceted, and dynamic, by means of which they construct both an overarching national Iranian and a subcultural Iranian identity. On the one hand, this popular culture is informed by politics, themes, language, and products of the homelands and, on the other hand, it borrows syncretically from the host society's technology, consumer ideology, marketing techniques, and forms and practices of narration and aesthetics. The fluctuations in Iranian popular culture and its transformation from political to cultural reflect and are a constitutive part of the exiles' ongoing dialectics of *authenticity and descent* and *identity and con-*

sent.[18] The delicate balance between home and host cultures cannot be maintained forever.

Liminality is flexible but fragile. As it recedes for many exiles, the infusion of the host into the syncretic mix becomes stronger, gradually replacing much of the original contents with consumer ideology and products. This is because popular cultures are structurally linked with and promote consumerism. If the exilic popular culture so successfully bleeds into the mainstream culture, the host society's popular culture, which depends on novelty, change, and crossfertilization for its continuing vitality, is likely to incorporate it by aestheticizing and commodifying exilic difference and otherness into a nonthreatening ethnic and multicultural gloss.

# 3
# Structure and Political Economy of Exilic Television

## Producers and Production

*Parviz Kardan, producer and host of* Shah-re Farang, *had been a well-known actor and entertainer in Iran before his emigration first to England then to the United States. I interviewed him on a warm mid-morning in his shoe shop. He was the owner of and at the time the sole salesman in the store, located in a nondescript mall near the Los Angeles airport. The mall itself was eerily empty of customers, as was the shop, lined with rows of nondescript shoes. During my two-hour interview only one customer came, and he left empty-handed. Kardan spoke of the plays he had staged in London and bemoaned the crass commercialization of exile television. His weekly show did not generate sufficient income, forcing him to make ends meet by running the shoe shop. Television, his love, had to be his sideline.*

*My interview with Hamid Shabkhiz, producer and host of* Iran, *was set for late at night after the airing of his nightly show. It was a warm California night cooled by a gentle breeze. We met at his TV studio, which was also his house, a large ranch-style home in the San Fernando valley with a swimming pool in the back. He greeted me at the door and took me through his control room out into the backyard where I met his wife and his advertising agent. The lights from the rippling pool cast a variegated blue shade everywhere. The atmosphere was congenial and informal. Fruit and soft drinks were*

*offered and I interviewed Shabkhiz while his wife in the control room
compiled a weekly version of* Iran *for syndication to other U.S. cities
(or as Shabkhiz would call them, provinces,* shahrestanha). *We were
often interrupted by frantic phone calls, taken at poolside or in the
studio. While Shabkhiz was on the phone, I interviewed Daryush
Mirahmadi, the ad man. High-pitched voices from the editing
machines shuttling forward and backward further punctuated our
conversations. One or two customers, bringing artwork for their ads,
came and went. Television was being made poolside: Our conversation, the editing of the syndicated show, and the business dealings
continued well into the night.*

*Homa Ehsan, producer and host of* Didar, *lived in an upscale security condo in Orange County—in one of those large gated communities (read "stealth communities") that have sprung up everywhere in
southern California. Her living room, where her show was usually
taped, was a typical ethnic room, neat, decorated with all kinds of
memorabilia from the homeland, from far-away family members,
and from a professional life in radio and television before emigration. She had just been forced to take her show off the air and she
was bitter about that, the sexism of the TV producers, and the loss of
a forum for exposing the fast-assimilating Iranian children to the
"authentic" culture of the homeland. Our conversation went on over
a working lunch in her kitchen.*

*Although many television shows are produced in studios, making
television programs in exile is often a home-bound activity, like their
viewing. Television production is part of the private lives of the
producers. As a result, exile television inscribes more fully than does
mainstream television the lives of its makers.*

## Minority Television

To maximize the size of its audience mainstream television has traditionally emphasized commonalities. Recent developments, however, have
encouraged specialization and audience segmentation, making the industry particularly responsive to ethnic, transnational, and exilic differences.
These developments include consolidation of cable television and its pro-
vision of lease-access to clients, including ethnic and exile communities,
and government regulation of the industry, such as requirements to provide public access and minority ownership of stations. To this set of industrial and regulatory measures must be added the availability of inexpensive but sophisticated technologies, which tend to "democratize"

television production and reception. Finally, the global news and information networks, program packaging consortia such as SCOLA, and videos imported from former homelands have created a very complex and intensified transnational traffic that feeds the nonmainstream form of television under study here.

These and other factors have enabled commercially driven television in the United States to surpass cinema as a vehicle of both the expression and the formation of minority identities. In Southern California, channel 18 (KSCI-TV), an independent station that dubs itself the "international channel," provides round-the-clock programming in some 16 languages produced by various diasporas in the United States or imported from their home countries.[1] There are also a number of local cable companies that air locally produced minority programs on a lease-access or public access basis. While there are many stations that target a specific ethnic or national group, KSCI-TV, by airing programs in so many languages, provides the most diverse ethnic and linguistic menu of any station in Los Angeles (and for that matter in the country).

In the following analysis, the menu of "minority television" is divided into three categories: ethnic, transnational, and exilic TV. Although these categories are flexible, permeable, at times simultaneous, and can merge under certain circumstances, there are distinguishing features that set them apart.

Ethnic Television refers to television programs primarily produced in the host country by long-established indigenous minorities. Black Entertainment Television (BET) is the primary example of this category, much of whose programming originates and centers on life and times in the United States. The homeland for these programs is ultimately located here and now, not over there and then. If its programming inscribes struggles, they are usually intracultural (within the United States), not intercultural. A good portion of the Spanish-language networks' programs also fall within this category.

Transnational Television is fed primarily by products imported from the homeland or those produced by American and multinational media concerns. Korean, Japanese, and Chinese programs fit this category. These programs locate their homeland outside the United States and they push to the background the drama of acculturation and resistance.

In some cases, reliance on imports gives a foreign government friendly to the U.S. administration direct access to program time, raising legal and political issues about unwarranted use of American airwaves for propaganda purposes (Holley 1986). The Korean-language broadcasts, for example, are produced by Korean Broadcasting Service in South Korea, a government-controlled body, and they are imported and distributed for broadcast in the United States by the government-owned Korean Television Enterprises. Station time is also subsidized by the government. As a result of such outside assistance, Korean producers of both radio and television programs have been able to block-book much of the prime-time hours of multiethnic stations in Los Angeles, pushing out other ethnic competitors. Spanish-language national networks in the United States (Univision, Telemundo, and Galavision) can be considered to be primarily transnational and only partly ethnic in that they are by and large produced by American or foreign multinational corporations and much of their programming is imported from Mexico, Venezuela, and Brazil.[2]

Exilic Television is by definition produced by exiles living in the host country as a response to and in parallel with their own transitional and provisional status. Television programs produced by Iranians, Arabs, and Armenians fall within this classification. Such programs are often produced by small-time individual producers, not by media conglomerates of the home or host societies. They tend to encode and foreground collective and individual struggles for authenticity and identity, deterritorialization and reterritorialization. Although they are relative newcomers, Iranians have been perhaps the most active users of television among all the minorities in this country. In fact, with the exception of Hispanic programming, Persian-language television tops all other locally produced transnational and exilic programming in the Los Angeles area. With the exception of *Aftab*, all Iranian programs aired in the area are produced outside Iran by entrepreneurs who oppose the Islamic government there.

Even though ethnic television, particularly BET and Jewish Television Network, is primarily focused on the culture, concerns, and personalities of a segment of the population in the United States, it can potentially reach mainstream audiences because it is spoken in English. As such, it is a form of "broadcasting." Transnational and exilic television, on the other hand, are examples of "narrowcasting" or "lowcasting" because they are aired in foreign languages.

In the process of developing infrastructure and experimenting with programming, a new exile genre of television has evolved, whose analysis will shed light on television's role as a facilitator of syncretic acculturation. On the one hand, exilic television creates a symbolic communitas in exile, and helps to consolidate collective solidarity based on descent; on the other hand, it procures cultural capital for the host society by reproducing its consumerist ideology, thereby obtaining the consent of its audiences to dominant values.

## Iranian Exilic Television in Los Angeles

The first Iranian TV program aired in exile was a thirty-minute program called *Haftegi-ye Pars* (Pars weekly), only one episode of which was aired in 1978 by channel 52 (KVEA-TV). The first regularly scheduled program was *Iranian*, which began in March 1981 as a thirty-minute weekly show, and later expanded to one hour. This program is also the longest continuous Persian-language Iranian program abroad, lasting to the present in the same time slot. Since these initial efforts, a total of 62 regularly scheduled programs have been aired, with the current number standing at 26 shows, totaling over 17 hours of airtime per week (Table 7). All of them are produced in Los Angeles.[3]

Although there has been a steady annual increase in the number of new shows (see Table 7), there has been considerable fluctuation in the fate of exile TV programs. Of the 62 regularly scheduled shows some 36 have disappeared. Every few months a television program dies to be replaced by one or more new shows—sometimes made by the same producers. This televisual ebb and flow is an index of the fluidity of life in exile—it parallels the ups and downs experienced by the other components of exilic popular culture. The fluidity is also related to the instability of funding sources and reliance on market forces. This fluidity hides a stable core of TV programs (*Iranian, Jam-e Jam, Jonbesh-e Iran, Sima-ye Ashna*), which are the oldest and perhaps the most watched shows, lasting for a decade or more. There are also a number of shows that have been on the air for more than four years (*Iran, Midnight Show, Jong-e Bamdadi, Pars,* and *Sobh-e Ruz-e Jom'eh*).

If exile TV was only regressive and nostalgic, as most Iranian intellectuals claim, one would expect its use to lessen with prolongation of exile and gradual acculturation. That the number of new TV programs has steadily increased and several programs have prospered indicates that exile TV is also an instrument of incorporation and acculturation, not just exilic identification. For a variety of sociopolitical reasons a great many Iranians seem finally to have accepted the physical fact of exile and reconciled themselves to a long period, perhaps a lifetime, of stay in the United States, prompting a gradual shift toward the host and away from the home country.[4]

Exilic television has been instrumental in both ushering in this shift and reflecting it. This is evident in that the authoritarian, univocal discourse of Iran and the past, the notion of the audience as an undifferentiated group of exiles, the rigid magazine format of programs, and the limited distribution system—which were so characteristic of the early period of communitas—have all begun to give way to certain structural features that organize the symbolic, ideological, and social milieu of exile in such a way as to encourage incorporation into the dominant universe of American consumer capitalism and its postmodern mode of cultural production. The chief direction that this new structuration has taken is toward rationalization of the production and distribution infrastructure and commodification of audiences, TV products, discourses, and fetishes of home and host cultures.

## Production, Transmission, and Distribution Structures

### Production

A number of TV producers have compared their output in exile to the output of the gigantic National Iranian Radio and Television (NIRT) during the heyday of its operation before the revolution, when it reportedly employed over 10,000 people. These producers (Manuchehr Bibian and Nader Rafi'i among them) contend that despite its size, NIRT did not produce a majority of its own programming. This is partially true—in 1974, for example, 40 percent of televised programs on NIRT consisted of foreign imports (Naficy 1981:358). In addition to producing the remaining 60 percent, however, NIRT created many hours of very expensive programs—serials, documentaries, and feature films—and it was engaged in a vast multidimensional effort to encourage and showcase Iranian performing arts nationwide. NIRT's programs, therefore, cannot be compared hour for hour with the simple and inexpensive magazine-format shows made in exile.

Although the producers' claim is largely self-serving, it is illuminating from a structural point of view. NIRT, like the TV broadcasters in many Third World and (until recently) Eastern and even Western European countries, was a centralized state-sponsored entity with a monopoly of national production and transmission. As a result, market forces were not a major criterion for programming; national developmental policies were.[5] Thus television producers learned to operate in an environment that was largely cushioned from budgetary constraints, direct market forces, and public tastes. Their programs tended to reflect the policies of the central government and the personal tastes of their makers.[6]

In exile, however, the situation has reversed entirely. Television production and transmission are not centralized; they are decentralized, indeed atomized, with 37 different producers creating 62 regularly scheduled programs in nearly a dozen years. Because exile programs are commercially driven, moreover, the producers are forced to be responsive to market forces, public tastes, and advertising dollars, as a result of which there is keen competition among them for advertising and suitable air-time. Despite this fragmented and conflictual relationship at the level of producers, there is a common technical, artistic, and commercial infra-structure undergirding the Iranian exile television industry, giving it a cer-tain cohesiveness. This consists of production and advertising person-nel—advertising agents, calligraphers, graphic artists, photographers, camerapersons, tape editors, writers, and musicians—who work simul-taneously on a freelance basis with a number of producers. What keeps these professionals together is not their employment by a centralized state agency such as NIRT but their economic relationship in the civil society as freelance talents and clients. Thus the economic and political relation-ships between above-the-line personnel (the program makers) and those below the line (technicians and craftspeople) is markedly different in ex-ile. Indeed, it is the gradual replacement of hierarchical relationships by economic relationships that is responsible for rationalizing and profes-sionalizing exilic television, and for its functioning as a facilitator of as-similation.

Of course, economic activity seeks coalition, and it polarizes around wealth-producing nuclei, which in the case of exile TV has meant those producers who own their own production and editing facilities or who engage in brokerage of time—people whom producer Homa Ehsan calls "televisual godfathers."[7] These so-called godfathers not only produce their own programs but also assist others by providing them with facilities and services. Indeed, these are among the few producers who earn their living solely from their televisual activities.

### Local and National Transmission

To accommodate the increasing population and the diversity of pro-grams, and to position the audiences to receive advertisers' messages, a wide-ranging, advertising-driven schedule has emerged, supported by a proliferating Iranian business community. This schedule has grown from an exclusively weekend time slot containing a single thirty-minute pro-gram in 1981 to one that distributes 26 programs across all days and nights of a week in 1992, from early morning hours to past midnight. (Table 8 shows the broadcast schedule of all current Iranian programs in Los An-geles as well as the type of programming under which they can be classi-fied.) With the exception of *Assyrian American Civic TV, Bet Naharin, Diyar, Iran, Melli, Mozhdeh, Negah*, and *Shahr-e Farang*, which are cur-rently cablecast, and *Aftab*, which is aired by KRCA-TV, all other pro-grams are broadcast by KSCI-TV.

It must be noted here that the reach of broadcasting stations and cable companies that air minority programs is not equal. A broadcasting station such as KSCI-TV, for example, has a larger area of coverage, reaching many more viewers than local cable companies. According to the station, KSCI-TV reaches over five million TV households in the Los Angeles and San Diego areas and is carried by more cable companies in Southern California than any other independent commercial UHF station. Because of high demand and increasing cost of transmission on broadcast TV, however, many minority producers are forced to cablecast their programs. To reach a wider audience in a number of communities, these producers are forced to lease time on multiple cable channels, a logistically burdensome and expensive process.

By now Iranian television programmers can target their audiences and deliver them to advertisers more frequently at more propitious prime-time hours than before. Saturdays and Sundays are not considered prime time for mainstream American television, but are considered so for ethnic, transnational, and exilic television because of the supposed extended-family structure of the immigrants and exiles, and their habit of collective viewing on those days.[8] This is reflected in KSCI-TV's rate card, which charges the highest amount for time on weekend nights, weeknights, and weekend days, respectively.

The broadcast schedule of exilic television is very fluid. KSCI's printed schedule in *TV Guide* is not very reliable. Century Cable's own lease-access channel in West Los Angeles, KCLA, does not publish a printed schedule because of its fluidity. Iranian programs have suffered from excessive changes in the schedule, often caused by the stations themselves, which seek to maximize their revenues by leasing time to the highest bidder. For example, in 1987 *Iran* was aired by KSCI-TV daily in the early evenings, then it was moved to twice a week in prime time, then to Sunday evenings, and finally canceled altogether. (Korean broadcasters, as previously noted, were able to block-book KSCI-TV's prime-time hours.) *Iran* was the first regularly scheduled show to be forced to move to cable and establish a beachhead there. Such a changing schedule interferes with audience loyalty and creates much anxiety among producers, emphasizing their exilic, not ethnic, status. As independent producers, most Iranian programmers must rely solely on advertising dollars from businesses to survive, although there are rumors that a few of them receive regular funding from factions opposing the Islamic Republic. Most of them must hold other jobs to make ends meet.

With the exception of early-morning news and magazine programs (*Sima-ye Ashna, Jong-e Bamdadi, Cheshmandaz*) and late night talk and phone-in shows (*Emshab ba Parviz, Harf va Goft*, and *Sokhani ba Ravanshenas*), which are usually transmitted or taped live, all other pro-

Fig. 7. *Jong-e Bamdadi*'s newscast.

grams are taped and edited, then transmitted. All live programs are transmitted from KSCI-TV's studios in Los Angeles. Taped programs must be
submitted hours before transmission to the TV stations or cable companies. Since Los Angeles is such a vast geographic area, it cannot be reached
by any single cable company; as a result, those wishing to reach simultaneously the entire area via cable must make multiple copies of their programs for transmission by multiple cable channels.

In the early 1990s, the parent company of KSCI-TV created the International Channel Network, the nation's first and only twenty-four-hour,
seven-day-a-week multilingual network, offering programs by satellite in
sixteen different languages. The network is fed by two sources: programs
imported from home countries, which constitute the bulk of the materials
(100 percent of Korean and 70 percent of Japanese programming), and
those produced in the United States. The network figures show that it
reaches some thirteen million ethnic households nationwide, and the network touts the affluence of this audience, particularly the Asians, by stating that it "delivers a loyal, upscale audience with a concentration of
households headed by a professional or independent businessperson."[9]

It urges both cable operators and advertisers nationwide to use the network to penetrate the traditionally hermetic non-English-speaking markets, which are increasing rapidly and "which have higher levels of disposable income than the U.S. population as a whole."

Among the many languages broadcast nationally by the International Channel Network are Iranian programs, including morning programs (*Sima-ye Azadi, Jong-e Bamdadi, Cheshmandaz*), late-night programs (*Emshab ba Parviz, Sokhani ba Ravanshenas, Harf va Goft*), and *Aftab*. Together, these add up to nearly 10 hours of Persian material per week, more programming than is done in Arabic, Russian, Hebrew, Italian, Armenian, German, and Hungarian. With the exception of *Aftab*, much of whose content is imported from Iran, all other Iranian programs are produced in Los Angeles and are transmitted live via satellite in their Los Angeles time slot. This means that morning programs aired at 7:30 A.M. and late-evening programs shown at 12:00 midnight in Los Angeles are seen on the East Coast at inconvenient time slots of 10:30 A.M. and 3 A.M., respectively.

The network has pushed its Asian audiences more than any of its other constituencies. As a result it has obtained national advertising for Asian programs from multinational companies such as AT&T, United Airlines, Bank of America, Mazda, Proctor & Gamble, Home Savings, Toyota, Japan Airlines, McDonald's, and Columbia Pictures. Iranian programs have so far received irregular advertising support from national American or Iranian businesses.

### Syndication

Iranian producers from the start created a syndication network which involved distributing tapes of their programs for rebroadcast by local stations in cities with large Iranian populations across the United States, Europe, and the Middle East. (Table 9 provides a list of programs produced in Los Angeles that are currently in tape syndication. The table does not include programs transmitted by satellite.) A few producers claim that after traveling a circuitous route their programs reach inside Iran. Manuchehr Bibian of *Jam-e Jam* TV, for example, stated in an interview with me that copies of his program find their way into Iran by way of Persian Gulf countries without his involvement, sometimes with the commercials and other offensive materials removed. Likewise, Ali Limonadi contended that tapes of his *Iranian* program are smuggled from Europe into Iran by truck drivers who remove the tape from its cassette casing during transit. Once in Iran, the cassettes are reassembled and duped. According to Limonadi, some parts of his program, such as the satirical skits critical of the Islamic government, are removed in Iran before duplication and distribution.

In terms of contents, syndicated programs differ to some extent from those originally aired in Los Angeles. In the case of *Jam-e Jam, Iranian*, and *Iran*, for example, the Los Angeles-based commercials and news are removed and replaced with either other program matters or blank spaces to be filled in by local producers and advertisers elsewhere. The newscasts present special problems for tape syndicators because news is so ephemeral. The usual solution is to create weekly roundups of recent news. Another difference between Los Angeles and syndicated programs is in their varying broadcast schedules. *Iran*, which is aired daily in Los Angeles, is broadcast on a weekly basis in other cities. This necessitates assembling a special weekly program for syndication.

## Political Economy of Exilic Television

### Time Brokerage Network

At the same time that exile television producers have expanded their national reach through satellite transmission and tape syndication, they have worked to deepen their penetration within the local Los Angeles market. A type of brokerage network has developed by which a time broker contracts for more than one broadcast slot from the television station airing Iranian programs. Now, the broker can place in that slot a program that he or she has produced, lease that time to someone else for a profit, or lease the time to another programmer but reserve the right to insert a few minutes of ads into that program. This is a very good way of generating additional income and is one factor that complicates the accounting of the producers' income. Of the four time-leasing brokers in 1989 (Naficy 1990b:211–12) only two have remained. Over the years, Parviz Qarib Afshar, certainly a televisual godfather, has been able to put together a strong time-leasing brokerage operation, renting airtime from KSCI-TV and leasing it for profit to the shows *Cheshmandaz, Emshab ba Parviz, Harf va Goft, Jonbesh-e Iran, Jong-e Bamdadi, Sima-ye Ashna*, and *Sokhani ba Ravanshenas*.

In general, because of the relative smallness of the capital involved and low audience figures, syndication and network organizations are extremely rudimentary and financially unstable. By opening themselves to the host society's mode of competitive consumer capitalism, Iranian producers and brokers have also made themselves vulnerable to the vagaries of the marketplace, which means rapid fluctuation in their own fortunes as well as in the schedules of their broadcasts. In 1988 *Omid*, managed by veteran broadcaster Iraj Gorgin, attempted to become a multimedia organization by producing a daily radio program (*Omid*), a quarterly magazine (*Faslnameh-ye Omid*), and a daily morning and daily evening TV show (*Jong-e Bamdadi* and *Omid*). The daily cost, however, of producing and airing the evening show ($1,500) continually exceeded its advertising revenue ($1,000), and it folded within a few months.[10]

Despite such inherent instability, over the years a solid unchanging core of programmers has flourished, chiefly by astute programming, obtaining national advertising, and combining leasing of production facilities and airtime with syndication and networking. Potentially this can enhance their earnings sufficiently to place them someday in a position to deliver large, heterogeneous ethnic audiences in a number of locations nationwide to what could become national Iranian-American advertisers. Qarib Afshar's time-leasing brokerage and the satellite transmission of all his programs have already brought him within range of that vision.

### Television's Exilic Economy

Most programs are run on a commercial basis, and clusters of advertisements frequently interrupt the flow of television texts. In fact, the amount of time devoted to commercials on Iranian TV increased so dramatically that by mid-1987 it reached an all-time peak of over 40 minutes per hour of programming. After much criticism from viewers, KSCI-TV and the program makers agreed on a limit of 20 minutes per hour of commercials, which seems to be holding with periodic violation.[11] Some programs contain many more minutes of indirect advertisements for products, however, especially in the field of entertainment.

The financial dimensions of the ad-driven schedule's political economy, supported by proliferating Iranian businesses, are also far-reaching, turning Iranian television into not only an exilic but also an ethnic economy. In fact, a number of producers, among them Manuchehr Bibian of *Jam-e Jam*, Nader Rafi'i of *Midnight Show*, and Hamid Shabkhiz of *Iran*, in their interviews with me credited Iranian television for making the community in Los Angeles become socially visible and economically viable. Bibian, for example, claimed that "wherever we started a new television program, Iranians increased in number." Although there is no definitive evidence in support of such a direct cause-and-effect relationship, exile television programs, Iranian businesses, and Iranian emigres have all proliferated in Southern California over the years. It is their generally high level of income, education, self-employment, and professional skill that allows Iranians as audiences, providers of advertisements, producers of programs, and consumers of products and services to have turned exile

Fig. 8. Television ad for wedding gowns.

television into an economic and symbolic engine which will ultimately transform them from exiles into ethnics, and which injects millions of dollars annually into the U.S. and Iranian economies.

Businesses place commercial announcements for their products within television programs and pay between $3 and $6 for each second of the commercial,[12] depending on frequency of broadcasts, perceived popularity of the program, number of times an ad is repeated in one show, length of the period during which the ad is aired, and personal connection between advertiser and programmer. On average, a thirty-second commercial can cost between $90 and $180. If half-hour programs are assumed to contain a minimum of 10 minutes of advertisements and hour-long programs a minimum of 20 minutes, then producers of half-hour and one-hour shows earn for each show $2,700 and $5,400, respectively. My calculations show that the existing roster of 26 programs earns over six million dollars per annum from advertising (Table 10). Of course, from this figure the cost of production and transmission must be subtracted.

There are other sources of income for producers that are not included in this calculation, such as financial contributions from political factions opposing the Islamic government and income earned from syndication of programs, because these figures are impossible to substantiate.[13] A few producers who own their own studios generate additional income by renting their facilities to other producers.[14] Based on these considerations, it can be safely said that the overall annual gross income of Iranian producers far exceeds six million dollars.

Iranian producers in four consecutive years, between 1989 (Naficy 1990b:194–98) and 1992 (Tables 11 and 12), spent over 1.2 million dollars annually to rent airtime from KSCI-TV and various cable companies to transmit their programs. Although these figures are not definitive because station rates vary, especially those of cable companies, and because stations may charge programmers rates slightly different from their standard schedule, they are close estimates. The cost of transmission for all Iranian programs since the beginning of exile TV will have to be in the tens of millions, but the cumulative figure is difficult to estimate because of the frequency with which programs have appeared, changed channels, or disappeared.

The figures for the cost of producing the programs are even harder to compute because producers use a variety of production houses with varying and personalized fee structures. The cost of production is high and the flow of ads, at least at first, was too slow for producers to make money, and a number of them lost money and went out of business.[15] Clearly, financial backing other than advertising revenues seemed to have been necessary for a program to survive long enough to become self-supporting. Indeed, this might have been a key reason, during the politically heated postrevolutionary period, that a few producers sought funding from exiled political factions—which were in need of legitimation through media exposure. Even though such politically motivated funding and such commercially motivated politicization have declined over the years, they have been significant features of the political economy of Iranian exile television. What sets Iranian programs apart from Korean, Japanese, and Chinese programs is the source of financing as well as programming. While Iranians rely almost completely on exile sources for programs and financial help, their Asian counterparts depend chiefly on programming and assistance from their home countries or their multinational corporations. As a result, Iranian programs are financially less stable, more prone to manipulation by exile groups, more responsive to market forces in exile, and more reflective of the conditions of exile.

## Station Politics

In the last decade, broadcast stations such as KSCI-TV, KDOC-TV, KRCA-TV, and a number of cable companies have carried Iranian programming.

The possibility of using more than one station to air programs theoretically must increase the ability of producers to engage both in counter-programming and in reducing the cost of airtime by playing one station against the other. As is evident from Table 8, however, Iranian programmers have so far refrained from programming against one another. They have elected to access different channels, however, in order to get around the stations' attempts at censorship. A case in point is the *Sima-ye Azadi* program produced by the Mojahedin guerrilla organization. The program was taken off the air by KSCI-TV in 1986 but soon it found a new home in KDOC-TV, where it continued to broadcast until mid-1989. It returned to Los Angeles airwaves a few years later by broadcasting on KSCI-TV again.[16]

It is worth spending some time on examining these shifts by *Sima-ye Azadi* because they tell much about the ways that broadcast diversity can be obtained or curtailed in the United States, especially with regard to exile politics, which may not match U.S. foreign policy; the kind of cat-and-mouse game that political exile organizations play in gaining access to U.S. public opinion; and the relationship between broadcasting stations and exile producers.[17] *Sima-ye Azadi* was first aired in 1986 on KSCI-TV but it was taken off because, according to the station, the producer had failed to fulfill contractual obligations. These obligations appear to have been formulated by the station in cooperation with the U.S. State Department. In a 1986 letter, the State Department informed KSCI-TV that the Mojahedin was a "terrorist" organization and that all the following organizations "represented" it: Council of Resistance, Muslim Iranian Student Society, Iran Relief, and People's Mojahedin Organization of Iran. With this in mind, the station signed a contract (dated 1/9/1986) with Star Productions, producer of *Sima-ye Azadi*, in which the company promised it would

> not air either in program content or commercial announcement, the activities or philosophy of the following groups:
> a. National Council of Resistance
> b. Moslem Iranian Student Society
> c. Iran Relief
> d. People's Mojahedin Organization of Iran
> e. Any group related to the organizations listed above.
> This includes, but is not limited to, on-air fund raising, invitations to rallies, demonstrations or meetings, editorial statements, etc.

The State Department apparently monitored the programs because two months later in a letter it informed the station that a few of the aired pro-

Fig. 9. *Sima-ye Azadi*'s newscast: Program logo, dove of freedom, is keyed into the background.

grams had contained interviews with three Mojahedin members who were tortured by the Islamic Republic. It continued:

> During the interview, there is frequent praise of the PMOI [Mojahedin] leader, Rajavi. No explanations were given as to the nature of PMOI, its role in bringing Khomeini to power, its ideology, or its extensive use of violence. Although the tapes contain no specific appeals for support for the PMOI, nevertheless, they appear fully within the PMOI's current propaganda line which goes roughly as follows: "the Iranian government is bad, the PMOI is against the Iranian government, the Iranian government represses the PMOI, therefore, the PMOI and its leader Rajavi are good and worthy of support."

The letter clearly posited that Star Productions' claim of no political affiliation and its promise to refrain from political proselytization were untrue. Because of this and the generally volatile politics of Iranians at the time, KSCI-TV hired an Iranian monitor to review for contents and amount of commercials all Iranian programs the station was airing. The monitor filed reports detailing contents of programs, including one for *Sima-ye Azadi*. Following the State Department's finding and the monitor's report, KSCI gave the organization four weeks' notice after which the program would be canceled on account of the "sensitive material thus far included." Less than four weeks later, KSCI-TV "reaffirmed" its decision to cancel the contract since the management did not "feel it is in the best interest of the station to continue airing" the program. Although Star Productions agreed to follow the policy standards outlined in the station's manual, and further promised "not to promote or encourage, or make representations political in nature so as to jeopardize licensing," the station stood fast and let the contract expire. In all fairness it must be noted that in fact the program continually proselytized in support of the Mojahedin ideology and the organization's political and military tactics against the Islamic government in Iran. Whether it was pressure from the State Department, the Mojahedin's violation of their contract, or the station's fear of losing its license at renewal time, the result was that the only anti-Khomeini program that was not also royalist was denied access.

After a period of hiatus *Sima-ye Azadi* resumed operation by moving over to channel 56 (KDOC-TV), where it continued its regular transmission until mid-1989. Although the program's contents had not changed, before each broadcast an announcement appeared stating that the producer was not a supporter of the Khomeini government in Iran. One inference that can be drawn is this: the Mojahedin had succeeded in dissociating itself from anti-American terrorism, which the State Department had worried about, while it continued to advocate anti-Khomeini terrorism, which the State Department was apparently not worried about. With this shift in the definition of "terrorism," *Sima-ye Azadi* was able to continue to air its programs until some time in 1989, when the organization relocated its headquarters from Paris to Iraq and suspended its propaganda activities in the United States to concentrate on military operations against the Islamic Republic.[18] In late 1991, the Mojahedin resumed its propaganda operations in the United States, including airing *Sima-ye Azadi* on its original channel, KSCI-TV. It is possible that the U.S. government's continued anti-Iranian foreign policy and the Mojahedin's relocation reassured KSCI-TV that leasing time to *Sima-ye Azadi* would no longer jeopardize its license.

The antiterrorism mindset in America in the late 1970s, of course, was consolidated by the taking of 52 Americans hostage in the American embassy in Tehran in 1979 and holding them for 444 days. The atmosphere in this country was poisoned for Iranian exiles and television producers. Limonadi, producer of *Iranian*, stated in an interview with me that in 1979, before the hostages were taken, he had signed a contract with KSCI-

TV to air his program. With the taking of the hostages, however, the station became fearful of a backlash from American citizens for having given access to Iranians (citizens of a "terrorist" country) and it postponed the fulfillment of the contract until the hostages were released.

The State Department's labeling of a country (Iran), a group (Mojahedin), and a government (Islamic Republic) as "terrorist" acts somewhat like the Motion Pictures Association of America's labeling of films. It encourages compliance through self-censorship. The label warns the broadcasters about sensitive issues whose exposure may endanger the stations' license renewal.[19] In the same way that license renewal produces compliance and deference by television stations, the lease-access contract, containing a 28-day cancellation clause, recruits consent from exile producers. Access to multiple broadcast channels helps the producers, who are at the mercy of the stations that lease time to them, to manipulate the stations or attempt to get around one particular station's attempts at censorship.

### Intermedia Rivalry

Although during the liminal period of Iranian exile television served to create exilic cohesiveness and national solidarity, it also nurtured a certain amount of political discord within the transplanted community. The chief reasons were economic and political competition and personal rivalries among various media producers, particularly those between publishers of periodicals and producers of television programs. Because of the Federal Communications Commission's regulative power, exile television programs are more circumspect than the periodicals in attacking each other, or in taking on the periodicals. Economic competition, however, appears to be the most significant reason for antagonism. According to a KSCI-TV official, the periodicals-television rivalry "comes down to economics," with both publishers and producers wanting larger shares of expanding advertising dollars.[20] One reason for the duration and nastiness of the rivalry may lie in the perceived effectiveness and desirability of television advertising over that in periodicals.

What complicates this economic rivalry is the fractious politics of exile groups working against the Islamic Republic. With the exception of the Mojahedin, none of the other opposition groups—which range from various shades of monarchism to Marxism—produce their own official television programs. Instead, they are said to clandestinely fund programs and periodicals in one or more of these ways: direct financial contribution to the owners; reimbursing TV producers for their travel expenses; paying producers and publishers for carrying "news" interviews with political figures;[21] and favoring a particular producer or publisher by placing advertisements with them. In its most insidious form, clandestine political sponsorship undermines the journalistic credibility of exile television because it not only politicizes but also commercializes their newscasts as well as the rest of their discourse. But this form of sponsorship serves the interests of exiled politicians: by appearing on television, they gain prestige and are recognized as leaders, thereby increasing their chances of obtaining funds from foreign governments opposing the Islamic Republic (such as Iraq, Saudi Arabia, or the United States). On the one hand, operating from behind the scenes confers on them power and the mystique of anonymity and removes them as targets of direct attack and criticism. On the other hand, audience perception of under-the-table machinations increases the sense of such politicians' power—although dislike of it is also present.

The manipulation of the news and interview processes through commodification, however, is not limited to politicians. Entertainers promoting their new albums and upcoming concerts and lawyers informing audiences about immigration laws often pay for the privilege of being interviewed on television. As a result of these financial and political practices, the line separating the program (text) and advertising (supertext) becomes blurred. Such textual ambiguity may be appreciated from a hermeneutic standpoint but it does tend to reinforce the negative public image of television producers as political or commercial hacks.

Another significant source feeding the intermedia discord is interpenetration of the private and public interests of producers. There is a duality in most people between self-interest and public interest.[22] The producers have resolved this duality by resorting to cleverness and deception—which is no different from the tactics used by non-Iranian producers. What makes the difference is that the producers attempt to raise funds by invoking sensitive and emotional issues: combatting the Islamic regime in Iran, nationalism, exilism, and serving the cause of displaced refugees and war children. As a result of these practices, television producers are accused of supporting the Islamic government under the guise of patriotism, receiving financial support from political factions in exile opposing the Islamic government while claiming otherwise, presenting views of one or another of the exile political factions while contending to be objective, and promoting personal gain while asserting service to the exile community.[23] There is always suspicion concerning corrupt practices[24] such as organizing allegedly fraudulent public service fund-raising events such as telethons.[25] The personal conduct of some producers reinforces the somewhat negative perception of them among many Iranians.[26]

One pathological symptom of the conflation of personal economic interest with public social interest is the manner in which exile TV producers, charged with allegations of the sort noted above, have used public airwaves to settle private scores, defend themselves, and launch direct countercharges against their detractors. These public contestations over personal integrity, sometimes fanned by periodicals, have had negative effects.

The regular program format has sometimes been disrupted to allow for the airing of charges and countercharges. When in April 1988 *Arya* TV charged that Homa Ehsan, producer of *Didar* (the first woman producer to air her program), had allegedly taken for her own personal use the money she had collected for Iranian immigrants, Ehsan abandoned her regular program format to deny the charge and defend herself.[27] Up to that point, *Didar* had been concerned with the familial self, and allowed expression of emotions more than did other television programs. It was focused on lifestyle, poetry, domestic issues, interviews with women, child-rearing practices, and children's performances. The set of *Didar* was domestic, resembling a comfortable Iranian guest room, suitable for rituals of hospitality (the show was taped in Ehsan's own living room). To defend herself, however, Ehsan felt obliged to shift from the private to a public, political orientation. Interviews with women and children and the display of children's performances gave way to Ehsan's own direct address to the camera, and her vernacular language also changed to more formal public utterances. The program lost much of its distinctiveness and soon ceased operation altogether, due to a drastic reduction in commercial sponsorship (particularly by physicians). With the demise of *Didar*, the women's voice was removed from the scene for some time.

The second negative effect of mixing personal benefit with public interest is the lessening of public trust in TV programs as organs of legitimate commercial enterprise and, in particular, of public good.[28] For a community whose psychology is so focused on sincerity, and which perceives cohesiveness to be more essential for its survival than differences, distrust may be very destructive. Farzan Delju, host of *Jonbesh-e Iran* (11/27/1988), warned in an emotional commentary that the "city of the angels" has become the "city of chameleons," in which Iranians often change colors. Whatever the ethical practices of *Jonbesh-e Iran*, this commentary was a call for upholding Iranian core values of sincerity and inner purity.

While anti-Islamic Republic politics, televisual fetishization of Iran, and disavowal of exile allowed television programs to create an exilic economy and, for some time, a symbolic collective unity, the commercialization of their political relations transformed them into intensely divisive, exploited, and exploitative political and commercial institutions. This is a clear indication that exilic ambivalence is structural. A few producers are themselves aware of this ambivalence. Rafi'i and Shabkhiz, of *Midnight Show* and *Iran*, noted in their interviews with me that exile TV programs created economic cohesiveness by linking consumers with ethnic businesses but they failed to produce political unity. Iraj Gorgin, producer of a series of cultural programs, emphasized this point in his interview:

> The role that Iranian television programs have played is perhaps a negative one, because they have created political polarization, not cohesion. This is because they are politically partisan and are always engaged in public feuds over personal interests. All these affect viewers negatively.

Such a tight imbrication of money and politics was more prevalent in the overheated liminal period following the arrival of the Iranians in America, when political factions were hoping to return triumphantly to Iran in the very near future. As the Islamic regime consolidated itself, however, and exile turned from a temporary sojourn into a long-term, perhaps permanent stay, financial and political divisiveness eased.

It surfaced again in 1992 with the advent of *Aftab*, a two-hour program that appears to be linked with governmental cultural institutions in Iran. The program positions itself as nonpolitical, but unlike all other exilic shows, the bulk of its contents (serials, plays, feature films, and cartoons) is imported from the state-run broadcasting networks and film organizations in Iran. Because of the higher quality of these materials, the program's emphasis on culture instead of politics, and its national transmission across the United States via KSCI-TV's International Channel Network, *Aftab* quickly attracted audiences and criticism. Royalist broadcasters and periodicals in Los Angeles vehemently criticized the program, accusing it of being an "agent" of the Islamic government. But when *Aftab* sought to attract advertisers, their begrudging tolerance turned into outright belligerence. Calls for boycotting the program and those who advertise on it were sounded, but to no avail, as businesses from Los Angeles to New York to Houston placed advertisements with it. Media frenzy against the "infiltration" into exile of a voice from inside Iran was so shrill that a respected Iranian communications expert, Kambiz Mahmudi, who himself opposes the Islamic government, was moved to criticize the exile media, challenging them to compete with the pro-Islamic program in the marketplace, leaving the ultimate judgment to audiences (1992:10). A number of TV producers, too, expressed support for *Aftab*, as for them the program (whose title translates as "sunshine") represented a ray of light in the claustrophobic discourse of exile television.

The response to *Aftab* indicates that at least a portion of Iranian audiences, businesses, producers, and critics have learned to separate per-

Fig. 10. Hamid Shabkhiz hosts *Iran*: Program logo is keyed into the background.

sonal politics from economic interests. It also shows how they can use their economic prowess and control of what they watch to pressure exilic media into a degree of compliance with their interests and wishes. At a more fundamental and personal level, this newfound tolerance for opposition viewpoints is a sign of democratization and assimilation. It is also an index of the gradual professionalization of exilic media and its critics, who are willing to follow codes and routines of journalism to gain ascendency in the "civil society" of the host country instead of relying solely on promotion of personal and political connections, as was customary in the "traditional society" and "state society" of the homeland.

## Political Demography of Exilic Television

### Program Producers

Until 1992, all Iranian television programs opposed the Islamic Republic in Iran. In addition, they were all secular and predominantly royalist. These political tendencies turned most of the programs into partisan

channels for antigovernment propaganda. As late as April 1992, representatives of the Iranian Mass Media Society of California took part in an anti-
Islamic Republic political convention held in Los Angeles not as journalists *reporting* on the convention but as politicians *organizing and
participating* in it.[29] Several reasons stand out for such partisan politics
and attitudes. The first is that TV programs reflect the anti-Islamic Republic views of the exile community in Southern California. Many, but by no
means all, of the producers, segment producers, program hosts, musicians, pop stars, and political figures who appear on these programs
openly admit to being against the Islamic Republic and in support of rein-
statement of some form of constitutional monarchy in Iran under Reza
Pahlavi, Mohammad Reza Shah's eldest son. Many producers envision an
exclusively political mission for exilic media; in the words of Manuchehr
Bibian of *Jam-e Jam* TV, this mission is to "wage a campaign against the
current government in Iran and to offer the public political information"
(Moslehi 1984:115). Iranian producers appear not to follow journalistic
values in the West of "objectivity" and "fairness," which tend to conceal
the politics of information and news. The high level of secularism among
Iranians in exile, particularly the Muslims, also tends to separate exiles
from the Islamic Republic. The separation of church and state has become
a chief political demand for the exiles, who have tasted the bitter fruits of
theocracy personally.

Another related reason for the politics of exile television might be that
many program makers belong to minorities persecuted in Iran. Of the 46
different TV producers in Table 13, 28 are Muslim, 12 Christian (6 Armenian, 5 Assyrian, 1 Protestant), 2 Jewish, and 4 Baha'i. Given that over 95
percent of the population in Iran is Muslim, the disproportionate
representation of Iranian minorities among producers becomes clear.
These minorities are also represented among technical personnel, ad
agencies, and performers. The reluctance among American mainline media to accept programming supporting the current government in Iran is
also a factor.[30]

Highly politicized exile programming partly results from the producers' general lack of formal training in journalism or television production. Of all the producers listed, less than four could be called journalists,
trained to see the world through news values such as "objectivity" and
"fairness." The irony of exilic television is that the news magazine format,
which is the most prevalent, demands the application of these values that
are in such short supply, rendering programs highly unreliable as sources
of news. Although most producers had what we might call "show business" or media-related backgrounds before emigration, only seven of
them had professional training in radio or television production and two

in film directing. The liminal condition of exile also produces emotionalism and extremism of all kinds. In the case of exilic television, extremism expresses itself chiefly in conservative partisan politics.

The end result of the producers' fierce opposition to the Islamic Republic was an unfortunate and politically dangerous conflation early on of anti-Khomeinism with anti-Islam or anti-Shi'ism, leading many programmers to replay the same mistake made during the Shah's reign, that is, ignoring or dismissing Shi'i religion as a significant and legitimate fact of Iranian political life. The fetishistic iconography of program logos may be cited as an index of this monovocal politics. In the first ten years of exilic television, almost all program logos referred in one way or another to the Iranian map, flag, colors of the flag, secular and pre-Islamic monuments in Iran, and Iranian cityscapes and landscapes to the point of fetishizing them. During this period, however, none of the logos contained a visual that referred to the Islamic aspects of Iranian art, culture, and architecture. Any sign of Islam was effaced from representations of Iran.

In addition, the same partisan and extremist news values that caused them to misrepresent the politics of Iran pushed some exile producers to misrepresent the politics of Iranians in exile as well, thus rendering their audience the manipulated objects and themselves the manipulating subjects of exiled political factions. For example, when in May 1992 a brother of the late Shah of Iran was arrested by the Los Angeles police on the charge of dealing narcotics, royalist media refused to report the news and pressured others to comply with the ban. In the same month, *Jonbesh-e Iran* accused *Iran* and *Sima-ye Ashna* of being "errand boys" for the Iranian government apparently because they had inserted in their newscasts footage from Iran available by satellite to all broadcasters.[31] These partisan Los Angeles media seem to fear the penetration of any information into their discourse that does not match their royalist and anti-Islamist ideology.

The virulent anti-Islamic Republic and pro-monarchy discourses have gradually lessened, and there are a few producers who do take a more or less independent stance, regardless of the criticism they receive. A few television programs (for example, *Emshab ba Parviz* and *Cheshmandaz*) reported the news of Pahlavi's arrest despite warnings not to do so.[32] Independent-minded producers will inevitably come under criticism from all sides, from those in Iran and those in exile, from the political left to the right. Despite setbacks and detours, this move toward diversification, professionalization, and democratization is part of the creeping assimilation within the Iranian community, and it will steadily gain momentum.

### Audience Demography

None of the rating services, such as Nielsen and Arbitron, compile regular statistics on viewing habits and preferences of so-called ethnic viewers, with the exception of Hispanic audiences. As a result, there is much uncertainty about the size, demographic profile, and preferences of audiences of transnational and exilic television. One source that provides a clue is the research conducted by individual stations airing these programs. According to the latest figures released by KSCI-TV, in 1987 the Iranian viewing audience in Los Angles was approximately 70,000 weekly households and 240,000 weekly viewers.[33] Iranian producers themselves claim much larger audience figures, based on inflated estimates of Iranians abroad (Naficy 1990b:171). The producer of *Jonbesh-e Iran* claims that more than two million Iranians worldwide watch his program (Ketab Corp. 1989:362) while the producer of *Sima-ye Ashna* stated in an interview with me (3/21/1990) that his program is seen by half a million Iranians from San Diego to San Francisco. Many also claim wide circulation abroad. The producers of *Jam-e Jam* and *Iranian* contend that copies of their shows are seen in Canada, Western Europe, Persian Gulf countries, and Iran itself.[34] The viewership worldwide is even harder to substantiate.

In the absence of an independent, reliable, and systematic rating service, both Iranian television producers and the stations that broadcast the programs must rely for audience reaction on letters and telephone calls from audiences, critical letters and columns appearing in exile periodicals, and personal contacts (especially in social gatherings and at parties). A few producers employ additional feedback methods, such as contests that encourage viewers to call in hope of winning a prize.[35] Advertisers, too, rely on similar methods, as well as on their own sales volume, to determine the effectiveness of ads.

The notion of viewers as groups of spectators (differentiated by age, gender, ethnicity, religion, and class) who can be addressed separately evolved gradually. Throughout most of its life, exilic television construed its audience as a homogeneous group of people uprooted from home and without roots here. It was seen to be not only homogeneous but also familial, as befits the Iranian self-perception and the condition of exile, both of which engender a desire for reunion and collective social constructions. A majority of producers in their interviews with me indicated that their target audience is foremost the entire "family." From the contents of their programs it becomes clear that the concept of the family encompasses not only the biological, nuclear, and extended family but also the social, national family of all Iranians in exile—both of which tend to suppress the individuality and differences of their members.

However, the survey of Iranians in Los Angeles County conducted in 1987–88 by UCLA sociologists Sabagh, Light, Bozorgmehr, and Der-Martirosian problematizes this notion by demonstrating the heterogeneity of Iranian exiles, and their varied reactions to programs based on class, education, age, and ethnoreligious affiliation. The survey included in-person interviews with 671 Iranian heads of households of four ethnoreligious groups (195 Armenians, 87 Baha'is, 188 Jews, 201 Muslims). Among other issues, they were asked about the types of videos and television programs they watch. The results show that the entire biological or national "family" may have been the producers' target, but each member of it was not addressed or reached equally.[36] The analysis that follows should be seen in the context of the profile of Iranian community in chapter 1.

Among factors that create differentiation within the exile "family" is internal ethnicity. Table 14 shows that of those surveyed, Armenians generally watch television more than any other ethnoreligious group, whether it is American, Iranian, or Armenian TV. This viewing pattern, however, is not neutral. It seems to express on the one hand the high ethnic affiliation of Armenians and on the other hand their strong desire to assimilate into the dominant host society. Corroborating the ethnic affiliation theses, the table shows that nearly 64 percent of Armenian-Iranians surveyed watch Armenian programs produced by non-Iranian Armenians (all Armenian-Iranians produce Persian-language shows that generally ignore Armenian nationalism, ethnicity, or issues). Supporting their assimilationist tendency, the same table shows that more than any other subgroup Armenians watch American TV (nearly 80 percent). This tendency toward the host culture is also substantiated by Table 15 which shows that 80 percent of Armenians watch English-language videos and only 3 percent watch Persian-language videos. But ethnically, Armenians do not have only a dual identity (Armenian and American); rather, as indicated by the high percentage of them (48.7) who watch Persian-language TV, their identity is a hybrid of three interethnic identities: Armenian, American, and Iranian.

Based on their television and video viewing patterns, Jewish Iranians seem to identify with Iranian ethnicity more than do Armenians, and they appear to favor assimilation into the host culture less than do Armenians. More Jews watch Iranian exilic TV and Persian-language videos, chiefly imported from Iran, than any other internal ethnic group (Tables 14 and 15, respectively).

Muslim respondents said they watched Iranian television less than any other group (Table 14), perhaps pointing to their dissatisfaction with underrepresentation of Islamic values or the overly partisan anti-Islamist politics of the programs. Muslim Iranians may, however, be more acculturated than the other three subgroups, thus not in need of assistance from exilic television in that process.

It has already been noted that compared with native-born Americans or other high-status immigrants, statistically, Iranians in Southern California have an unusually high level of income, education, self-employment, and professional skills—all of which are indexes of their higher class status and necessary components of a viable exilic economy that can support television programs. In the UCLA survey of Iranian viewership, the data from education and income in Tables 16 through 19 together are taken as indexes of class. The higher the class aspiration, the more attractive assimilation appears. That education is associated with assimilation is clearly indicated by the figures showing that those with higher levels of education watch less Persian-language and more English-language videos. Corroborating the general trend in the United States, the tables also show that the lower the level of education and income among Iranians, the higher is the amount of TV watching. Clearly, education is not only a source of class difference among the exiles but also an agent of their assimilation into the host society.

Income figures show that the lower the income of all Iranian ethnic groups, the more they watch videos and television, thus confirming the link established in the larger American society between lower income and higher TV watching. Low-income Baha'is, Jews, and Muslims watch more Persian-language television, while those with higher incomes watch more English-language television, thereby affirming the link between higher income and the turn toward the dominant host culture. The pattern of viewership of Armenians of all income levels—more U.S. television, followed by Armenian and Persian-language television—seems to corroborate their gravitation toward both Armenian ethnicity and American assimilation.

Taken together, the data on education and income suggest that the higher the class status of the exiles, the more they aspire toward the dominant culture, although when income reaches a certain high level, as among some rich Jewish Iranians, assimilation to the host society becomes less important.

The viewership data was obtained from heads of households only, about 90 percent of whom were male, thus removing from consideration children, young people, and to a large extent women.[37] Data in Tables 16 through 19 show that middle-aged and older Armenians (41–60 years) watch more Persian-language videos, followed by Armenian, American, and Persian-language TV, in that order. Elderly Armenians (60 years plus) watch more Persian, American, and Armenian TV, respectively. These figures confirm the expectation that the older generation's attachment to

Iran and to Armenian culture is stronger than that of the younger groups. They also indicate that the older generation lacks knowledge of the English language and must rely more heavily on native languages. The trend for the younger generation (25–40 years) is similar in that it prefers Armenian, American, and Persian programs, in that order.

The older the Baha'is and the Jews, the more they tend to watch Persian-language videos and Persian-language broadcast television. Younger Baha'is and Jews watch more English-language TV followed by Persian-language TV. Among the Muslims, the older group (41–60 years) watches more American television followed by Persian television, while the younger group (25–40 years) watches more Persian-language videos than any other subgroup (Table 19). The reason for the unexpectedly heavy use of Persian-language television by the younger Muslims may be sought in differences in income and other differences among Iranian internal ethnics. Generally, younger Muslims may be said to be economically poorer than their Armenian, Baha'i, and Jewish counterparts, and unlike them, they lack the kind of ethnoreligious networks and economic institutions that these minorities had formed in Iran and brought with them into exile. As a result, the younger Muslims more than other subgroups may be using Persian-language videos as a marker of their exilism and ethnicity.

From the analysis of the UCLA survey, it becomes clear that the target audience for exilic television—the Iranian exile "family"—is neither biologically nor demographically homogeneous, and its use of ethnic, exilic, and mainstream television varies depending on ethnicity, education, income, and age. An additional factor of diversity among Iranian exiles, which television producers have ignored, is language. With the exception of Assyrian programs and *You and the World of Medicine*, all other programs have been in Persian. Since Iranian minorities generally know Persian, this attempt at monolingualism has served to reinforce an Iranian solidarity in exile based on language. Such a solidarity, however, tends to exclude an important and growing population—that is, young people who have spent all or most of their lives in the United States and who do not know Persian or who prefer English.[38] Table 20 illustrates this point by showing that interest in Persian-language videos and TV programs increases with age. This information leads us to conclude that if teenagers had been surveyed they would have shown even less interest in these programs than the 25-year-olds who were surveyed.

The ethnic, religious, class, and generational diversity of Iranians flies in the face of the assumption of homogeneity of audiences that seems to have driven much of exilic television during most of its existence. The widespread dissatisfaction voiced by Iranians in conversations, on radio, and in periodicals about television must partly be attributed to the failure of program producers to take into account the diversity of their target audiences. Just because they all share the fact of displacement, a national language, and, to a large extent, opposition to the Islamic Republic does not mean that they have no differences. But until the late 1980s exile producers exploited the commonalities of their audiences and suppressed their differences for their own economic gain, and to enlist political solidarity favoring monarchist nationalism. As such they have acted more to consolidate Iranian ethnicity than to promote assimilation.

Since the late 1980s, however, a series of factors have contributed to modifying the homogenized notion of the audience as a unified biological or national family: proliferation of producers and programs; emergence of women producers; availability of multiple transmission channels, particularly cable television; specialization through targeting of microaudiences based on gender, age, education, profession, religion, and language; termination of the Iraq-Iran war; reduction in the bellicose mutual rhetoric of Iranian and American governments; and the reduction of the culture of politics and ascendency of a politics of culture among the exiles.

All the women producers began (and ended) their shows in the late 1980s (*Didar, Ma, Sima va Nava-ye Iran*). Live phone-in shows, transmitted nationally via satellite, began during this period (*Emshab ba Parviz, Harf va Goft, Sokhani ba Ravanshenas*). Exile-produced serials increased in number and quality. A few shows, such as *Tapesh* and *Diyar*, attempted to target young audiences by programming music videos. The program *You and the World of Medicine* became the first regularly scheduled Iranian program in the English language. The political discourse of exilic television also widened, with the introduction in this period of the antigovernment guerrilla show (*Sima-ye Azadi*), the Assembly of God religious program (*Mozhdeh*), and the somewhat pro-Islamic cultural program (*Aftab*). Clearly this diversity of programming targets hitherto unaddressed constituencies, or creates constituencies where there were none. Such transformations show that one of the keys to the survival of Iranian exilic television will be its ability to keep up with its audiences and act as a means for both assimilation and exilic identification.

Over the past decade, Iranian exilic television has developed certain structures for production, transmission, syndication, time-brokering, cross-fertilization, advertising, and audience segmentation that have helped to create an ethnic economy and an Iranian national and exilic identity. At the same time, by rationalizing the industry and introducing market forces into production, transmission, and consumption, these structures have helped exilic television to facilitate the assimilation of its audiences.

4

# The Exilic Television Genre and Its Textual Politics and Signifying Practices

## How the Shows Are Seen

*For many Iranian exiles, Sunday lunches are big affairs, an occasion for the entire nuclear or extended family and friends to get together for a late meal. Up to the mid-1980s, many restaurants offering Iranian food in Los Angeles had installed in a prominent place a television set or a video projection system. On these screens, the customers could watch old music videos and TV serials made before the revolution and imported from the homeland. They could also watch exile-produced TV shows such as* Iranian, Jonbesh-e Iran, *and* Jam-e Jam, *which have for years been aired on Sundays in one block from 11 A.M. to 2 P.M. The narrow rooms typical of the restaurants and the symmetrical seating arrangement created a kind of classical quattrocento perspective, with the television screen forming its vanishing point. No matter where you sat, at least one side of the restaurant faced the screen squarely and you were forced to look at it. Even though the volume was often turned up so high as to interfere with conversation and the image broke up frequently, no one seemed to mind. It was as though the customers were facing an electronic altar or qebleh (prayer niche) that displayed sacred icons of an idealized homeland and an irretrievable past.*

*Watching the Sunday shows during social functions, however, was not limited to public occasions and places. In homes, too, these pro-*

89

*grams provided a moving background for Sunday lunches and children's birthday parties. Television thus became part of public and private rituals. Even during the inevitable dances and obligatory singing of the birthday songs, the set would remain on with the sound turned down. During periods of crises, such as the bombing of Iranian cities, Scud missile attacks, and waves of assassinations and executions at home, television would suddenly move to the foreground. The news headlines or a particular film clip would bring a quick hush to the crowd. Eyes would be glued to the set, the silence broken by an occasional angry outburst. The celebration would resume, infected by the news of home.*

*Interestingly, not all viewers of Iranian programs are Iranian or are of Iranian descent. Shared cultures and history allow cross-viewing among not only Iranian subethnics but also other Middle Eastern populations in diaspora. My friend's mother, an elderly Jewish emigre from Palestine, likes to watch Iranian programs even though she does not understand Persian at all. It seems the nostalgic music and visuals of exile music videos remind her of her own childhood and homeland.*

## Exilic Television as a Ritual Genre

The approach to the analysis of television adopted here considers exile television as a genre, with its own televisual flow, textual strategies, and signifying practices. This might be called a "generic ritual" approach, since it seeks to understand not only the genre itself but also its interplay with the evolving community that produces and consumes it. For a community living in the liminality and anarchy of exile, the television that it produces and consumes is a vehicle through which the exilic subculture and its members, collectively or individually, *construct* themselves in the new environment. Television for them not only reflects but also constitutes and transforms the community. The televisual exile genre is without precedence, as it is produced and consumed by people outside of their own culture and society. The long time frame, the critical apparatuses, and the common grounds necessary for codifying and internalizing the genre conventions are largely absent.

As a ritual genre, exile television helps to negotiate between the two states of exile, *societas* and *communitas*. Societas is the rule-bound structured world both of the homeland from which the exiles are separated and the host society to which they are acculturating (Turner 1969). Communitas, on the other hand, is the formless, liminal state in which the rules and structures of both home and host societies are suspended, and aspects of sacredness and religiosity—here, ritual—take their place. When social structures are threatened, communitas emerges, and helps the exiles maintain similarity through elaboration of differences based on ethnicity and locality. This is a concept that appears to fly in the face of attempts made by structuralists to negate the concept of community in favor of universal structures. We are in a historical period characterized by waning of traditional universalist ideologies such as colonialism, neocolonialism, and communism and we are witnessing the world over, in preindustrial and postindustrial nations alike, people continuing to aggressively assert their locality and ethnicity through marking their boundaries.[1] Such boundaries are largely symbolically constructed, sometimes imperceptible to outsiders, redefinable by the members of the community itself, and maintained through manipulation of symbols of that community.

Rituals gain additional prominence when the actual social boundaries of the community are undermined, blurred, or weakened. Communal celebrations (weddings, barmitzvas, batmitzvas, discos, political demonstrations, anniversaries, calendrical festivals) occupy a prominent place in the cultural repertoire of the exiles, and commercially driven exilic television as a ritual functions in parallel with these social rituals to maintain individual, communal, and national boundaries.[2] It introduces a sense of order and control into the life of the viewers by producing and replicating a variety of systematic patterns that set up continually fulfilled (or postponed) expectations: narratological and generic patterns (program format, formulaic plots, stock characters, regular hosts and newscasters, a familiar studio set), patterns of consumption (scheduled airing and repeated airing of programs, interruption of the text for commercials, household environment, and viewer activity), and patterns of signification (subjectivity, mode of address, iconography).

Together all these narratological, consumption, and signification patterns produce an electronic communitas, which creates for exilic producers and viewers alike a sense of stability out of instability and commonality out of alienation. Part of the work of exilic popular culture, including television, is to produce a repository of symbols and a web of signification with which exiles can think and through which they may differentiate themselves from the host society. That is why exile is such an intensely symbolic and semiotic space and exilic television so integral an element in it.

As ritual, exilic television not only aids in creating an exilic communitas but also facilitates the transformation of the communitas toward the host societas. As such, exilic television helps the exiles maintain a dual subjectivity and a syncretic identity. There are many characteristics that set apart the exilic genre from other televisual genres. At the level of texts and intertexts, the exile genre is characterized structurally by nested texts, flow, and schedule, and by the magazine format; narratologically and ideologically by the narratives and iconographies of fetishization and ambivalence; thematically by nostalgic longing for a reconstituted past and homeland and the metaphoric staging of return to the origin; and politically by the construction of a particular imaginary nation-at-a-distance in exile.

## Televisual Texts

Determining what the unit of analysis for television should be and what a televisual text is has proven to be a problem largely because television texts are so multipurpose, polyvalent, and amorphous. Raymond Williams formulated the television text as a rather hermetic and seamless "planned flow" in the construction of which viewers play a more or less passive part (1975). Horace Newcomb's concept of the "viewing strip," on the other hand, foregrounded the active role of viewers in constructing the texts they watch (1988). In an effort to move away from text-based analyses toward locating television within the political economy of production and consumption, Nick Browne proposed the concepts of the "supertext" and the "megatext" as textual units of analysis. The supertext includes the program and all the interstitial materials surrounding it—teaser, titles, credits, advertisements, station identifications, program promotions, and public service announcements—its position within the schedule, and the relation of the schedule to the "socially mediated workday and workweek." The megatext consists of "everything that has appeared on television" (1984:177). Although these concepts take into account the television's textual environment and advance our understanding of the way the texts are linked with the political economy of consumerism, they fail to account for viewer activity, which, as will become evident, is much more complex in exilic than in mainstream television.

Much of the cultural studies work conducted in Britain, beginning with the work of Centre for Contemporary Cultural Studies at Birmingham University, focused on establishing links between the production of television texts and their reception by audiences. The ideological, ethnographic, and feminist analyses that followed explored the links between the signifying practices of production and the socially structured audiences, thus turning television texts into writerly (in Barthes's sense, 1975), open (in Eco's sense, 1979), and producerly (in Fiske's sense, 1987b) thereby accounting for multiple readings.

"Liveness" characterizes the televisual flow and its textual components. Even when the event is prerecorded, its simultaneous transmission and reception affirms its live ontology and the ideology embedded in it, which Jane Feuer has defined as "the ideology of the live, the immediate, the direct, the spontaneous, the real" (1983:14). This ideology dominates the magazine and the talk-show formats, the quintessential forms of both mainstream and exilic television. The liveness of exilic television, however, has a fundamentally different character in that it unfolds in a liminal space, activating memories of elsewhere, and it is received in an exilic household.

## Nested Exilic Text, Flow, and Schedule

The "text" of exilic television is what might be called a "nested text," in the sense that it is an exilic supertext nested within an exilic flow that is embedded within an ethnic flow which itself is nested within the mainstream television's megatext. The exilic supertext itself is a split or a double text because the program (text) is infused with sounds, images, and discourses primarily driven by the values, culture, and language of the homeland while the interstitial materials, particularly commercials, are driven chiefly by the consumerist ideology, values, and culture of the host society. Thus exilic television supertext is an instance of Derridean "double reading and writing," in which neither of the adjacent texts obtains primacy, as each resonates with or against and deconstructs the other. Split subjects produce split texts, and exilic supertexts both inscribe and erase cultural, racial, ethnic, historical, and linguistic differences and tensions which can be read when attention is paid to their interpermeability and resonances. The result is that the cohesiveness of the communitas created by televisual texts is threatened constantly by the implosion of the dominant host values by means of both the commercials interrupting the texts and the commodification practices of exile television itself.

Exile television programs are usually broadcast by television stations not as single entities but in clusters, forming an exilic flow. Los Angeles cable companies schedule *Iran* and *Shahr-e Farang* programs back to back on Friday nights and *Negah* and *Diyar* on Sunday nights; KSCI-TV schedules a series of Iranian programs from 7:30 A.M. to 9:30 A.M. on weekdays and from 11 A.M. to 2 P.M. on Sundays (see Table 8). These exilic flows are themselves nested, particularly in the case of KSCI-TV, within an ethnic flow containing clusters of programs from many national, ethnic, and linguistic groups (programs in 16 languages are aired). The majority of these programs are imported from home countries. Chinese programs occupy the afternoon and early evening slots, Korean shows dominate the prime-time hours on weeknights, and Japanese shows the prime-time hours on weekends (Table 21).

This conception of a multilingual nested ethnic televisual flow is radically different from the monolingual, monochannel, monocultural flow television scholars have formulated and studied. What is more, this ethnic flow is not insular. Through viewer activity and channel selection, it is inserted yet again into the larger megatext of television, which includes all broadcast channels. Exile television programs, therefore, are consumed within a triple-tiered viewer-strip selected by the audience. Exilic and ethnic viewers can travel across these nested flows (exilic, ethnic, and mainstream) because they are generally familiar with more than one language. For a majority of the monolingual viewers, however, the exilic and ethnic flows remain generally unreadable.

The ethnic flow at multiethnic stations is characterized not so much by seamlessness as by segmentation. It is also intensely hermeneutic, as varied politics, nationalities, ethnicities, religions, cultures, languages, classes, news values, narrative strategies, modes of address, physical locations, tastes, gestures, faces, sights, and sounds clash with one another.[3] This segmentation penetrates to even below the level of nationality as many emigre and exile communities are themselves not homogeneous.

The diversity of the Iranian population in terms of internal ethnicity, religiosity, and language allows its members to access not only Persian and English-language programs but also Armenian, Arabic, Assyrian, and Hebrew programs not necessarily produced by Iranians. Access to multiple texts produced in multiple languages by multiple nationalities and ethnicities makes the flow not only interethnic but also intraethnic. This textual access means the ethnic flow is replete with excess and alternate meanings, going beyond either intent or hegemony.

The oppositional use of this excess is made possible by the differences and contradictions among the exilic, ethnic, and dominant texts, which access brings to the fore. This semiotics of excess turns the viewer activity into a rather complex and intertextual one, both along the exilic and ethnic flows (syntagmatic intertextuality) and across the nested texts (paradigmatic intertextuality).[4] Because the exilic supertexts are nested within an ethnic flow, viewers are constantly made aware of the minor status of the exilic texts themselves and their own minority status as an audience in exile. A syntagmatic viewing of the exilic supertexts can serve to consolidate a sense of cohesion and hermeticity around the notions of exile and nationality. A paradigmatic intertextual reading of it, which places it within its commercial environment, the ethnic flow, and the mainstream megatext, however, creates multiple splittings and deconstructive nuances across all the texts, which serve to continually problematize the cohesive exilic, ethnic, and nationalistic readings. The exilic supertext and flow are thus not only excessive but also ambivalent and unstable.

Mainstream television establishes its relationship to the real world through the schedule, keyed to the workday and the workweek. As a result, the schedule tends to reproduce and naturalize the "logic and the rhythm of the social order" (Browne 1984:176). However, the exilic and ethnic television schedule—at least that produced by multiethnic stations—reproduces a radically different logic. Multiethnic stations lease their time not to the most popular shows but to the highest bidder, regardless of the type of programming. The majority of exile and ethnic programmers, in turn, do not make their programs with the schedule in mind, since the stations can change their airtime or bump them off the air on short notice. As a result, Iranian exile morning programs are not vastly different from afternoon or evening programs. The schedule then reflects the exile's own liminal condition, its formlessness, the endlessness of its time, its ambivalence.

## The Magazine Format

The magazine format dominated exile TV in the first decade of its existence. Like most genres and rituals, the magazine format is not unchanging; here, it is a symbolic construct that changes with time as it responds to and inscribes the evolution of individual subjectivity and collective identity of the exiles. In this sense, exilic television by definition is both processual and contradictory as it encodes the tensions of exilic evolution, adaptation, and resistance. In the magazine format, the program unit typically consists of a collection of usually single-topic miniprograms linked by commercials. Historically, the format's use in the public affairs area resulted in talk shows and news magazines (the latter will be highlighted here).

The magazine format is one of the most proliferating and least studied forms of television and it is central to my analysis of the exile genre.[5] There are many variations, but in its classic form, the news magazine consists of several important structural features that set it apart from daily television newscasts and talk shows.[6] Like its printed namesake, a television magazine is transmitted on a specific day and at a specific time on a daily, weekly, or monthly schedule. Like printed magazines, it contains several self-contained segments, which are much longer than a typical item on a newscast. Unlike talk shows, which are usually studio-bound, the news magazine's segments are usually shot on location. Television magazines rely on a regular cast of anchors and reporters—stars of the format—who supply it with a public image, a sense of continuity, calmness, knowledge, authority, reliability, and humanity.[7] The enunciative strategy of the format is generally as follows: the regular in-studio anchors or hosts introduce a segment, which is then reported by a correspondent in the field. In some cases (*60 Minutes*) the anchor and field reporter are the same, in others (*20/20*) they are different. Advertisements follow the completion of one segment, to be followed by another in-studio introduction to the next segment.

The magazine's mode of address is live and direct, with anchors and correspondents facing the camera and speaking directly to the invisible audience at home. The program's guests, likewise, speak without a written script to the hosts who act as intermediaries between them and the audience. The phatic banter and the "ritual of hospitality" between the in-studio hosts and guests or between anchors and field reporters enhance the "liveness" of the medium. All this is undergirded by the currency, urgency, and "realness" of the social issues the format usually tackles. The news magazine format can thus be characterized by immediacy, intimacy, and intensity.

A side effect of the ritual of hospitality is the creation of a sense of familiarity and familiality at the level of enunciation. At the reception end, too, these familiar and familial attributes are mobilized again by reception of the program within the home environment and by the pattern of viewing, which is often collective.[8] The direct address and the direct gaze of the anchors and reporters tend to suppress individual subjectivity obtainable through the primary process and suture. Instead, they foreground a kind of collective subjectivity, made available through the secondary process and through language.

The magazine's narrative regime is presentational, not representational. It is also self-reflexive and self-referential, and does not use the realist illusionism that dominates dramatic programming. Unlike these programs, the magazine does not hide its narrative and enunciative apparatuses (direct address and presence of reporters, cameras, microphones) or its own existence.[9] While dealing with the individual and social issues that real (empirical) people face in their daily lives, magazine shows do not ignore drama. News magazines generally do not use reenactments (although there are recent tabloid exceptions in mainstream programming), but they inject drama into the treatment of their "stories" by selecting sensational topics and exciting, villainous, or heroic personalities, and by employing classic dramatic structure. Further, although the magazines subscribe to the standard values of "objectivity" and "fairness," they do allow the expression of a wider and deeper range of opinions than do newscasts.

The magazine format's relationship to advertising was spelled out most clearly in the inception of the format by NBC in the early 1950s. Unlike the single-sponsor programs, then usually produced by advertising agencies, the "magazine concept" promoted the idea of inserting spot ads by multiple sponsors within programs produced by the networks themselves (Barnouw 1978:47). This arrangement allowed the networks to retain control of both the contents and the revenues. It is this same arrangement that drives exilic magazine programs.

## The Exile Magazine

Structurally and narratologically, the exile magazine format is a composite genre combining features of both hard-news and tabloid magazine formats. At the same time, it contains certain elements that differentiate it from both of these forms of mainstream television and mark its exile status. Typically, the exile magazine contains the following seven elements: a program opening containing a visual logo and a musical signature; greetings by the program host and introduction to the program; advertisement, chiefly for ethnic products; then a newscast featuring news of the homeland, the world, and the United States, delivered often by regular news readers different from the host. While news usually is defined as political news, when it comes to news of the community in Los Angeles, it is often limited to entertainment news. Various types of news are separated by advertisements. A segment containing one or more of these constituent elements follows: a comedy skit, a segment of a continuing satirical or soap-opera serial, news commentary, interviews with people in the news or with experts in law, medicine, real estate, and financial matters. This segment may contain more than one commercial break. Then come current stocks, weather, sports, and fashion reports, and then one or more musical numbers, including music videos. Often the musical numbers are preceded or followed by a publicity interview with the performer.

From this taxonomic listing of elements of the magazine supertext, it becomes clear that the exile magazine, unlike its mainstream television counterpart, is an extremely heterogeneous, composite genre, combining both fictional and expository narratives and their various subgenres. In essence, this is a "montage" genre in which a number of genres and discourses meet head to head. Its principle of cohesiveness is not continuity but clash, not seamlessness but segmentation.[10] The hosts and commercials are the chief producers of continuity within the exilic supertext and flow.

The segmentation of the format, and the multiple ownership of programs by one producer, provide a built-in mechanism for intertextuality and self-referentiality, whereby producers and hosts can refer to and promote across a number of programs (and even media) the various programs in which they have an interest. This enhances discursive exposure, and

Fig. 11. Sportscast on *Iranian*.

also the earnings of the producers. That the "magazine concept" forces the exile producers to rely on spot ads instead of single sponsors means that they are not theoretically very susceptible to economic influence from a few powerful commercial sponsors. However, the exigencies and vulnerabilities of exile, at least in its early phase, open the producers to heavy political (even financial) influences brought on by powerful political factions.

## Program Types

Throughout much of the 1980s and 1990s, the magazine-style supertext dominated, although there were programs that did not fit into the form as tightly as others. Reflecting the processual nature of the exile genre itself and of television in general, which must continually change to find new audiences, during this period producers attempted to differentiate their programs from one another by varying the mix of the seven format elements noted above. This resulted in a gradual emergence of a number of types within the exile magazine format, which are listed here with one sample from among the current programs:[11] newscast (*Jong-e Bamdadi*), news-feature magazine (*Sima-ye Ashna*), news commentary magazine (*Cheshmandaz*), cultural talk show (*Harf va Goft*), news magazine (*Iranian*), variety magazine (*Jam-e Jam*), pop music magazine (*Diyar*), satirical magazine (*Shahr-e Farang*), serial magazine (*Negah*), live phone-in magazine (*Emshab ba Parviz*), women and family magazine (*Didar*), religious magazine (*Mozhdeh*), ethnic magazine (*Bet Naharin*), medical talk show (*You and the World of Medicine*), guerrilla magazine (*Sima-ye Azadi*), and program-length advertising magazine (*Sobh-e Ruz-e Jom'eh*). It must be noted that each type of program may not necessarily contain all of the elements of the magazine format, but it will contain many of them in varied combination. For example, a news magazine may contain more news than a variety magazine but it will also contain at least one musical number. Likewise, the variety magazine contains some hard news. In the same vein, the interview on the news magazine may be focused on news and current affairs, while that of the variety magazine would deal with the entertainment field.

Gradually, several programs became so specialized that strictly speaking they can no longer be called magazines, but even these retained some of the features of the format. In the 1980s and early 1990s, for example, *Negah* devoted much of its half-hour broadcasts to airing two engaging soap-opera serials produced in exile, but it retained some of the format elements: opening logo and musical signature, greetings by the host, phatic banter with co-host, news, interview with a psychologist about the topics raised by the program, and advertisements. In 1992, the Assembly of God religious program, *Mozhdeh*, came on board. Although the program is commercial-free and devoted to proselytizing, it uses a number of hosts, choral and musical religious numbers, and interviews with and testimonials from Iranians who have converted to Christianity. The basic structure of the magazine has remained remarkably intact principally because it is a flexible format capable of responding to and encoding the shifting and multiple exigencies of exile. This flexibility has allowed it to give access to diverse voices, even though the magazine's familiar format, regular daily or weekly broadcast schedule, and longevity (some programs have been on the air in the same time slot for over a decade) have served to regulate and contain the flux of exilic liminality.

Variation in the mix of format elements helped to recast the concept of audience from an amorphous, familial, and homogeneous mass to a number of different targetable clusters. The principles of variation were the broadcast time of the program and gender, age, politics, and ethnoreligious affiliations of audience members. Significantly, language differences were suppressed. This is understandable; the first step in identity formation for most exiles is to differentiate themselves from the host society by reducing their own internal differences. Due to the absence of a reliable rating system, the producers were guided in this targeting practice more by trial and error than by demographic studies.

The exilic and ethnic television schedules are in considerable flux and although they are unable to closely replicate the social order of the work-week and the weekend, the producers of exilic television attempted throughout the years to link their shows to the time of broadcast, however loosely, and to the life patterns of their increasingly assimilating audiences.

## Program Contents

The two daily morning programs are current affairs programs. *Jong-e Bamdadi* presents hard international, national, and local news, including extensive coverage of Iran and of Iranians abroad, while *Sima-ye Ashna* is chiefly a news magazine, emphasizing soft feature stories and film clips from around the world. Both programs target adults who view the programs before leaving for work. The morning medical programs (*Pezeshg-e Khub-e Khanevadeh, Mardom va Jahan-e Pezeshgi*, and *You and the World of Medicine*), in relaxing talk-show and interview forms, offer medical and health tips to the eldest members of the family, those men and women who stay at home during the day. *Sobh-e Ruz-e Jom'eh* is an infomercial or advertising magazine, in which the host, using a talk-show format, talks amicably and persuasively to the camera or with a guest about an Iranian product or service, interspersing his presentations with well-known poetry and proverbs. These interviews and presentations are interrupted by prerecorded spot commercials for products and services.

Prime-time programs are generally more entertainment-oriented and can potentially attract audiences different from those of the morning shows. Of these, *Iran* seems to be targeting a younger viewer. Its younger host has an informal and hip style and his program is loose in form, upbeat in tone, feature-oriented, music-dominated, and less concerned with the politics of home. The program has featured a number of television serials, such as the satirical serial *Da'ijan Napele'on* (Uncle Napoleon), produced in Iran before the revolution, and the drama serial *Amir Kabir*, made in postrevolutionary Iran. *Shahr-e Farang* is a satirical variety magazine. Its host is a well-known comic who mixes satirical commentaries about current events and personalities in Iran and the United States with dramatic serials he has produced on life in exile.[12] *Iran va Jahan* is currently chiefly a variety magazine, containing news, news commentary, music videos, and tourist films about Israel. The religious program *Mozhdeh* carries no

Fig. 12. Newscast: *Jong-e Bamdadi*'s Nureddin Sabetimani.

commercials but uses its magazine format to proselytize for the Assembly of God church.

Weekends for Iranians are traditionally occasions for visiting friends and for extended-family get-togethers. As a result, daytime Sunday programs provide a very diverse mixture of adult and family programming. *Iranian* and *Jonbesh-e Iran* provide news, interviews with Iranian political and cultural figures, and one or two music videos, while *Jam-e Jam* provides news and many entertainment segments, particularly music videos. *Negah*'s most innovative feature has been the airing of a series of well-produced soap operas (*Ro'ya-ye Emrika'i* [The American dream] and *Payvand* [Connection]) that explore the tensions of Iranian families and young couples in the process of acculturation. Sometimes the serial is followed or preceded by an interview with an expert on immigration or family counseling. *Diyar* is a musical variety magazine targeting younger viewers, and it is devoted entirely to entertainment news, interviews with Iranian entertainers, and various types of music videos. *Aftab*, much of whose programs are imported from Iran, attempts to stay away from straight political news and to operate instead in the cultural domain.

Each week its host presents commentaries that attempt to link Iranians living abroad with those who have remained at home. The magazine format and the two-hour time slot allow him to present a melange of segments: dramatic and satirical serials, portions of feature films, and animated cartoons for children. (Although, over the years, a few of the exile programs tried to target Iranian children, they failed to attract them because of a dearth of existing programming, the high cost of producing new materials, and the impossibility of competing with American mainstream children's programs.)

Following the model of American mainstream television, late-night exile programs employ chiefly the talk-show form of the magazine, with the recent addition of the phone-in feature. Clearly, the intended audiences for these shows are adults. In *Emshab ba Parviz*, aired live nationally, the host interviews one guest each time about a single topic and takes phone calls from viewers. *Sokhani ba Ravanshenas*, too, is a live call-in show, during which audience members discuss with the psychiatrist-host of the show their personal and familial problems. *Harf va Goft* is a live interview show in which the host talks with one or more individuals about some aspect of culture and life in exile. Often films or other works of art are shown and the contents explored with the artist or a critic. *Midnight Show* is the longest-running talk show, the format of which is flexible enough to allow its host to interview his guests either in the studio or on location and to cover news and cultural events of interest to Iranians. *Pars* is a variety magazine, containing music videos, news, hard news, entertainment news, and news commentary. *Agahi-ye Behtar* is a program-length commercial for ethnic products and services, produced and hosted by the same person who runs *Sobh-e Ruz-e Jom'eh*. Although the guerrilla magazine, *Sima-ye Azadi*, does not carry advertisements for consumer products, the entire program is a commercial for its producer, the Mojahedin guerrilla organization, which is engaged in armed struggle against the Islamic government in Iran. This program, too, utilizes a magazine format presided over by a host who links the various segments, including a newscast, videotaped reports of the Mojahedin activities, speeches by the organization leaders, musical numbers, and antigovernment music videos.

Although women have produced three programs (*Didar, Ma*, and *Sima va Nava-ye Iran*), none has survived. Women's issues and tensions in the family structure in exile were foregrounded in *Didar* and *Sima va Nava-ye Iran*. The former dealt with them in a variety talk-show form while the latter used the soap-opera format as well.

Iranian ethnoreligious groups have in the past produced a number of programs. *Mozhdeh* is entirely devoted to preaching Christianity, while

Fig. 13. Interview show: *Midnight Show*'s host, Nader Rafi'i (*right*), interviews Reza Pahlavi.

Assyrian programs tend to focus on issues related to the Assyrian ethnic and religious communities in diaspora. Although various ethnic and religious minorities are represented among producers of other programs, it cannot be said that these programs are openly ethnic or religious. Rather, because of fear of bad publicity and persecution, ethnicity and religious affiliations have become submerged presences encoded at a latent level in the programs. For example, the overall discourse of *Jam-e Jam* and *Iran va Jahan*, both produced by Jewish Iranians, is not religious or ethnic, but news and news commentary about Israel forms a greater part of their newscasts and they seem to carry more advertising from Jewish businesses. Satirical segments produced by the Armenian Rafi Khachaturian (*Jan Nesar* and *Khub, Bad, Zesht*) are not ethnic or religious. In fact, they are highly political, against the Islamic regime in Iran, and they poke fun at the foibles and frailties of all Iranians. Programs produced by Iranian Baha'is, too, do not foreground their religion or ideology, although they may favor Baha'i concerns. For example, *Mona's Execution*, a harrowing music video recreating the execution of a Baha'i girl in Iran, was aired by

*Cheshmak*, produced by an Iranian Baha'i. Finally, during much of the first decade of programming, none of the Muslim producers highlighted Islam in their discourse. Its presence was limited to references to the politics of the Islamic Republic in the news or the periodic condolences or congratulations offered audiences on the death days or birthdays of major Islamic religious figures. In the early 1990s with *Aftab*, the creation of an Islamic Center in Beverly Hills by Iranian Muslims, and the gradual acculturation, depoliticization, and democratization of the exiles, Islam and Islamic issues began to surface. *Sobh-e Ruz-e Jom'eh* dared to feature in June 1992 a religious sermon (*rowzeh*) to commemorate the death of imam Hosain, the slain martyr of Karbala.

The ethnic flows and the megatext of KSCI-TV and the cable companies in which exilic programs are nested place at the disposal of Iranian ethnoreligious minorities ethnic programs produced by others with whom Iranians share cultural, linguistic, or religious affiliations. Jewish Iranians may watch *Israel Today, Phil Blazer*, or the Jewish Television Network; Armenian Iranians may watch *Armenian Teletime* or *ANC Horizon*; Assyrian Iranians may view *Bet Naharin*, Arab Iranians may watch *Arab American TV, Alwatan*, or *Good News*; and those interested in the religion and practices of Islam may watch *Islam*.[13]

The basic magazine format has endured, although many variations in the mix of its elements have been introduced. These variations and the differing signifying practices of the aforementioned programs clearly demonstrate that the conception of Iranians as a homogeneous mass of exiles or as a cohesive biological or national family is no longer tenable. Programmers have succeeded by trial and error in segmenting and targeting their audience by age, politics, religion, profession, interests, ethnicity, and gender. They do not usually couch their programming strategies in the cold and calculating terms of commerce, however. Instead, they often differentiate themselves and justify their format variation by claiming a greater stake in and allegiance to an "essential" and "authentic" Irani-anness.

## Subjectivity and Mode of Address

Televisual and cinematic signification differ from one other on a number of levels. The most significant of these is the process by which viewer subjectivity is formed. Theories of cinematic spectatorship have highlighted the function of vision and voyeurism in the constitution of the subject (Mulvey 1975, Metz 1982). This function is said to be driven by the primary process, which Freud associated with the prelanguage unconscious and with the pleasure principle. It is chiefly concerned with affect and sensory data, particularly visual. The primary process is remarkably single-minded and insatiable and does not distinguish between real objects and persons and their images. If it is blocked from attaching itself to one object, person, or memory, it will seek another. As I have shown elsewhere in this study, it is this process that is responsible for the fetishistic iconography of exile television, whereby the lost or absent homeland is recovered through overinvestment in the signs that stand for it (such as the flag and its colors, the map of the country, dead and tortured bodies, and national monuments). It is also the same process that drives the nostalgic narratives of return to the homeland and to nature. These processes are operative chiefly in the magazine format's logos, music videos, and narrative portions which rely on vision and affect more than on words.

Freud also posited the secondary process, which works in tandem but in opposition to the primary process. This process, associated with the preconscious and the reality principle, tends to tame and hold in check the impulsiveness of the pleasure principle by "binding" it chiefly to language (Silverman 1988:69). By submitting the unbounded pleasure principle to linguistic structuration, the secondary process tends to reduce the intensity of the affective and sensory values of the mnemic traces. This is the process that forms the basis of televisual subject positioning, particularly in the case of the magazine genre, which is driven chiefly by words and the direct address. Since the exile magazine contains both expository and fictional forms, however, it encourages a split subjectivity that must oscillate between the primary and the secondary processes, between affective sights and sounds and linguistic structuration, and between fictional and real-world issues. If the former promotes fetishization within the visual track, the latter encourages fetishization within the audio register. This is because while subject formation in the case of the narrative portions may occur primarily through scopophilia, in the case of expository sections it is driven primarily by epistephilia. This textual and subjective duality is undergirded by a further split (explained earlier) in which program matter is largely encoded by home while the ads inscribe host cultural values. These multiple dualities and splits resonate sympathetically with ambivalent identities—which typifies exilic liminality.

The direct address of the hosts, reporters, interviewees, and commercials, which bare the device of enunciation, enhance the overall sense among viewers of being continually addressed. The direct address, moreover, tends to suppress individual identification by situating the viewers not only within language but also within the home. The "leaky," segmented, and contradictory supertext of television as well as the extratextual environment of the home in which it is received (telephone calls, doorbells ringing, lighted rooms, presence of children, availability of a kitchen nearby, neighborhood noises) tend to suppress the intensive gaze characteristic of cinematic viewing. Instead, a type of distracted and cursory gaze, what John Ellis has called "glance," is encouraged (1985:137). In the case of ethnic and exilic television, the viewer's glance not only takes in the television set but also the home interior, which is ethnically and exilically coded by souvenirs, photographs, flags, maps, carpets, paintings, food, aromas, art objects, and handicrafts from the homeland. The reconstitution of the television signal by viewers within such a highly coded environment tends to enhance the collective experience of being (dis)placed, in exile.

Viewers read exile television programs not merely as textually positioned subjects but also as historically and socially located individuals who bring to their viewing their national, cultural, ethnic, and ideological orientations.[14] Spectatorship cannot be disengaged from the viewers' preconscious and conscious activity.[15] Neither can it be divorced from the viewers' rules of social interaction, nor should we universalize the Western psychic structure, which is based on a strongly individuated self. Cinematic techniques of spectator positioning, such as shot reverse-shot—in film the armature of suture—are not universal and can be culturally coded and read. If rules of the Iranian system of courtesy (called *ta'arof*) are applied, for example, an over-the-shoulder shot in television can be read as an impolite gesture, because one character has his back to the viewers. Turning one's back to someone, especially a stranger, is considered very impolite in the discourse of ritual courtesy. An example of this type of reading is provided by *Zendegi-ye Behtar* (2/12/1990), in which the host interviewed a real-estate agent and the pop singer Martik. During both interviews, the host was taped from over his shoulder or from a three-quarter angle, with the result that his back was to the audience for much of the time.[16] Noting that he had violated one of the key codes of courtesy, at the end of the program the host faced the audience and apologized for having turned his back to them.[17]

The spectator is positioned not only by the text but also the orientational schemas of the society, which in the case of Iranians includes ritual courtesy, modesty of vision, and veiling and unveiling practices. These schemas and practices have a profound effect on the constitution of a communal subject in cinema and I have discussed them at length elsewhere (Naficy 1991a).[18] The familial and communal structure of the self among Iranians also works against the notion of television and cinema creating a unified, stable, and individuated subjectivity.[19]

### Epistephilia and Collective Subjectivity

Words are necessary to express and shape both the fear of and the fact of the changed consciousness that exile engenders. Exilic television (along with independent transnational cinema, feminist films, and politically radical documentaries) relies greatly on such words. Epistephilia and the direct address of the exilic supertext destroy the distance and absence necessary for gaze-driven voyeuristic scopophilia. Instead, they institute glance-driven viewing, based on presence and on language. As a result, while in fictional narrative cinema the spectator is engaged through sexual pleasure, in expository nonfictional magazines the viewer draws pleasure through social engagement. Bill Nichols noted this difference in his discussion of documentary films:

> The engagement stems from the rhetorical force of an argument about the very world we inhabit. We are moved to confront a topic, issue, situation, or event that bears the mark of the historically real. In igniting our interest, a documentary has a less incendiary effect on our erotic fantasies and sense of sexual identity but a stronger effect on our social imagination and sense of cultural identity. (1991:178)

In exile words play an important role in creating social imagination and cultural identity. There is an insatiable drive among Iranians in exile for information, knowledge, and the exchange of ideas and words. Epistephilic desire is well suited to the television magazine because the magazine's expository form invokes and promises to gratify the desire to know. This desire and its expectation of fulfillment in exile sets into motion a generic contract between viewers and television producers that is not only binding but also spellbinding. This may partially account for the behavior of Iranian audiences, who complain constantly about the number of commercials interrupting the programs (sometimes totaling over 40 minutes in an hour-long show) but who apparently cannot help but continue to watch. The spell, however, is cast not only by epistephilia but also by the segmentation of the televisual supertext itself, which tends to psychologically intensify the desire to watch, thereby making spectators continually available for commercial messages (Houston 1984). In exilic television, each commercial interruption or delay in obtaining epistephilia constitutes a lack that tends to intensify the desire, thus encouraging continued viewing.

The status of the gaze requires further elaboration. As already noted, television suppresses the probing voyeuristic gaze and promotes the cursory glance. Moreover, the exilic magazine format, integrating a variety of genres and styles including documentary and nonfictional footage, accommodates a variety of what Nichols has called "ethical looks," which link the style of filming and looking to the moral and political points of view of the filmmakers and to their ethical implications. This is because the subjects in documentary cinema are usually social actors who live in history, not screen actors inhabiting the diegesis. What the viewer sees in this type of cinema is a record of how filmmakers look at and regard their fellow human beings. There is considerable tension between an ethical and moral standard requiring those who film real events to place the public good uppermost, and the exigencies of producing commercially viable television, particularly in exile. The fact remains, however, that the magazine format's reliance on concern with the real, the social, and the collective means that its credibility rests upon some fulfillment of public good.

### Collective Address and Collective Subjectivity

Television's direct address is a strategy of presence, while cinema's narrative address is one of absence. The narrative space of classic narrative cinema effaces the presence of the spectators and encodes it as absence; the expository space of the television magazine recognizes and highlights the presence of the viewers. The televisual direct address has an added dimension of nowness, promoted by the technology of the apparatus, which removes the distance between transmission and reception at home. As a result, the subjectivity that the television magazine cultivates, based on its live ontology, the copresence of image and viewer, direct address, epistephilia, and the primacy of language and thus the secondary process is collective and in the present tense, while cinematic subjectivity, based on the separation of enunciation and reception, and the image and thus the primary process, is individualistic and in the past tense.

Because of its composite form, the exilic magazine encodes both absence and individual and presence and collective subjectivities. Collective subjectivity tended to dominate because of producers' previous conceptions of audience as a mass of homogeneous exiles, and because of the collective mode of address, which targeted neither individuals nor segments of the population but the entire family and exilic community. Early on, then, most exile programs attempted to provide materials suited to all family members, including cartoons and special segments for children. In terms of the manner of address, many of the program hosts continue to use either a collective term of endearment to address the audience such as "you dear ones" or a familiar, poetic form of address reserved for intimate friends, such as "greetings to you, my lovely, my fellow countryman, my unique one."[20] Likewise, many program hosts use collective transitional phrases when going into commercials, such as "let's watch the following messages *together*," "*we'll be together* again after these messages" (emphases added). These types of formulaic, collective, and poetic forms of address, repeated many times during a show, encourage a familiar, familial, complicit, copresent discourse in which the relationship between program hosts and viewers is not so much based on individual psychological identification driven by scopophilia as on a collective communitas developed by means of epistephilia, in the formation of which both the hosts and viewers participate. The direct address of the commercials, too, which regularly aim their sales pitches at what they call "the Iranian community," further emphasizes the collective conceptualization of audiences. In this it can be seen that Iranian exilic television is intensely communitarian.

Such efforts at creating a community of address are enhanced by the nature of the magazine format itself, characterized by what Michael Arlen has called the "ritual of hospitality" between the hosts and guests (1981:310–12). In this type of program, in-studio hosts invite guests to visit the set, which is often made to look like a living room. In the case of exilic magazines, both the set and the ritual of hospitality are informed by the exiles' traditions and cultural orientations. Many early shows were staged in a set that resembled a typical Iranian drawing room in which nonfamily visitors are received formally: a sofa, a few comfortable chairs, a coffee table, a large bouquet of flowers on the coffee table, and large plants in the background. The exilic format relies on life-size close shots, an expository form of enunciation, formal dress, composed posture, a formal style of communication characterized by literate language (not vernacular), and appropriate invocations of rules of ritual courtesy in introducing guests, speakers, and program segments. These rules require that, as guests who come to viewers' homes via the magic of television, the hosts camouflage their personal emotions under a veneer of politeness and civility. Programs always begin with the hosts greeting the viewers, sometimes in effusive terms (which displays humility and ritual courtesy). Even when Los Angeles-produced programs are syndicated to other cities in the United States, greetings specific to each city are inserted at the head of the program.[21] When viewers perceive that codes of courtesy have been violated, they complain to the producers:

> Sir, right now I am watching an Iranian television program and I see that the news anchor is appearing in front of the camera with a T-shirt. As long as I remember, television anchors have read the news to the camera wearing a proper suit, tie, and a clean shirt. (*Sobh-e Iran*, 2/3/1989, p. 15)

Fig. 14. Interview setting: *Jam-e Jam*'s 1992 New Year program.

When there is bad news to impart, the system of courtesy authorizes the display of personal emotions, particularly sadness and grief—core values for Iranians. In April 1988 during the bombing of Iranian cities by Iraqis, the news anchor of the morning program *Jong-e Bamdadi* (Nureddin Sabetimani) began his newscast not with news about the incident but with a personal metadiscourse on the news designed to prepare the audience for the bad news he was about to read. He said:

> I would have preferred to begin the carefree hours of the morn-
> ing with the most pleasant and comforting love poems instead of
> with disturbing news. But how can we sit back and witness our
> country becoming such an arena of battle for traders of
> war? . . . Has this spring morning in Iran begun with delicacy
> and freshness that we should begin ours with tranquil-
> lity? . . . Are we separate or different from the Iranian nation?
> So let me begin with a poem about spring, a spring without
> pansies.

Then he read a highly emotional, elegiac, and patriotic poem about his homeland before presenting the news. With these statements he not only cushioned the bad news but also made himself vulnerable by revealing his inner self and his own personal emotions to his unseen audience—that is, he displayed intimacy and sincerity instead of objectivity and clever-ness.[22] When bad news is not properly processed through politeness it can lead to audience displeasure. Ali Limonadi, producer of *Iranian*, told me of an engineer who called him after a broadcast and threatened to sue him on the grounds that his newscast had caused his mother to faint and go into convulsions (2/4/1989). In the case of Sabetimani, who did deliver the news with appropriate processing, one would expect a sympathetic response. I do not know how the audience reacted to his presentation, but the only public reaction, printed in *Rayegan* magazine (4/22/1988, p. 22), corroborates the expectation. In an editorial, the weekly not only quoted the newsman and his poem at length but also praised him lavishly for his display of sincerity and patriotism.[23]

Such a collective feedback completes the circle of courtesy, for ritual courtesy is not only a "social contract" between interacting people in a face-to-face situation but also an "implied contract" between viewer and program,[24] where the contract is implied not by the traditions of the text, as in film, but by the social context—the cultural orientation of both pro-gram makers and viewers. In such a conception, every narrative may be considered to be a medium of exchange "determined not by a desire to narrate but by a desire to exchange" (Barthes 1974:90). What is being ex-changed is not only textual pleasure but also social relations between two interactants: the viewing public and the film-television texts. This interac-tion, however, is not between two equal sides, since in an Islamist reading of the spectatorship the screen occupies a hierarchically more privileged position.[25] Nor is it between familiar partners, since in such a reading the screen is considered to be unrelated or a stranger (*namahram*) to viewers (Naficy 1991a). Ritual courtesy, designed to deal with hierarchical and for-mal relations, must be inscribed as a component of viewing, particularly in television and its most collective form, the magazine format.[26] Televi-sion cannot then violate the protocol of formal relations between strangers without incurring the discomfort and criticism of its audience.

Even though formal and polite in its presentational mode, the exile magazine creates a familiar and familial community of address. What turns the formal into the familiar is exilic space, which in its liminal stage finds the formality of the ritual courtesy of the homeland to be comfortingly familiar. This is enhanced by the familiar form of address that some hosts occasionally use. What turns the polite into the familial is the sense that hosts and audience share not only the copresence of the television medium but also a common language, culture, value system, and orienta-tional framework. This concern with collective cultural institutions, particularly with the family structure and the native language, which are perceived to be threatened, tends to enhance the communitarian structure and discourse of exile television. I will deal first with the configuration of the family structure and then the native language as methods by which exile television creates a type of community of address.

Exile media repeatedly and regularly focus on the threat to the constitution of the family. Deterritorialization problematizes, even severs, the bonds with tradition, culture, ethnicity, language, status, family, and nation that tend to interpellate individuals as subjects within ideologies and politics and locate them within the state or civil societies of the homeland. That many exiles enter the host society without their families elevates the threat of severance and deepens the sense of tragedy and loss.[27] Even for those who leave their homeland with their families, the familial tensions are great because of the conflicts that exile sets into motion between generations and gender roles within the family, and the discrepancies it creates between here and there and now and then. These conflicts and discrepancies cause some Iranians to regard family life in exile as unmanageable and altogether undesirable. Consider, for example, the following desolate imaginary picture of a family in exile, which appeared in the weekly magazine *Javanan* (12/2/1988, p. 3):

> Whenever I was alone at home [in Los Angeles] I would imagine that I was married, that my wife would return home from work tired, take a shower without my noticing it, and cook her own meal and eat it alone. I would imagine my son dancing and stomping his feet with his girlfriend upstairs and when confronted with my protest he would shut his door and urge me to be quiet. I would imagine my daughter arriving home drunk and stupefied at midnight, turning the key in the door, and stumbling down the hall to her room. I would imagine the phone ringing the next morning and the school counselor calling me for a new round of counseling, the police summoning me for investigation, and the psychologist urging me to pay his office a visit.

Since, in the case of Iranians in America, the exiles are moving from a familial culture to an individualistic culture, the self is under tremendous pressure to transform accordingly—a process fraught with fear and loathing. The symbiotic, reciprocal, and emotionally intimate relationship that some nostalgic exiles think characterized family life in the homeland comes under serious questioning in the new environment, particularly by women and children, who seem to be the primary agents of acculturation and change. The self cannot maintain an intact sense of "we-self," and because of the change of social context, it loses the grounds on which contextual ego-ideals and successful hierarchical relationships are formed. Familial tensions in exile are so great that many exile periodicals and radio programs carry regular sections in which psychologists and counselors answer questions from readers and listeners about family problems. These professionals also appear regularly on exilic television for short interviews or full-hour discussions with in-studio audiences. *Sokhani ba Ravanshenas*, which began in 1992, is entirely devoted to phone-in questions and answers between audiences and the in-studio psychiatrist-host of the program. The Christian program *Mozhdeh* has attempted to deal with family tensions from a religious point of view.

The use of the native language is another significant marker in exile television's construction of a collective community of address. As I have noted, until recently, with the exception of Assyrian-language programs, all other Iranian programs in Los Angeles were in Persian. Exclusive use of the native tongue is caused not only by Iranians' recent arrival here (they are still liminars) and their nationalism, ethnocentrism, and resistance to assimilation, but also by their desire to validate and consolidate an essentialist Iranian subjectivity in exile. In the discourse of Iranian ritual courtesy this is tantamount to "raising" the exiles to a privileged status. Ignoring the native language causes negative audience reaction, particularly from the older generation. For example, when in the mid-1980s *Iranian* aired a five-minute English-language news commentary for six months, the producer received many negative comments from viewers, forcing him to discontinue the experiment.[28] Overreliance on the native language, however, discourages younger people from watching exilic television. Based on my interviews with program producers and analyses of audience demography elsewhere in the book, it is evident that middle-aged and elderly people form the largest segment of the Iranian television audience. Young people, in their conversations with me, have shown a clear disinterest in television programs that fail to address them and their problems directly. Manuchehr Bibian, producer of *Jam-e Jam*, summed up the dilemma of generational division that television producers face:

> Young people who have learned the English language obtain their music and news from American television channels. Children watch cartoons on American television with which we cannot compete. But there are people who were 25 years or older when they left Iran; they are accustomed to Persian music and proverbs and they cannot speak English as well as their mother tongue. There are those among this group who cannot believe they will die in exile. Our television programs give these people what they want. (Interview, 3/4/1989)

Fig. 15. Discussion show: Parisa Sa'ed hosts *Ma*.

By foregrounding the Persian language, television producers cater to the older age group who are their most loyal viewers, and leave the young people to the assimilative power of American pop culture.[29]

The ways exile producers and viewers use the magazine format to engage in collective social construction and negotiation of reality turns exilic television into what Newcomb and Hirsch have called a "cultural forum" (1983). Such a forum can disseminate information, express shared beliefs and values, and assist the producers and viewers in their acculturation, and their construction of individual and collective identities. The magazine form can both present ideologies and comment on ideological problems. By adding the live phone-in format, the magazine has evolved into a multivocal cultural forum in which a variety of views by various peoples of different ethnoreligious affiliations are exchanged in varied accents. In the process, perhaps more questions will be posed than answered—even about exilic television itself—but this is precisely a chief function of television as a cultural forum, particularly in liminality, when there are more questions and criticisms than answers.[30]

The notion of cultural forum and collective subjectivity necessitates a reverse flow of communication, from viewers to programmers. Such an exchange does occur in exilic television, more directly and intimately than in mainstream American television. Exile productions are often very small, one-person operations in which the producer is often host, director, and advertising sales manager. To obtain advertisements and audience feedback, exile producers, unlike their mainstream television counterparts, urge advertisers, businesses, and viewers to contact them personally through the phone numbers that are flashed on the screen. In their interviews with me many producers pointed to viewers' calls as significant indicators of the size of their public or the popularity of certain topics or personalities. This type of direct interaction increases discursive traffic and assists in establishing a personal and collective link between program producers and their viewers.

Cultural productions not only air the tensions of communitarianism and fragmentation, ethnicity and acculturation, liminality and incorporation, but also often disavow or displace them by ideological rearchaization and reconstitution under the sign of some type of essentialist collectivity, which may predate history and time. The story of the Simorgh is invoked in exile as a way of reconstituting a communal self and a national Iranian identity. This ancient story is best told by the great twelfth-century Iranian mystic poet Faridoddin Attar, in his allegorical epic *Manteq al-Teyr* (The conference of the birds), which tells the story of thousands of birds on a quest for a legendary king of the birds called Simorgh (literally "thirty birds"). After much hardship only thirty birds survive and arrive in the Simorgh's palace, only to discover that the Simorgh they were searching for is none other than the thirty surviving birds themselves, reflected in a mirror (Attar 1971). This and other mystical allegories are so well known to Iranians as to have become encoded into their consciousness. One way to decode it is this: the Iranian self is a communal one—all are one and one is all—and every one is potentially the bearer of a singular, unified truth, or capable of absorption into the unique supreme Being.[31] The homogenizing work of the Simorgh paradigm in Iranian culture far surpasses Attar's allegory, as it shadows over myths and ideals of selfhood, heroism, and nationalism that are drawn upon heavily in exile (Naficy 1990b:231–33). The use of the paradigm in exile, where literary and business establishments are named after the Simorgh, would seem to either disavow the threat of fragmentation of individual and national identities by exile or rearchaize these identities by reconstituting them under the essentialist Iranian communal self, the Simorgh ideal.

The music video *Ma Hameh Irooni Hastim* (We're all Iranian), sung by Andy and Kouros, the duo rock stars of Iranian exiles, provides a rich televisual example for both fragmentation and reconstitution of the communal self and the collective national identity in exile.[32] The video consists of a fast-paced collage of an Andy and Kouros concert in front of a tumultuous audience. It creates an alluring narrative charged with sex, mystery, power, and wildness by means of huge, short-duration close-ups of body parts, musical instruments, and a frenzied audience (mostly females) in an atmosphere saturated by rolling fog, flashing lights, and chiaroscuro lighting. The two singers sing an up-tempo song in Persian that first differentiates Iranian exiles by naming the diverse regions of the country from which they have originated, and then reconstitutes them as a homogeneous population united in their desire for a return to the homeland:

> You are a native of Khuzestan
> You are a child of Abadan
> You are a native of Kermanshah
> You are a native of Kurdestan
> You are a native of Azarbaijan
> You are a child of Kerman
> You are a native of Baluchestan
> You are a child of Sistan.
> Regardless of where we are from,
> We are all Iranians
> Waiting to go back home.

Having united the exiles in their desire to return, the singers proceed to further unify them by suppressing regional differences. Here, the video becomes dialogic: the singers query the audience about their native regions, and the audience responds to each query en masse.

> SINGERS: Who is from Khuzestan?
> AUDIENCE: We are from Khuzestan.
> SINGERS: Who is from Kurdestan?
> AUDIENCE: We are from Kurdestan.
> SINGERS: Who is from Tehran?
> AUDIENCE: We are from Tehran.
> SINGERS: Who loves Iran?
> AUDIENCE: We love Iran.

This video posits that regardless of regional and ethnic differences, Iranians are all members of the same nation and national family. It becomes a modern reworking of the ancient Simorgh paradigm, at a time that the ideals encoded in it are threatened. In the liminality of exile, nationality supersedes ethnicity. It is only much later, and in order to gain political power in the host country, that the exiles will turn to ethnicity.

It is ironic, however, that exilic television tends to reconstitute the

familial self and communal identity largely as a consuming self and identity. This is because the magazine format is disproportionately filled with
expository materials and commercials for products and services, which
impede individual subjectivity but aid the formation of collective subjectivity based on consumerism. In this case, it is not so much the intense
emotional relations among family members and significant others that are
responsible for creating unity as it is economic relations and the pleasures
of consumption.

Exilic television's relationship with the familial self and its treatment of
the family unit is made more complex because collective subjectivity,
which television creates and caters to, is neither fully stable nor unitary.
In it an individual subjectivity is unfolding. This is an uncertain, liminal
subjectivity, one that is not always already in place. By and large, in its first
decade, Iranian exilic television ignored the drama of this unfolding individual identity and the reconfiguration of the traditional patriarchal family structure demanded by it. Television was dominated by forms, such
as the magazine, that usually give access to the public self, and there were
very few examples of forms, such as dramas, more suitable for expressing
emotions and exploring the dramas of self-fashioning and identity formation. With the exception of music videos and occasional serials—*Ro'ya-ye
Emrika'i* (The American dream), *Payvand* (Connection), and *Faseleh*
(Distance)—none of the other components of the magazine format explored in any extended, dramatic, or narrative form the interior world of
emotions, affect, and the evolving self or the nuances of family life.[33] In
*The American Dream* serial the unit of analysis is a transplanted family
consisting of a young couple who must deal with their ties to the home
country, their relatives abroad, and their own relationship with each
other in the new society—all in the context of their status as foreigners
forced to live in a society that is hostile to them and stereotypes them
negatively. Among other issues, *Distance* also deals with a mother-
daughter relationship in exile. By focusing on the dynamics of the family
relations and by pitting the collective national identity against the individuating hybrid exilic identity, these shows express the instability and
complexity of that identity.

## Aesthetics of Exilic Repetition

In cybernetics redundancy and repetition ensure accurate transmission of
signals. Redundancy reduces variability, indeterminacy, and unpredicta-
bility. If in times of normalcy humans seek the thrill of the unexpected,
in times of chaos they seek certitude—the expected. Exile as a time of
chaos demands stability, which can be found in television as ritual, fetish,

Fig. 16. Serials: Mother-son drama in exile in *The American Dream*.

and nostalgia. Exilic television produces discursive and symbolic order and rigidity in the face of personal and social disorder and fluidity.

Repetition and redundancy are encouraged by the exile magazine format and its postmodern pastiche style, which tend to suppress narrative singularity in favor of expository diversity and segmentation. Repetition takes many forms. Images are either replicated synchronically within the frame itself or repeated sequentially and diachronically within the flow. This is especially true of the commercials and certain fetishized and stereotyped icons, which are repeated a number of times during any one program.

In exile, repetition is a way of reassuring the self that it will not disappear or dissolve: "It is as if the activity of repeating prevents us, and others, from skipping us or overlooking us entirely" (Said 1986:56). Two contradictory processes seem to be involved: one an affirmation of the "old" identity in the homeland (relatively unified, usually familial), the other a confirmation of the "new" identity in exile (syncretic and generally individuating). The nostalgic tropes of home that are circulated repeatedly within program logos, texts, and music videos in exile represent an affirmation of the old

Fig. 17. In-frame repetition: Fattaneh's image in her music video, aired by *Jam-e Jam* in March 1992.

self, a way of reminding ourselves not to overlook ourselves. The validation of the new self figures the individual as a consumer; an individuating self in exile; and a member, if not of a physical community, at least of a symbolic community (communitas) in exile.

The formation of the new self as a consumer is evident predominantly in commercials. Recently arrived in this land of affluence and waste, the average exile from the Third World, who in the past more than likely cycled and recycled all products, from food cans to old tires, requires indoctrination through repetition to become a guiltless consumer. The incessant repetition of commercials on Iranian television not only makes economic sense for the advertisers and program makers but is productive ideologically, inculcating consumerism. The high educational level and financial resources of recently arrived exiles from Iran make them more receptive than some to the ideology of consumerism, and more adept at integration into that ideology and economic system. In postmodern consumer ideology the adoption of a consumer lifestyle and consumption of products extend to the creation and consumption of media for communication, propaganda, and advertising so globally widespread and locally intense that it has been dubbed "mediolatry" and "semiotic fetishism" (Mitchell 1986:202). The active Iranian popular culture in Los Angeles, which within less than a decade has produced the following varied menu of media, provides an instance of such mediolatry: nearly 80 periodicals, 62 regularly scheduled television programs, 18 regularly scheduled radio programs, and 4 telephone newscasts were produced. During this period, some 180 feature films were screened in public theaters in Los Angeles and 26 features produced. By 1992, over 700 music cassettes had been produced in Los Angeles, half-a-dozen discos with a mixture of Iranian and Western music were in operation, and Iranian rock concerts were being staged in such bastions of American pop culture as the Shrine Auditorium and the Hollywood Palladium. The menu was rounded off with a plethora of poetry reading nights and academic and semiacademic conferences, seminars, and lectures.

The affirmation of the individuating self in exile can be seen in many aspects of televisual production: changing program format, from a general magazine catering to all family members to more specialized formats; evolution of the notion of audience from a homogeneous mass to targetable clusters; development of an advertising-driven schedule; syndication and networking of programs; and increasing professionalization, involving division of labor and inscription of aesthetics and ideological systems of mainstream cinema and television. The self in exile, however, is not an autonomous, always already individuated self; rather, it is a self in process of formation and differentiation and as such it is hybrid and ambivalent. The textual practices of the heterogeneous, segmented supertext and flow of exilic television inscribe and promote these multiple subjectivities.

The confirmation of the new communal identity, as a national group uprooted in exile or an ethnic group with roots within the host society, is also complex. The liminality and ambivalence of exile produce profound crises of identity and "ethnic anxiety." Living with such crises is painful, and they must be resolved. One way to accomplish this, suggests Michael Fischer, is through repetition of the individual experience, which "cannot be accounted for by itself" (1986:206). It must be repeated in order to establish its realness, its validity. Moreover, since the unitary experience of a single individual is deemed insignificant and insufficient in exile, televisual repetition is needed in order to establish the truth of living as a community in exile. By circulating fetishes of there and then and the nostalgic narratives of return, television tends to affirm the old "authentic" self, and by repeating representations of consumer lifestyle here and now it tends to confirm a new emerging "consumer" self.[34] Taken together, it can be seen that television assists the exiles in constructing a hybrid self and identity, not by producing absences but by multiplying presences of the home and the past and of the here and the now through the magazine format and its ontology of liveness and copresence.

This exilic recapitulation (affirmation of the old and confirmation of the new selves) is part of an aesthetics of seriality and intertextuality fostered by the postmodern world of late capitalism, characterized by dissolution of centers, amorphousness of texts and boundaries, indeterminacy of meaning, and multiplicity of subjectivities. The pleasure of television's system of intertextual seriality and simulation is not so much derived from innovation and "shock of the new" as it is from pull of the permanent, and "return of the identical" (Eco 1985:178).

These multiple notions of repetition characteristic of Western postmodernism provide the context in which the exiles, through their cultural productions, can stage repeatedly their own imaginary returns to their own originary schemas and values. For them, however, this "return" is not wholehearted; it is charged with potential choices about which there is much ambivalence: a return to the old originary identity, or a turn toward consumerist subjectivity, or a move to construct a third, syncretic identity. Thus the repeated circulation of narratives and fetishes that embody both the exilic search for the schema and for the permanent, and the craving for the current and the new not only rewards our ability to textually foresee narrative developments but also serves to reinforce the internalization of a split subjectivity and of a syncretic identity in exile.[35]

## The Ideology of Professionalism

With the development of structures of commodification and assimilation such as advertising-driven schedules, varied magazine formats, live transmission nationwide, time-brokerage, syndication, and audience segmentation, there has emerged not only a certain diversity in televisual discourses but also an ideology of professionalism—both of which have begun to gradually erode the authority and the univocality of the discourses of the first years of liminal exile. Stuart Hall defines professionalism as "practical technical routinization of practice" (1977:344), and it can be seen in the division of labor and the variety now becoming evident in Iranian television programs. One person no longer produces, tapes, edits, hosts, and distributes a program by him- or herself. The number of producers has increased, as have the number of hosts, who are not necessarily producers any more. A single program may contain a number of segments, each produced and presented by a different male or female host, thereby increasing not only the variety of faces and voices but also the polysemy of discourses. Likewise, the division of labor has extended to technical personnel, which have been growing in number, experience, and specialization. In addition, in Los Angeles a number of advertising agencies have emerged that obtain and place the majority of the ads on Iranian television.

Variety is another element in professionalization, which is undergirded by the diversification of program types and formats. The rigid magazine format evolved into other types, with many shows emulating mainstream American TV. Experimentation with narrative forms led to the airing of over a dozen satirical serials and soap operas about exile.[36] A new genre of exile-produced music videos influenced heavily by American music videos also emerged, which provides a discourse as well as a metadiscourse about assimilation and consumerism.[37]

Professionalism entails internalization of ideological, narrative, and aesthetic codes of the profession. In Los Angeles, Iranian television is being produced, transmitted, and consumed in a highly media-conscious and media-sophisticated context, whose codes and values have gradually been internalized by exile producers (and audiences). At the most obvious level, this entails simulation and imitation of the predominant televisual formats of mainline media. For example, *Midnight Show* seems to pattern itself after ABC's *Nightline* (in an ad its host is called "Iran's Ted Koppel"), *Ma* (whose host is sometimes labeled "the Iranian Barbara Walters") was modeled after the syndicated *Oprah Winfrey Show*, *Arya in L.A.* in much of 1989 resembled KABC-TV's tourist magazine show *Eye on L.A.* (taking its audience to various tourist spots around town), *Jong-e Bamdadi*, with its heavy news emphasis, is like *CBS Morning*, and *Sima-ye Ashna* resembles ABC's *Good Morning America*.

Internalization of American ideologies of liberal democracy and consumerism and the codes of professionalism, intellectual property, and ways of seeing and narrating the world does not occur automatically or naturally, especially for exile producers from non-Western worlds with vastly different cultural frameworks. They require training, which is often provided by the stations broadcasting exilic programs. KSCI-TV's procedure for training, and in effect interpellating, foreign-language producers is inscribed in the Foreign Language Program Monitor Form, quoted in full below.

KSCI-TV's Foreign Language Program<br>Monitor Form

Title of Show:                          Date:
Airtime:                                Length:

If the answer to any of the following questions is YES, please explain on reverse side.

DID THE PROGRAM DEAL WITH A CONTROVERSIAL SUBJECT OF
PUBLIC IMPORTANCE?

DID THE PROGRAM CONTAIN OFFERS TO THE VIEWER INVOLVING
LOTTERIES OR GAMBLING?

WERE THERE ANY PERSONAL ATTACKS?

WAS THERE ANY OBSCENITY?

WAS THERE ANY OFFER TO THE VIEWER THAT MIGHT BE A
FRAUDULENT SCHEME?

DID THE PROGRAM HAVE ANY POLITICAL CONTENT, SUCH AS
PRESENTATIONS BY CANDIDATES FOR PUBLIC OFFICE?

WAS THERE ANY ADVERTISING THAT MIGHT HAVE BEEN FALSE OR
MISLEADING?

WAS THERE ANY ADVERTISING WHOSE SPONSORSHIP WAS NOT
CLEARLY EVIDENT?

HOW MANY MINUTES OF COMMERCIALS WERE SHOWN?

BRIEF DESCRIPTION OF THE CONTENTS:

SOURCE: KSCI-TV.

This form is given to the foreign-language monitors whom the station
hires to view and evaluate ethnic programs as they are being aired. If a
programmer continually receives negative evaluations from the monitor,
his contract can be terminated by the station with a month's notice. The
items in the questionnaire are in effect the station's standards and norms
of professionalism disguised in an interrogative form, and the monitors
are asked to carefully judge adherence to them. According to a KSCI-TV
official, Iranians were particularly singled out for extended monitoring on
a regular basis because of the volatility of their politics; the antagonistic
competition between exilic periodicals and television programs; and the
excessive airing of commercials, far beyond the station's standard 14
minutes of ads per hour-long program (extended to 20 minutes for Iranians). In addition, extended monitoring was motivated by a desire on the
part of the station to avoid jeopardizing its broadcast license.[38]

The criteria embedded in this form and the station's power to ter-
minate a show with a one-month notice place the programmers in a relatively vulnerable financial and political position, with the result that they
discourage substantial investment due to fear of short-notice termination,
and encourage short-term tactics to maximize immediate profits. Timidity
regarding controversial matters and a reduction over time of partisan poli-

tics are also a result.[39] Those U.S. laws dealing with copyrights, libel, slander, and obscenity are enforced by this regime,[40] and "professionalism" is inculcated in producers by the fostering of appropriate routines and procedures of television production. All of this naturalizes the codes and values of the dominant host culture.[41]

The ideology of professionalism involves employing the dominant codes and rules of narration and representation. Increasingly Iranian television programs have began to subscribe to the routinized rules of the host country's discourses, encoded in the four narrative and programming regimes of mainstream television: classical Hollywood cinema style for narrative and dramatic serials; seamlessness and segmentation of the televisual flow; objective news value for newscasts and public affairs programming; and variation as a principle governing programming, counterprogramming, presentation, and format differentiation—all devices used to establish individual program identity not through sameness, as was the case in the early phase of exile when home infused the discourse, but through difference. In effect, by adopting and routinizing these regimes of professionalism in their practice, Iranian producers (and viewers) are interpellated unknowingly into American consumer capitalism, individuated subject positioning, and representative democracy. Significantly, however, the presence of such professionalism not only signals the incorporation of Iranian exilic television into the dominant cultural mode of production but also masks that incorporation by naturalizing it.

Iranian exilic television in its first decade structurally reflected and shaped the lives of its producers and audiences. Reflecting the formlessness of liminality, it first emerged as a hermetically sealed collection of audiovisuals put together with great individual effort by producers and addressed to what was thought to be a homogeneous audience. A ritual exilic genre of television was developed with its own generic conventions, strategies of signification, viewer positioning, and transmission and consumption patterns. The emergence of these strategies of structuration and commodification signals the evolution of Iranians from liminality toward incorporation, and from exile into ethnicity. This process, however, is neither linear nor consensual as much of the traditional sociological literature would seem to posit. It is, rather, a conflictual and dialectical process involving resistances, differences, reversals, and leaps forward, during which features of both liminality and incorporation may coexist for quite some time—a truly syncretic culture. These tensions, ambivalences, and syncretic practices characteristic of exile are more evident in the programs themselves and in the intertextual interplay between them and their interstitial materials, a subject discussed in the next chapter.

# 5
# Fetishization, Nostalgic Longing, and the Exilic National Imaginary

## Returning to the Homeland

*The warm midnight air of August that suddenly hit me was the first sign that I had arrived in Iran. As I stepped out of the plane onto the ramp—the last person to get off—I encountered this incredibly warm air, so thick and warm that it had become a material thing into which I stepped. Ghosts of other planes seemed to silently float in that dark thickness like grey whales in water. I was remarkably calm. For a moment I flashed back on the image of the Pope years back landing in his homeland of Poland, or that of the American hostages held in Iran returning home, kneeling down on the tarmac to kiss the ground. I dismissed the idea immediately as too sentimental. I also had no sense of panic or fear of the pervasive security system, even though I had worried about it earlier. It had been thirteen years since my last stay in Iran in 1978, the year the revolution took out the Shah. I did not know whether my name would be on the list kept by the airport security and this began to gnaw at me as passengers lined up for the first of what turned out to be four checkpoints. At the first, the customs agent asked what the address of my residence in Iran would be. For a moment I panicked because I could not remember the house number. I told him I had been away for many years and could not remember it. My candor brought a smile to his face. "How about 280," he said. Considerably relieved, I said: "That'll do."*

*He entered the fictitious address on the form. This was my first en-counter with the Iran I knew, and the first of many realizations that the monolithic monster the exiles in Los Angeles had created of the current Iran was a much more nuanced and complex organism. I felt at home, realizing at the same time that not all people—especially not those on various blacklists—would be treated so kindly. On learning how long I had been away, the last agent waved me on without checking my luggage, saying: "Welcome to your homeland, enjoy your time." I felt welcomed, simultaneously realizing in the treat-ment of returnees the Islamic government's attempt to reverse the loss of skilled people caused by the revolution and by its own subsequent policies.*

*My sister Nahid had given a party to celebrate my arrival. After the party, upon leaving her house, the atmosphere was somehow charged as if I was leaving the country. Earlier that night my sister's kids had asked me to talk into a tape recorder for them. After relat-ing a few jokes and childhood anecdotes I broke into singing Rumi's famous poem, "Song of the Reed." I began hesitatingly but my voice gradually gained confidence. Emboldened, I closed my eyes and abandoned myself to the exilic lament of the poem and was amazed at how much of it I was able to recall after so many years. At a few points I forgot the lines and paused, but my father who was sitting near me quickly fed them to me. In the end, I opened my eyes to see that I was not the only one overwhelmed with tears. The bittersweet realization came to me again that return can never be fully consum-mated. To be sure, I had returned, and was with my loved ones again, but it was temporary and, besides, we were in the grip of other exiles. If exile be a palimpsest, I had reached only one layer. Many more remained.*

*Earlier that morning I had attempted to reach another layer. Ac-companied by my mother and sisters, I had visited my childhood house, now turned into an elementary school. It was after school hours and the students were gone. I examined all the interstices of the old house and was filled with a deep sense of attachment to this place. Yet there was a strange sense of detachment and incomplete-ness. In that conflicted moment I realized again why the impossibility of reunion with childhood makes its metaphoric and nostalgic restag-ing through literature, cinema, and video—especially from exile—so appealing.*

*Our tears at my sister's house were, on the one hand, from happi-ness at consummation of this small exile—my temporary return—and on the other hand from knowing that many more exiles, separations, and losses remained to be bridged, longed for, and recovered by each of us—and some of them would be impossible. We are always already in exile.*

## Television as a Fetish

Syncretism and hybridity are similar in some respects but not the same by any means. Syncretism involves impregnating one culture with the contents of another in order to create a third, stable culture while hybridity involves an ambivalence about both of the original cultures, thereby leading to creation of a slipzone of indeterminacy and shifting positionalities. This is a state of unbelonging, in effect a form of freedom, nomadism, homelessness, or vagrancy—even opportunism—because it settles on nothing but difference itself. The dominant host culture does not interpellate the exiles unproblematically. Host-exile power relations produce psychological and ideological ambivalences that, when unresolved into syncretism, can lead to defensive hybrid strategies of disavowal, self-deception, fetishization of the homeland, nostalgic longing, and chauvinistic nationalism.

Fetishization in exile results when the exiles invest heavily in constructing certain cathexted images of homeland and the past while knowing deep down that those are forms of disavowal, or of partial representation, because they are fixed and frozen. This "duality in the mind" stems from one of the major contradictions that one faces in exile: to remember the past and the homeland or to forget them—both of which are painful. As such, fetishization is a homeostatic mechanism by which exiles attempt to transform an unstable *societas* (empirical exilic community) into a stable *communitas* (symbolic exilic community).

For reasons I have discussed elsewhere (Naficy 1991b), film cannot be considered to be a fetish, but photographs can. Television, too, has an ontology and a use that allow it to both play on fetishism and become itself a fetish. The conditions in which television is received are usually private. (This parallels the usual way of looking at a photograph.) Moreover, the ability to record and replay programs at will, from any point and in any mode and speed, help to denarrativize the sounds and the images. The conditions of transmission, too, including the repeated airing of programs and the electronic manipulation of sounds and images, tend to lower the narrative line by overfamiliarization and abstraction, rendering the sound and images susceptible to fetishistic uses.

For the exiles, the television set itself may achieve the status of a fetish, or what D. W. Winnicott has called a "transitional object." A child in infancy may form a special attachment to an object (such as a blanket) that helps him make the transition from overreliance on his relation with the primary care-giver to developing relationships with others. Such comforting objects of illusion "start each human being off with what will always be important for them, i.e., a neutral area of experience which will not be challenged" (quoted in Laplanche and Pontalis 1973:465). Television in exile appears to act in a similar way, since the fetishized images and narratives of the homeland aired on it give the set an aura that instead of challenging tends to comfort those who are caught in the liminal and transitional spaces of exile. In addition, like all transitional objects, television facilitates individuation.

The pervasiveness and versatility of TV sets and VCRs, the ease with which they can be operated, and their now pocket-sized portability, render both television hardware and software into potential fetishes that like photographs can be transported to any location and held in the hand as well as in memory. Visual fetishes and nostalgic narrative, driven by the primary process, form a major component of the iconographic and narrative segments of the magazine format. This includes program logos, news photos, film footage, and music videos. The newscast itself is a narrative in whose construction fetishization and longing are inscribed.

## Fetishism and Liminality

The fetishism of exilic popular culture, including television, helps control the terror and the chaos of liminality, but if one submits to the process, these fetishes become controlling agents themselves. Fetishism thus is always already ambivalent. In psychoanalysis, fetishism is defined as a form of perversion that results from the threat of castration posed by the absence of the penis in the mother. Two contradictory attitudes arise in the male child. One is a recognition of the lack. The second is a disavowal of the lack through fetishization of the difference, resulting in the splitting of the ego (Freud 1969:58–61). The fetish blocks the view of the lack but, paradoxically and inevitably, in its own existence it points to the absence, it becomes an index of the absence. The fetish as a substitute, therefore, memorializes the absence (Freud 1961b:154). The person thus alternates between belief and disbelief and this is precisely a major source of the ambivalence in fetishism. If for Freud fetishization based on the threat of loss is a crucial moment in forming male sexuality, for Lacan it is a general process of sexual formation in both sexes. While many film scholars have focused on fetishism as disavowal of lack, Gaylyn Studlar (1988) formulated it as disavowal of separation from the object of desire, the mother. While in the former model the pain of the lack is turned into sadistic pleasure by mastering the woman and controlling her fetishes, the pleasure in the latter stems from identification with the woman, submission to her fetishes, and ultimate symbiosis with her.

Despite the differing formulations and the disparate spheres of human activity for which Marx and Freud developed their notions of fetishism, they both invoked the religious conceptions of fetishism prevalent in eighteenth-century anthropology of religion, positing that human beings invent fetishes and invest them with powers and spirits only to ultimately submit to them by forgetting their manufactured inception—as if the source of power was some transcendental entity beyond human community. As Linda Williams explains, these two thinkers shared yet another insight:

> Both Marxian and Freudian fetishes locate illusory and compensatory forms of pleasure and power in the gleam of gold or the lacy frill of an undergarment. . . . For both, fetishization involves the construction of a substitute object to evade the complex, but ultimately empowering, realities of social and psychical relations. (1989:29)

The exiles locate the "illusory compensatory forms of pleasure and power" not in gold or undergarment but in images of the homeland and of the past. As a fetishized substitute for the homeland, these images—like any other fetish—must encode unequal relations of power and be ahistorical, stereotyped, and simplified.[1] As liminars, exiles face two types of immanent and imminent threats simultaneously: the threat of the disappearance of the homeland and the threat of themselves disappearing in the host society. Fetishization in this case entails disavowal of both of these threats by means of condensing all the meanings of the home and the host societies into substitute fetishes and frozen stereotypes. Thus, in the game of power exercised by the exiles, the fetish objects are invested with extraordinary power and allure. While fetishization tends to empower the hitherto powerless exiles and reduce the threatening spell of the two lands, the overcathexis of fetishes positions the exiles to become victims of their own creations. This is particularly true when Freudian and Marxian notions of fetishization meet, that is, when fetishes are turned into commodities and images that serve to sell products and ideologies in the marketplace.

In exile, fetishism based on disavowal of both lack and separation is operative, as a result of which the exiled subject vacillates between being active and being passive, between control and submission, stability and instability. Fetishization is a contradictory process in yet another way: during the liminal phase of exile, it aids in the formation and consolidation of exilic identity by circulating illusions that stand for the homeland but that either disavow the threat of, or invite nostalgia for, the homeland; at the same time, the electronically mediated circulation and commodification of fetishes helps to imbricate the exiles within the dominant host's ideological and socioeconomic systems. The use of televisual fetishes to produce stability will be explored in this chapter. Its inscription of instability will be examined in the following chapter.

## Fetishization and the Production of Stability

In exile, separation from the mother country is a severing of deeply held ties, and is a source of trauma and pain. During the liminal phase, the exiles seem to form an "affective fixation" to the traumatic experience of separation, and they relive that experience as though they were "not finished with the traumatic situation, as though they were still faced by it as an immediate task which has not been dealt with" (Freud 1977:275–76). The shock of the new culture further enhances the trauma and the pain. This is, I believe, the general condition of liminality shared by all emigres, but each culture brings its own specificity to the situation.

In the case of Iranian exiles three factors deepened the trauma of separation and the pain of the absence of home. The first was the 1978–79 revolution that drove the majority of them out of the country and constituted for some a great personal loss—of property, status, power, and links with family members. This loss was made more painful because many Iranians at home, particularly the official media, denounced those who had chosen exile as traitors who had deserted their homeland in a time of trouble.

The second factor was the ravages of a terrible war at home.[2] The long and deadly war with Iraq, which began shortly after the revolution in September 1980 and lasted until cease-fire was declared in August 1988, for many exiles constituted a profound national loss—of human, natural, and economic resources and national honor and world prestige. The destruction and loss caused by the war, the inability to affect its course from a distance, and the guilt of living in safety and relative opulence in the West all compounded the inherent trauma of exilic dislocation.

The third was the act, and the repercussions, of taking 50 Americans hostage in the American embassy in Tehran in November 1979 and holding them until January 1981. This indefensible act, which turned the newly formed Islamic government into an international pariah, aroused widespread chauvinistic sentiments in the United States, fanned by two presidents, Carter and Reagan, and by a generally deferential media.[3] The media and politicians labeled the hostage-takers, and by implication all Iranians, variously as students, militants, terrorists, kidnappers, criminals, and barbarians. Mediawork, the combined operation of the signifying institutions, commodified these messages further: T-shirts bore slogans such as "Nuke Iran." Demonstrators carried banners saying "Camel Jockeys, Go Home." Pop records such as "They Can Take Their Oil and Shove It" became national hits on radio. Jokes about Iran and Iranians cropped up regularly on *Saturday Night Live*, Johnny Carson's *Tonight Show*, radio talk shows, comedy clubs, improvisational theaters, and Las Vegas acts (Naficy 1989a:232–33). Iranians in the United States came under considerable financial and legal pressures as well: President Carter canceled the visas of all Iranian students, forcing them to reregister, and deported those found in violation. The severing of all diplomatic and economic ties between the two countries made the transfer of funds and legal documents, travel, and communication into ordeals. Many Iranians were taunted and beaten up in counterdemonstrations, refused service, denied apartments, and jailed (one for stealing a single grape from a store). Both the "news" and their own personal experiences deeply embarrassed and humiliated the Iranians living in the United States. There was also a sense of outrage at being subjected to shame for actions committed by the clerics, whom the majority of the exiles disliked.

## Aesthetics of Fetishization Based on Loss

While the revolution and the later war made separation from home and loss of homeland painful, the hostage situation and the consequent loss of face and prestige in a foreign land made life in exile unbearable. The end result was that Iranian exiles, like many others, suffered from multiple exiles, or from what Maya Jaggi (1988:164) and Abdolmaboud Ansari (1988:14–16) have respectively called "double exclusion" and "dual marginality," meaning that the exiles were accepted neither at home nor in exile.

It is the recognition of these multiple losses that televisual fetishization of home as an unchanging stereotype disavows, masks, and ultimately turns into pleasure. Exile television, in its first decade, produced fetishized stereotypes by fixating on Iran prior to its tripartite "loss"—to the Islamic Republic, to the war, and to exile. Fixation on prewar Iran and on pre-Islamic iconography are ways of repressing the trauma and shielding the self from the effects of exile. They are also forms of ideologically repressing the current Islamic state. The psychic process involved in the transplantation of an emigre can be analogized to the entry of the child from the Imaginary (homeland) into the Symbolic (exile), which reduces the mother to a memory that, in the words of Mulvey, "oscillates between memory of maternal plenitude and memory of a lack" (1975:14). This formulation is apt for Iranians; they think of their homeland in feminine terms, as motherland (*mam-e vatan*), and of their exile as separation from this mother. (These concepts are widely circulated in exile popular culture.) Excess and oscillation characterize the memory that the motherland evokes, as exiles repeatedly and alternately recall their homeland as a nurturing mother or a tortured mother whose body (in the words of a political activist) is being torn asunder by "the wolves and the hyenas" now ruling Iran (Mofid 1987:27). While television newscasts and news commentaries tended to emphasize the lack by focusing on the bad new times, music videos in particular highlighted the plenitude by dramatizing the good old times.

Through identification with these fixed images the splitting of the subject in exile is thwarted, as he/she returns to the narcissism of the Imaginary, united with the motherland. In this way, during the liminal stage, the exiles remain psychologically whole and home remains partially repressed as a fetish. Through controlling "there" and "then" the exile can control "here" and "now."[4]

At this point a crucial political question must be asked: Who is doing the controlling and who is benefitting from this process? The answer is that those who want to gain political power attempt to regulate the flow of fetishes. Jean Baudrillard notes:

> As power that is transferred to beings, objects and agencies, [the fetish] is universal and diffuse, but it crystallizes at strategic points so that its flux can be regulated and diverted by certain groups or individuals for their own benefit. (1981:89)

In the case of Iranian exile, it has been the royalist factions who have been the most successful both in regulating the flux of fetishization and in controlling Iranian politics and political discourses in California. They have accomplished this by promoting an anthropomorphized notion of the motherland as an indigent and suffering mother. The overdetermination of this notion in exilic media fetishizes "motherland," and chauvinistic nationalism results. Intense focus on and overinvestment in the fetish demand that the fetish and its synecdoche remain pure, unambiguous, irreproachable, and authentic. When the fetish involves a nation and its history, such views can lead to jingoistic nationalism and to racially prejudiced stances, both of which are evident and implied in the discourse of Iranian exile media, which insist on distinct authenticity, historical antiquity, and racial difference. In this way the media, especially television, produce in exile a cultural artifact, an imaginary nation, or (as formulated by Benedict Anderson) an "imagined community" (1983:14–16).[5]

In the discourse of Iranian exilic television, nothing is more sacred than

"Iran" itself, a homeland that has actually undergone rapid fundamental changes under the Islamic Republic, but whose televisual simulacrum in exile remained generally stable, at least during the war with Iraq. In terms of power relations, this "authentic" homeland, memorialized through fetishization and nostalgic longing, was usually projected as a secular, non-Islamic community. This was accomplished by using fetishes that continually referred either to the secularized Pahlavi era prior to the Islamic revolution of 1978–79 or to the far-distant pre-Islamic past of the seventh century. It seems that the more the exile community was incorporated into mainstream American culture, although its position was marginal, the more exilic television clung to a fetishized construct of homeland and of the past that failed to take into account the reality of changes taking place in Iran. As the original present-day Iran was found wanting or receding, this myth of a secular Iran continued to act through televisual surfaces like a series of Lacanian mirrors within which exile members (mis)recognized themselves. Iranian exiles thus not only found themselves located in the social imaginary of a "nation in exile" but also negotiated for themselves positions as televisual subjects. Simulacrum thus ended up replacing lack.

The televisual iconography of this imagined homeland is a prerevolutionary Iranian flag flying high, waving with a gentle breeze against a blue cloudless Iranlike sky. Often this nostalgic visual is accompanied by patriotic songs, such as in a video by Aref that had the following refrain: "People always people, Iran always Iran."[6] In 1988, with the intensification of the Iran-Iraq war and the bombing of Iranian cities, the status of the flag became a major issue among the exiles, with each political faction attempting to monopolize or modify it in order to regulate its use for its own benefit. One arena in which this semiotic and ideological battle was waged was the public demonstrations held by Iranians in Los Angeles. Those supporting a return to constitutional monarchy in Iran carried the flag used during the Shah's era: three horizontal stripes (red, white, and green) with a lion in the center white stripe, holding a sword in a raised paw, while a rising sun shines behind him. Those on the left, who opposed monarchy, opted for a flag made of the three colors but without the lion, the sun, and the sword. Some advocated a white flag as a symbol of freedom and peace.[7] During the bombing of cities, the choice of the flag became a hot topic of debate, sometimes leading to physical skirmishes. Exilic periodicals and radio and television broadcasts reflected and encouraged this debate. The most graphic example on television was the animated film *Shir va Shamshir* (The lion and the sword), made by Bahram Basiri.[8] To fully appreciate the ideological and the semiotic skir-

mishes encoded in it, a schematic representation of the soundtrack and
the visuals is provided.

| Sound | Images |
|---|---|
| A strong wind is blowing. Then, we hear voice of Shah Mohammad Reza Pahlavi, televised on the eve of the revolution: "I want all my dear fellow countrymen to think about Iran. We all think about Iran. In these historic moments, we all think about Iran. I, too, have heard the message of your revolution." | Close-up of lion holding a raised sword, tail raised high, sun is behind him.<br><br>Zoom back to reveal lion's location: in center (white) stripe of the flag.<br><br>Suddenly, lion's head is bowed down. |
| Revolutionary slogans: "Death to the Shah," "Long live Khomeini." Then, rapid gunfire. Khomeini's voice: "How can I thank this nation which gave up everything in the path of God?" Then, one after another we hear the national anthems of England, the U.S., and the U.S.S.R. | Lightning, thunder. Lion loses sword. Sun disappears from behind him. Lion is gone. A sword appears with British Union Jack embossed on it, another carries U.S. Stars and Stripes, the Soviet Hammer and Sickle is added. Swords disappear, leaving hammer and sickle and the red color in back. |
| Suddenly, the lion roars angrily, we hear machine guns, tumult, then a patriotic Iranian march: "O Iran, O Bejeweled Land." | A furious lion attacks superpower signs, causing the sun to reappear behind him and the sword to appear in his hand. He vanquishes all foes and assumes same position of pride in the Iranian flag as at beginning. |

A decade of complex history and politics is condensed in a system of
signs in this chauvinist narrative, which predates the breakup of the Eastern bloc and of the Soviet Union. Its importance lies in the manner in
which history is spoken through what Luce Irigaray has called an "overcathexis of vision" (1985), a visual fetish for Iran: the flag and the map of
Iran. Pahlavi Iran is seen by male-dominated exilic television as stable and
as the reference point for historical interpretation and reconstruction.

Fig. 18. Semiotic battle: Iranian lion attacks the signs of foreign powers, from *The Lion and the Sword*.

The revolution and the monopolization of power by the Islamists are interpreted as having been engineered, or at least aided, by the superpowers of the day, eventually leading to the formation of a communist Iran. Finally, the Shah himself is symbolized as a fallen lion whose vision of a glorious Iran is restored by a royalist uprising, untainted by superpower assistance. Clearly, exile produces not only nationalism but also chauvinism, not only power but also delusions of power.

Most program logos likewise highlight the link to the secular, fetishized past by borrowing either from ancient pre-Islamic Persian motifs (Persepolis palace in *Jam-e Jam*, a 4,000-year-old golden bowl in *Omid*) or from the Pahlavi era's official culture of spectacle (the Shahyad monument in *Iranian*). Further, clips from Albert Lamorisse's highly visual film on Iran, *The Lovers' Wind* (1969), are either used in opening and closing titles of programs (*Jam-e Jam, Iranian*) or within program texts and music videos when a reference is made to Iran. In fact, this single film, produced under the Pahlavi government as part of its official culture, which shows the Iranian landscape and people filmed from a roving helicopter, has be-

Fig. 19. *Iranian*'s logo: Lion in the center surrounded by a parallelogram bearing the green, white, and red colors of the Iranian flag.

come so closely identified by exilic television with the "authentic" but "lost" or "vanishing" (hence imagined) Iran that it can be said to be occupying all three Peircian definitions of the sign. By constructing a limited selective representation of Iran, this film and clips from it have come to reproduce in exile an anomalous ideological structure: a royalist official culture in exile without royalty. Almost entirely absent from TV logos in the first decade of exile television were any images of the magnificent Islamic buildings and monuments. This iconographic absence corroborates the point made previously, that exilic television initially conflated anti-Khomeinism with anti-Islamism, thus ignoring a bedrock of current Iranian culture.

Titles of shows, too, testify to the desire among producers to posit in exile some sort of Iranian authenticity, antiquity, and nationalism. Terms such as "Iran," "national," "the nation," "Pars," and "Aryan," which are repeated in show titles in various iterations and combinations, reverberate with these themes.[9] Through this sort of iconography and titling, exile television constructs Iran in the past tense. In so doing, it contains the threat of the slipping away of the homeland, and it recoups through rearchaiza-

Fig. 20. *Jahan Nama*'s logo: Program title is in the center of the map of Iran, itself placed on the tricolor flag in the background.

tion the "loss" of that homeland to those it considers to be usurpers and hijackers of Iranian discourse—Islamist "fundamentalists." As an ahistorical fetish, "homeland" can now be held in memory and captured and reworked on television without pain.

Program titles also point to a contrasting way in which exilic television symbolically constructs the community in exile. Titles abound that connote friendliness and togetherness.[10] These titles emphasize both an imaginary familial self and a cohesive community in exile, a veritable "electronic communitas." The majority of the shows in this category are recent and focus more on life in exile than on conditions in the home country. Finally, both titles and show contents construct life in exile in the present tense, life in the process of being lived, life full of action and interaction.

### Aesthetics of Fetishization Based on Separation

The temporary abandonment of the Karbala paradigm for grieving (founded on the death of imam Hosain, the originary event in constructing Shi'ism) may have led to dysphoria and the production of disavowed

CH 18  KSCI
LOS ANGELES

CH 48  KSCI
SAN DIEGO

ARYA IN LA

Every Monday at 12.00 Midnight

Fig. 21. *Arya in L.A.*'s logo: Aryan and pre-Islamic Zoroastrian motifs.

knowledges, particularly masochistic fetishism. This is seen in exile television's representation of the current Islamist order in Iran, which utilizes
the same mummification process as was applied to pre-Islamic Iran, with
one major difference: as much as the fetishization of the Iranian past was
celebratory, the fetishization of its present Islamist conditions is celibate.
Like Iranian intellectuals and writers abroad, exilic television's dominant
mode of discourse on Iran in the present is one of tragedy, in which
masochistic pleasure is produced by overemphasis on disparagement,
denunciation, disfigurement, destruction, and death—without invoking
the deeply traditional Karbala paradigm. Television constructs a representation of present Islamic Iran as a ruined motherland in the throes of
death, eulogizes the death of the present by mourning it, memorializes the
past by commemorating and celebrating it, and produces masochistic
pleasure by identifying with the tortured and dying country.

The masochistic aesthetic of exilic television befits the liminal state, as
programs draw heavily upon the "symbolic vocabulary of poverty and indigence" (Turner 1974:245) by foregrounding the hardship that has beset
Iran since the revolution. The symbolic value of the poor is enormous,
and many thinkers and politicians have used it. The power of Rousseau's
Noble Savage, Marx's proletariat, Gandhi's untouchables, or Khomeini's

dispossessed is great in mobilizing these discourses as well as political movements. Predominantly royalist and chauvinist exile television has used the symbolically constructed image of Iran as indigent to mobilize the exiles against what it presents as the sole cause of that indigence—the Islamic regime.

As part of this discourse, Iran was portrayed, especially before the cease-fire with Iraq, to be a total ruin and a vast cemetery, with the result that any reference to it concerned destruction and waste. A case in point is the episode of *Omid* aired on 3/7/1988, during which the host painted a harrowing verbal picture of Tehran as a ruin under the first wave of Iraqi bombs:

> Tehran is without water, without electricity, without doors or
> windows, and without gas in the cold of winter. But for years
> our people have gotten used to such things. Now, Tehran is be-
> ing transformed into a city empty of women, empty of men,
> empty of children, empty of laughter, empty of sweet little girls.
> A city which has no night, no dawn, no drop of tears, no songs.
> A city which is only a cry. What shame is greater than a city
> which is only a cry!

This depiction and many other similar ones during the war period that foregrounded the destruction were accurate enough; however, they overlooked the resistances and the resilience of Iranians in the face of this senseless and criminal war. This was because the point of view was external, not internal; it emanated from a position of exile.

The univocal tragic discourse evokes a sense of utter helplessness and passivity characteristic of masochism. Even when action or resistance is shown, it is injected with tragedy and powerlessness. For example, in the same program we see the footage of a demonstration by Iranians in Los Angeles against the so-called war of the cities. We see participants marching and making impassioned speeches. Then some of them break into tears, weeping publicly for what has befallen their country. At this point, over the visuals we hear an extradiegetic song added to the soundtrack whose refrain is "Lonely homeland, indigent homeland." Clearly this song represents the filmmaker's own commentary about the futility of action, which undermines the activism of the demonstrators.

Sometimes such visual or verbal invocations of home as a ruin are inappropriate and irrelevant but they serve to deepen a sense of loss and passivity. Again, the same program ran a segment of a film, *Ruyeshi Digar* (Another growth), which emphasized the destruction of the city of Khorramshahr by the Iraqis some seven years *earlier*, long before bombing of

Fig. 22. Iran as a ruin: *Jonbesh-e Iran*'s footage of destruction in Tehran caused by Iraqi bombing. The caption reads, "With tears and shouts, from Tehran to downtown Los Angeles."

cities became an Iraqi practice. This is tantamount to ahistoricization of the documentary evidence, unanchoring it from its particularity and tying it to unrelated materials: images from a particular situation (shelling of Khorramshahr) can be used in another situation at another time (air bombing of Tehran seven years later). It is here that the power of the fetish and the stereotype to ahistoricize, simplify, and therefore control the representation of the other is revealed. If Islamic Iran is a signified for "ruin," then any picture of ruins taken at any time might do as a signifier of the current Iran.[11]

The signifiers and the signifieds of ruin and destruction are circulated in music videos as well. Homaira's video *Bahar Bahar-e Emsal* (This is a year of spring times), aired in March 1988 by many television shows, provides a good example. Because of the complexity of the narrative, I will reproduce portions of the video in two columns below. Homaira herself does not appear in the video. The entire narrative consists of her voice accompanied by fast-changing images.

| Lyrics | Images |
|---|---|
| Do not call it a homeland, it is no longer a homeland. There are gallows in the alleys there, Murder is a profession there. This is a year of spring times. | Shahyad monument, built before revolution, fighting & struggle during 1979 revolution. Dead bodies hanging from gallows. |
| Equality and fraternity is a lie, there is a crowd lining up to die. The cemetery and the mosque are the Mecca A life is worth a blade of straw. | A flower in bloom, Persepolis monument, pictures of 2,500th anniversary celebrations. A young Basij Corps volunteer is saying goodbye to family and leaving for the war front, he and family members are weeping. |
| The Mongols have invaded again, frozen is the poor people's brain. Plague has filled the soul with dread walls are built with corpses of the dead. | Bearded men and veiled women crying in a cemetery over graves of loved ones. Footage from *The Lovers' Wind*, showing tribes & scenes of traditional mourning (*rowzeh*). The "fountain of blood" in Tehran cemetery. Martyrs' cemetery overcrowded with gravestones and flags. |
| You can neither move back nor forth, if you speak, you are no more. This is a year of spring times, now begins our labor times. | Men and women cry over graves, tears drip from a woman's nose. Royalist demonstration in Los Angeles against the war with Iraq. |
| Instead of sowing barley and wheat, they are planting gallows in the street. | Well-dressed demonstrators in Los Angeles carrying placards, flowers, signs, pictures of Reza Pahlavi. |

| | |
|---|---|
| This is a year of spring times. | Iranian flag with royalist lion |
| This is a year of spring times. | and sun insignia behind a |
| This is a year of spring times. | wire fence. |

The video posits that under the Islamic regime, the "motherland" has become a "ruined land," and it does so by mobilizing all the fetishized icons that have been discussed so far or will be in the course of this chapter. The significant feature in this video is not only the damning condemnation of the Islamist government but also the parallel that it draws between the two discourses, ideologies, and iconologies of "Pahlavi Iran" and "Islamic Iran." In this discursive and semiotic battle, the former is linked to Persian heritage, antiquity, authenticity, and to Iranian nationalism and monarchy; the latter is associated, in the words of Gholam Hosain Afkhami in another context, with "thanatos on a national scale" (1985).

The iconography of the masochistic mode of fetishization surfaces also in what Michel Foucault has called the "political economy of the body," whereby the body is made to be "both a productive and a subjected body" (1979:25–26). The bodies depicted on television are made productive economically and ideologically to the extent that they are shown to be subjected to the pervasive disciplinary technologies of the Islamic regime. Further, bodies are made productive iconographically by continually showing them maimed, tortured, and destroyed. Political activists who have managed to leave Iran appear on television to show either the scars left on their bodies or entire limbs removed from their bodies by torture. Mojahedin supporters who have been tortured in the prisons of the Islamic Republic and who have succeeded in leaving Iran appeared a number of times on *Sima-ye Azadi* to display their scars, burns, disfigurement, and dismemberment and to tell television audiences of their torture and escape. Accounts of various kinds of assassinations, hangings, and stoning and raping of women are also repeated in other television programs and inserted within music videos. This is especially true of atrocities and persecutions unleashed against ethnic and religious minorities, particularly the Kurds and the Baha'is. A rock video, *Mona's Execution*, recreates in a realistic narrative the capture in the classroom of a 16-year-old Baha'i girl, Mona Mahmudnezhad, her subsequent imprisonment, her interrogation during which she refuses to renounce her faith, her torture, and finally her execution by hanging.[12] Filmed in Canada with an English-language soundtrack, the video ends with people of various ethnicities and races placing flowers on Mona's grave. Both the Baha'i faith and their pain are thus universalized.

In this context, the tortured body, the exposed flesh, becomes a text,

Fig. 23. Body in crisis: The music video *Mona's Execution*. Mona defiantly places the noose over her own head.

indeed a "minor literature" (in the sense employed by Deleuze and Guattari), in which visions of power and resistance, of difference and transgression, are inscribed. As Michel de Certeau notes, torture is a mode of writing that memorializes on the text of the body the hieroglyphic scars of its inscriptions.[13] These inscriptions, in turn, become literal criteria for admitting individuals to political organizations such as the Mojahedin and the government in Iran.[14]

The Mojahedin guerrillas have capitalized on the art and spectacle of the tortured body, not only in their television programs but also in their publications and political demonstrations. Through the years the organization has publicly boasted about the number of its supporters who have willingly died for its goals. In 1985 the organization circulated a 181-page book listing in detail the manner of death of 12,028 "martyrs" killed in battle against the Islamic government (Mojahedin-e Khalq-e Iran 1985). Of these, 9,069 belonged to the Mojahedin, whose manner of death is a litany of cruelty and barbarism: 1,333 killed in fighting, 6,262 executed by firing squad, 210 executed by hanging, 305 tortured to death, 14 burned to death, 17 dragged to death, 21 assassinated, 907 not specified (Abrahamian 1989:226). In 1990 they claimed the incredibly high number of 90,000 dead bodies.[15] It is on pillars constructed of these piled-up tortured and decimated bodies that the Mojahedin has erected its edifice.

During the 1980s, the Mojahedin put on periodic public demonstrations and street performances in major American and European cities where scenes of imprisonment and torture were graphically reenacted on the sidewalks. Prisons and torture chambers were recreated in which prisoners were interrogated and tortured to death, and mock executions were reenacted, while Mojahedin supporters worked the crowd of spectators with thick albums of photographs of tortured, scarred, and maimed bodies. The discourse on torture and martyrdom produced by the Mojahedin was designed not only to promote group solidarity within the organization but also to arouse public sympathy in the West and generate financial contributions.[16]

Royalist television producers and entertainers in exile, too, have engaged in the discourse of indigence and the body in crisis, as exemplified by the music video *Sorud-e Hambastegi* (Song of unity).[17] Appropriately, this is a syncretic bit of cultural production in that it borrows an American vehicle for the expression of a specifically Iranian concern. The model for the work is the fund-raising video *We Are the World*, and it shows a group of well-known exiled entertainers standing in front of a giant Iranian flag (minus its recently added Islamic emblem) and singing a choral song whose haunting, oft-repeated refrain is "O spring breeze, tell me about friends, tell me about friends who are hanging from the gallows." The scene of singing in the studio is constantly interrupted by a parade of electronically processed images of death and destruction in Islamic Iran: people hanging from the gallows in public, fighting during the revolution, the Iranian flag waving against a blue sky, ruins of the ancient palace of Persepolis, the setting sun, the Iranian landscape and countryside, a flag-draped coffin, a map of Iran, a cemetery with women mourners crying and displaying pictures of their lost sons, execution by firing squad, and bodies of executed generals.

By recounting and displaying with precision methods of torture and manners of death, each side of the Iranian political divide attempts to gain legitimacy for itself and discredit its opponent. In the process, the tortured body becomes a text in which this gruesome discourse of power is inscribed and a medium in which it is enacted. By fetishizing and continually repeating these tortured images, exilic television invites identification and pleasure in the return to loss, thereby feeding into the masochistic economy of desire. Thus the divided, fragmented self in exile is made whole again through symbolic symbiosis.

Fig. 24. Body as minor literature: Electronically processed image of dead bodies hanging from the gallows, from the music video *Song of Unity.*

The production of unity out of the fragmentation and chaos of exile is also achieved by creating narcissistic models of beauty to be emulated, a process Baudrillard has called "a perfectionist vertigo" (1981:94) and in which exilic television participates with a vengeance. In this process, physical beauty is valorized. The beautiful body as fetish veils the essential split subjectivity of the exiles and negates the symbolic castration engendered by separation from home. Restoring wholeness, Baudrillard tells us, is no longer achieved "by endowing the individual with a soul or a mind, but a body properly all his own" (96). The fragmented, disappearing body in exile is restored to its former relative unity "properly all its own" through fashion, makeup, makeover, body building, diet, and reconstructive surgery—all of which are repeatedly urged in television commercials and in interviews with plastic surgeons. The wide use of makeup, hair dye, and plastic surgery among Iranians may stem partially from their desire—common among immigrant groups—to hide or remove marks of ethnic physiognomy, particularly when the host society is perceived to be hostile. Surgery, the most invasive of all the techniques to the body in exile, is curiously reminiscent of the torture that has wracked the body in Iran. Both plastic surgery and torture reconstruct the body. The difference, of course, is that the former is embedded not in a discourse of tragedy, indigence, and crisis but rather in a discourse of perfection achieved through "art" and "aesthetics." This aestheticized discourse is evident in advertisements for Iranian plastic surgeons. A large cover photo in the weekly magazine *Rayegan* (12/9/1988), for example, hyperbolically identifies the plastic surgeon Dr. Asurian as the "Michaelangelo of the twenty-first century" and the ad copy inside calls him an "artist," whose aim is to make his patients "more complete" by "recreating" their faces. Likewise, an ad for Dr. Hosain Najafi which for years appeared in Iranian exile periodicals carries the following breathless copy in English:

> Alter your ego. Reward yourself with a beautiful new you. Get the ultimate artistic results, achievable only by a gifted surgeon with aesthetic sense and imaging skills of a true artist. (*Javanan*, 9/22/1989:18)

The strategy of the beautiful body feeds into an ideology of a dual self: by altering the exterior, one may succeed in reconfiguring the interior. It is also a reflection of the transformation of that ideology and the formation of a new self in exile. The Iranian self is theorized to be different from the American-Western self in that it is not completely individuated; rather, it is a communal, familial self that involves one's significant others. This means that others are part of the subjective experience of the self. A recent study indicated, however, that acculturation in exile has increased individuation, intensifying fetishistic narcissism among Iranians in the United States (Moradi et al. 1989). Perhaps the seeming obsession with the beautiful body can be attributed partially to this newly "learned" individuation, which through narcissism can serve to veil the fractured exilic self. To this must be added the extreme concern among well-to-do Iranians with looks and style of dress—all of which can be considered to be strategies of self presentation, self-fashioning, and self-protection. In this regard, what Stuart Ewen has noted about the rural migrants and European immigrants moving into American cities in the early decades of this century rings true for recent immigrants from the Third World:

> In the face of this apparently "hostile" environment, style allowed one to put up a front, to protect one's inner self. As a kind of armor for city life, style taught people that they could gain comfort from self-estrangement, from erecting a visible line of defense for a subjectivity that often experienced a sense of jeopardy. As a basic message in modernization, immigrant and migrant workers learned to be "presentable," to rely on the tools

of presentation while navigating the treacherous waters of every-day life. True moderns, they were learning to internalize the dictum of Bishop Berkeley, that "to be is to be perceived."
(1988:77)

The culture of narcissism, of the beautiful body, of style, celebrated in a variety of media and locations (television commercials, music videos, rock concerts, nightclubs, parties, weddings, anniversaries) is a by-product not only of the modernization of the so-called Third World populations but also of the liminality of exile itself, which like other liminal states encourages synaesthesia. Because exile removes the native structures and constraints of the past and instead heightens fear and anxiety concerning the present and the future, the body in exile is not the same "old" body but a "new" one that must be reexperienced through synaesthesia and physical testing (dancing, body building) and reconstruction (makeup, makeover, diet, surgery). The reexperiencing of the new self in exile extends to experimenting with mind-altering drugs and to addiction, especially among the younger generation—a topic television programs frequently examine. Several effects ensue from opening up and celebrating the whole sensorium: the exiles obtain a new sense of the self, a wholeness that counterbalances the fragmentation of their life in exile; they create a homogeneous communitas in exile, liquidating internal divisions among themselves; and they differentiate themselves from the dominant culture of the host society.

## Nostalgia and Return to Origins

Nostalgia, a feature of exile, has in recent years become a common currency as postmodernity, neocolonialism, communism, totalitarianism, imperialism, and transnational capital have displaced peoples and cultures the world over. Fredric Jameson writes that this fragmentation and deterritorialization force us to experience time differently (1983); that is, we experience the present as a loss or, as Baudrillard would have it, as a phenomenon that has no origin or reality, a "hyperreality" (1983:2). For the exiles who have emigrated from Third World countries, life in the United States, especially in the quintessentially postmodern city of Los Angeles, is doubly unreal, and it is because of this double loss—of origin and of reality—that nostalgia becomes a major cultural and representational practice among the exiles.

Nostalgia, of course, is not just a feature of exile; it is a constituent part of human development and it serves to repair our discontinuous identities as both individuals and collectivities by appealing to origins and commonalities.[18] The nostalgia for one's homeland has a fundamentally interpsy-chic source expressed in the trope of an eternal desire for return—a return that is structurally unrealizable. Although the lost mother that is the goal of this desire for return is structurally irretrievable, the lost homeland *is* potentially recoverable, and it is this potentiality—however imaginary—that drives the exiles' multifaceted desire to return.

This is retrospective nostalgia; there is also prospective nostalgia for the future yet to come, which seems to be emerging particularly strongly in some of the science-fiction films of the late 1980s and early 1990s. In *Blade Runner* (1982) and *Terminator 2* (1991), the harrowing future of urban landscapes is tempered by the still recognizable vestigial cultural icons and value systems with which we emotionally identify. These are examined with deep yearning, as if they were part of our cherished past. It is as though the present cannot be appreciated without projecting it onto the future as a loss, which thereby creates a nostalgia for it. There are such exile-produced science fiction films—*The Nuclear Baby* (1990), for instance. This film, directed in the United States by Iranian-born film-maker Jalal Fatemi, inscribes a similar configuration of the future folded back on the nostalgia for the present. In it Fatemi envisions a post-nuclear-war period in which the iconography of the current Islamist Iran is en-coded with nostalgic longing. (If in this film the present is seen as the past, it is because the filmmaker-in-exile is expressing his longing to return to his homeland. In *Blade Runner* and *Terminator 2*, on the other hand, nostalgia is a function of temporal, not spatial separation, since both the present and the future occur in the same location, Los Angeles.)

It is important to consider the paradigm of exile as it operates within the exiles' native culture, because it is through that paradigm that they think and experience their lives in exile, feel nostalgia or desire to return. For Iranians, it is poetry, especially Sufi poetry, that provides the paradig-matic world view and language of exile, embodying many journeys, returns, and unifications. Such an assertion may seem implausible to readers unfamiliar with Iranian culture; a similar claim about any contem-porary Western culture might not be upheld. As historians, anthropolo-gists, literary critics, and any number of Iranians can attest, however, theirs is a culture suffused by poetry and shaped by the citation of canoni-cal, classical (and at times contemporary) poets in daily life; rich and poor can and do cite Ferdowsi, Sa'adi, Hafez, Rumi, and Khayyam.

The paradigm of exile is also indissolubly linked with the Hejri calen-dar, the Iranian version of the Muslim Hijrah (hegira), dating from the prophet Mohammad's emigration to Medina which was followed some years later by a triumphant return to Mecca. The exiled poet Nader Nader-pour (1986) has classified the notion of hegira (emigration) as a multilayered metaphor for exile (hegira from one's country), life itself (hegira from Eden), passage to adulthood (hegira from childhood), acquisition of knowledge and insight (hegira from innocence), and the daily passage of the sun (hegira from dawn to dusk). Exile is a palimpsest inscribed with many layers of meanings and is deeply rooted in the culture and psyche of Iranians. While Naderpour's formulation accords with the Iranian mystical tradition (Sufism), it nevertheless misses the importance of the central notion that turns migration into exile animated by the desire for return and reunion—a concept deeply encoded in Iranian mysticism and in the psychic structure discussed as *safa-ye baten* (inner purity).

This mystic paradigm of exile fits the Lacanian formulation of the permanent disruption of prelapsarian unified wholeness, or the Imaginary, by the entry of the child into the Symbolic order (culture and language); this disruption inclines humans forever after to seek to recover wholeness, to identify and to become one with the Imaginary. Classic figures of Iranian mystical poetry, such as Farid al-Din Attar and Jalal al-Din Rumi, have elaborated these notions of exile in their masterpieces.[19] Nowhere is the pain of separation and the longing for return and reunification expressed more passionately than in Rumi's famous "Song of the Reed," a portion of which, translated by William Jones, reads:

> Hear, how yon reed in sadly pleasing tales
> Departed bliss and present woe bewails!
> "With me, from native banks untimely torn,
> Love-warbling youths and soft-ey'ed virgins mourn.
> O! let the heart, by fatal absence rent,
> Feel what I sing, and bleed when I lament;
> Who roams in exile from his parent bow'r,
> Pants to return, and chides each ling'ring hour.
> My notes, in circles of the grave and gay,
> Have hail'd the rising, cheer'd the closing day:
> Each in my fond affections claim'd a part,
> But none discern'd the secret of my heart.
> What though my strains and sorrows flow combine'd!
> Yet ears are slow, and carnal eyes are blind.
> Free through each mortal form the spirits roll,
> But sight avails not. Can we see the soul?"
> Such notes breath'd gently from yon vocal frame:
> Breath'd said I? no; 'twas all enliv'ning flame.
> 'Tis love, that fills the reed with warmth divine;
> 'Tis love, that sparkles in the racy wine.
> Me, plaintive wand'rer from my peerless maid,
> The reed has fir'd, and all my soul betray'd.
> He gives the bane, and he with balsam cures;

> Afflicts, yet soothes; impassions, yet allures.
> Delightful pangs his amorous tales prolong;
> And Laili's frantick lover lives in song.
>
> (Arberry 1954:118–19)

This complicated, mystical, painful yet alluring paradigm of exile still informs and infuses the discourse of Iranians in the United States who, like the lamenting reed in Rumi's poem, long for a return to their homeland—a longing intensified by the inability of many to return.[20] The novelist Mahshid Amirshahi, who lives in France, uses a botanical metaphor to speak of the inevitability and the pain of this longing:

> More than belonging to the future, I am grafted to the earth. I am searching for a lost earth in which I am rooted, a sun in whose rays I have gained strength, and a water by whose grace I have matured. No matter how wasted this earth, how burning this sun, and how meager this water, I love them. . . . I will return to this land, this earth, this homeland. (1988:45)

The literary critic Farzaneh Milani, in a poem called "Zadgah" (Birthplace), draws a parallel between the inevitability of the longing of the exiles for a return to their homeland and the urge of salmon to return to their spawning grounds (1989:26). Both Amirshahi and Milani, however, like Naderpour, overlook an important feature of the exile paradigm, namely the fact that the unconsummated longing that is the motive force of exile would cease to exist if return and reunion are accomplished.[21] The impossibility of return and reunion are fundamental elements of human signification; as Susan Stewart has noted:

> The inability of the sign to "capture" its signified, of narrative to be one with its object, and of genres of mechanical reproduction to approximate the time of face-to-face communication leads to a generalized desire for origin, for nature, for unmediated experience that is at work in nostalgic longing. (1984:23–24)

The same inability to "capture" the homeland is operative in exilic discourse; without distance, without separation, the nostalgic longing so prominent in exile would not be: "It is in this gap between resemblance and identity that nostalgic desire arises. *The nostalgia is enamored of distance, not of the referent itself*" (Stewart 1984:145, emphasis added).[22] The "glorious return," the operative engine of actively maintained exile, must remain unrealized; in the words of Rumi, the exiles must roam and pant to return but never actually achieve it.

The nostalgia remains, then, and this nostalgia, this desire to desire, is staged narratologically in music videos frequently aired by exilic television. In one video, for example, aired by *Midnight Show* (on 3/27/1988), Sattar sings about departing from home but leaving his heart with his family, which has remained behind. As he sings in exile about loss and separation, a family group photo, apparently taken in Iran in his absence, appears behind him. At this point, the image of Sattar singing, which had dominated the foreground, gradually grows smaller until it fits in a spot inside the group photo in the background. The foreground fuses with the background. The gap between resemblance and identity is filled in. If reunion is not possible physically, it at least can be staged metaphorically. The ever-threatening loss is averted, the pain assuaged symbolically.

This nostalgic past is itself ideological in that, as Said writes in *Orientalism* (1979:55), it has become an "imaginary geography," a construction created by exilic narratives. But this construction is not hermetic, since the "real" past threatens to reproduce itself as a lack or loss: it is against the threat of such a loss that the nostalgic past must be turned into a series of nostalgic objects, into fetish-souvenirs that can be displayed and consumed over and over. Photo albums, letters, diaries, telephones, birds in flight, candles, rising smoke from cigarettes or from fog machines, the beach and the waves of the ocean—these are some of the nostalgic fetishes circulated in music videos. Images of people looking through photo albums, reading and writing letters in the light of a candle, of a burning cigarette smoking in an unattended ashtray, of loved ones conversing on the phone, of a lone singer singing love ballads by the sea—these are the recurring micronarratives of nostalgic return.

Such fetish-souvenirs, and the narratives in which they are embedded, have a dual role: they serve to authenticate a past and simultaneously to discredit the present. Their authenticating function can be understood better if a parallel is drawn with religious and secular rituals, during which, as Victor Turner has observed,

> often, but not always, myths are recited explaining the origin, attributes, and behavior of these strange and sacred habitants of liminality. Again, sacred objects may be shown to the novices. These may be quite simple in form like the bone, top, ball, tambourine, apples, mirror, fan, and woolly fleece displayed in the lesser Eleusinian mysteries of Athens. Such *sacra*, individually or in various combinations, may be the foci of hermeneutics or religious interpretations, sometimes in the form of myths, sometimes of gnomic utterances hardly less enigmatic than the visible symbols they purport to explain. (1974:239)

These souvenirs, fetishes, icons, symbols, and narratives, along with the Persian artifacts imported from home that dominate the interiors of many

Fig. 25. Metaphoric return: Sattar returns to his family album.

homes in exile, operate as cultural mnemonics, through the circulation of which the "habitants of liminality"—namely, the exiles—attempt to transmit to "novices"—that is, to their children, who are fast becoming American—the parents' native cosmologies and values, which they feel are threatened. What is more, to paraphrase Kathleen Stewart, the Persian artifacts that decorate the exiles' homes do not so much reproduce Iran as produce a world made of signs: "The point is not just to 'decorate' in itself but to signify the production, or at least the possibility, of meaning" (1988:233). The meaning that is produced involves establishing both cultural and ethnic differentiation (from the host society) and cultural and ethnic continuity (with an idealized past and the homeland); in short, what is at stake here is the construction of what Bourdieu has called the codes of "distinction and taste" (1984). These *objets d'art* and handicrafts and the Persian food available in grocery stores and restaurants help to produce and validate in exile a distinctively Persian taste culture.

By focusing almost solely on vision (and more recently on sound), film and television studies have failed adequately to develop theories that can account for the relationship between film and television viewing and the nonaudiovisual senses.[23] The exiles construct their difference not just through what they see and hear but through their senses of smell, taste, and touch. Indeed, these aspects of the sensorium often provide, more than sight and hearing, poignant markers and reminders of difference and of separation from homeland and therefore must be considered seriously.

## Nostalgia and Return to Nature

When return is not possible, and when its metaphorical and narratological staging is insufficient, other substitutes may be sought. Liminality itself, as Turner tells us, is a timeless condition, which places "enhanced stress on nature at the expense of culture" (1974:252). It does so by invoking the biological and the symbolic processes of the natural order. In the absence of the native habitus—that is, the former social, political, religious, familial, linguistic structures and authorities of home—the exile culture now is forced to seek the structures and the authority that only nature is thought to be capable of providing: wildness, timelessness, boundlessness, predictability, reliability, stability, and universality.

Although nature is universally important, each society is formed in specific ways by its own geography, terrain, and climate. Iran's geography has had not only a crucial role in forging its history and in forming the individual and national identities of its inhabitants but also a significant and signifying part in its visual arts and cinema. Iranian cinema and exile-produced television and music videos encode and express nature in certain privileged ways, through several "chronotopes" (in Bakhtinian sense) which are examined below. These must be seen not just as visual but as synaesthetic chronotopes involving the entire human sensorium.[24]

### Wilderness

Iranians, like many other peoples, revere nature. In particular, they consider wilderness to be the sacred space of uncontaminated wildness that contrasts with the profane spaces of civilization. However, wilderness also connotes a place of danger. In Iranian cinema, wilderness—particularly plains, deserts, and mountains—is heavily used, sometimes as a ferocious force to combat and tame and sometimes as a means to bridge the gap produced by the fall. In the first modality, wilderness is not used as a passive decor for foreground action or a semiactive presence, as is the case with American Westerns; rather, it is often posed as a formidable antagonist against which the human characters and communities must defend and define themselves. Parviz Kimiavi's films, *P-e Mesl-e Pelikan* (P as in pelican, 1972) and *Bagh-e Sangi* (Stone garden, 1976), Mas'ud

Kimia'i's *Khak* (Earth, 1974), and Amir Naderi's *Ab, Bad, Khak* (Water, wind, dust, 1985) are powerful examples of this active engagement of individual human beings and communities with the elemental forces of the wilderness (sun, wind, earth, water). Wilderness also seems to have left an indelible mark on the aesthetics, iconography, and narrative strategies of Iranian cinema. Indeed, it would be impossible to define an Iranian "national cinema" without considering the following wilderness-related tropes: a claustrophobic yet expansive landscape and atmosphere; a slow, deliberate pace accompanied by meditative and nostalgic music; a sense of repetitiveness and sameness; characters who are either intensely fragile or emphatically dogged; valorization of solitude and isolation; and a passion for water, green fields, and gardens.[25]

Wilderness in its nostalgic mode has provided the visuals for much of the Iranian television and music videos produced in the first decade of exile. In this mode, the wilderness is used strategically to link the inherited chronotope (space-time) of the homeland with the constructed chronotope of the exile. In this case, the space of Iran collapses into the time of exile. Program logos and music videos contain images of the land, mountains, fields, sky, setting sun, sea, and monuments so ancient that they have acquired the status of natural phenomena (such as the ruins of the Persepolis palace). The opening sequence of many exile television programs (such as *Jam-e Jam*) feature stills or footage of Persepolis and other monuments of antiquity that predate Islam, reinforcing the royalist politics of the exiles and also staking a claim to a kind of ahistorical and inherited moment of origin that predates culture. The land, literally the earth of Iran, also figures importantly in music videos. Homa Mirafshar's videopoem *Sarzamin-e Man* (My homeland) contains a compilation of clips from *The Lovers' Wind* showing a variety of Iranian landscapes and geological formations while the lyrics, recited by the poet, speak of undying love for the country and for the land:

> You are the best reason for my continued existence
> You are love's refuge, a warm roof over a home
> You are a love ballad, an eternal song
> Live long O land of Iran.[26]

Each nation imagines itself topographically: the topos of nation for the Greeks is the polis, for the English it is the island, and for Iranian exiles it seems to be the wilderness and nature itself, best condensed in the feature poetic documentary film *The Lovers' Wind* (*Bad-e Saba*, 1969), made by the French director Albert Lamorisse.[27] The film posits Iran to be, as is nature itself, timeless, boundless, permanent, wild yet tamed, and filled with wondrous and varied natural beauties.[28] Most of the footage, filmed from a hovering helicopter, represents Iran from the point of view of the various winds (such as the lovers' winds) that "inhabit" the land and who anthropomorphically "narrate" the film.

> The camera, defying gravity with smoothness and agility, provides a bird's-eye view, caressing minarets and domes, peeking over and beyond mountaintops, gliding over remote villages to reveal the life enclosed within high mud-brick walls, leaping along with the local wildlife, following the rhythmic, sinuous flow of the oil pipelines and train tracks, and hovering over the mirrorlike mosaic of the rice terraces that reflect the clouds and sky. (Naficy 1984:xvii)

As we see these images, we hear the mellifluous voice of a narrator who, speaking on behalf of each wind, narrates portions of the film in the first person. The images of the wilderness, "naturized" human-made monuments, and the narrative points of view of the winds all link Iran directly with natural elements and with nature itself, thus providing a testimonial to the obduracy and resilience of Iran and of its Iranian peoples. In times of exilic stress and self-doubt, such images are most reassuring, as the constant and continued plundering and plagiarizing of clips from *The Lovers' Wind* by producers of Iranian television and videos in exile serve to underscore. Program logos, music videos, videopoems, and documentaries on exiles repeatedly employ clips from this film.

### Sea

Exilic television, especially music videos, are frequently coded with visuals of the sea and lyrics about love, ambiguous enough to be interpreted as referring to love of any kind, that is, a universal love, resulting in longing for origin, home, family, country, and, since Persian pronouns are not gender-specific, either homosexual or heterosexual love. An example is a music video called *Parandush* (the name of a bird or a girl), sung by a female singer, Zoya.[29] We see the singer perched on the rocks overlooking the ocean, singing about the lost bird of the title, complaining that "the pain of separation from you has turned my heart into a sea." The lyrics are clearly about love—a love that can variously be taken to be for a bird, Zoya's family, her lover, her country.[30] Visually, Zoya is made one with the sea: her image is superimposed over the waves, either hovering faintly above the waves or washing gently to the shore with them. Her dissolution into the sea is enhanced by the soundtrack: her voice, the solo piano accompanying her, and the sound of waves washing or crashing against the shore are so delicately intermingled as to create a union. Another music video, *Ashena* (Familiar), sung by Davoud, shows him achieving a kind of visual and epistemological symbiosis with sea and clouds.[31] He seems to have become the ocean itself, his image alternately floating on the surface of the water or submerged just below the surface. Throughout, his image and that of the waves interact and interweave, while the love song intones, "Oh, always familiar, stay with me, tell me your thoughts, make me yours." Again, ambiguities make possible a number of readings, but clearly the preferred reading coded in the video is the union, through dissolution, with mother nature.[32]

As noted earlier, homeland is a gendered concept for Iranians. It is coded as feminine and maternal. The union with "mother nature" inscribed in these videos is a symbolic substitute for reunion with the "natural mother" and with the "motherland," not possible for many of the exiles (and for all the singers of pop music, because of the vehement opposition of the Islamic government in Iran to this music on account of its putative amoral and corrupting influences). Videos vicariously and nostalgically transfer the primarily bourgeois exiles to their childhood, to their past, and to the "good old days" by the Caspian Sea.[33] These references to nature might be read also as attempts at activating senses other than vision and hearing in order to reproduce that intangible "feel" of the homeland.

### Birds and Monsters

Animals figure more prominently in Iranian visual arts than in their Western counterparts. As art historian Richard Ettinghausen has noted, these animals were

> sometimes the animals familiar in agricultural use or in the hunt; elsewhere they were the symbols of deities, of royalty, or of cosmological elements. But whatever they represented, they formed the enduring themes of artistic production. (1979:xv)

Birds appear more often than any other type of animal in exile-produced television programs and music videos. As part of their iconographic encyclopedia of nature, both *Ashena* and *Parandush* show birds in flight, as symbols alternately of the journey, of escape, of freedom, of messages borne over long distances.[34] The image of a white dove as a signifier for peace is well known, an image used particularly effectively as an opening logo by the *Sima-ye Azadi* (Face of freedom) program. We see a white dove frozen in flight against a solid blue sky, and we hear the crescendo sequence of Strauss's *Also Sprach Zarathustra*, and the title of the show is keyed in. The semiotic and ideological skirmish at work becomes clear upon scrutinizing the political subtexts.

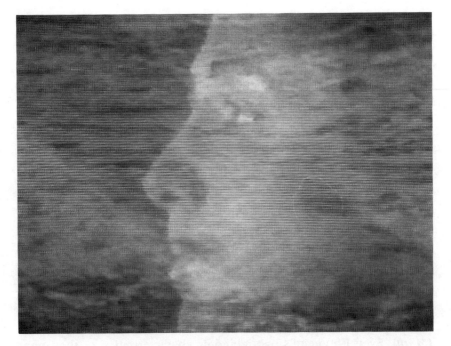

Fig. 26. Symbiosis with the sea: Zoya in *Parandush*.

The program is produced by the Mojahedin. The group is opposed both to the return of monarchy to Iran and to the present Islamist government; it claims itself to be the sole legitimate alternative. As a result, it can use neither the pre-Islamic, Achaemenid iconography monopolized by the royalists nor the Islamist one exclusively employed by the current regime. Since warfare is impossible without ideological and semiotic mobilization, the organization has opted for the white dove of freedom to differentiate itself and its politics from both the royalists and the Islamic clerics. In all cases, the supporters of the monarchy, the present Islamic government, and the Mojahedin are appealing to symbolism and iconography that predates the existence of the factions themselves and, in some ways, links them to the natural or cosmological order.

In the same way that a bird in flight is seen as a symbol of freedom, a caged bird signifies imprisonment—an image with a long-standing tradition in Iranian mysticism, literature, and cinema.[35] The caged bird as a symbol of constriction and claustrophobia contradicts the sense of wildness and vastness that wilderness and the sea provide. Such is the symptomatic contradictoriness of exile and its narratives! Many music videos and audiocassettes produced in exile refer to exile as imprisonment. One epi-sode of the avant-garde television program *Qod Qod-e Morgh* (Hen's cackle) constantly repeats a close-up image of a caged parakeet both in the background, behind the host, and in the foreground. As befits the style of the show, there is no commentary but periodically a hand reaches into the frame and pats the top of the cage, thus drawing attention to it. At times, it seems as though the host himself is inside the cage. At times, too, the cage is empty, and the perch swings back and forth, signifying flight and escape. The feelings of freedom, refuge, and imprisonment that exile implies all are inscribed in this episode of the show.[36]

"Naturization" can be an effective political ploy in the semiotic, ideo-logical, and cosmological power struggle in exile; this process has turned the Ayatollah Ruhollah Khomeini himself into a wild or dangerous mythi-cal beast. The exilic media have called him, among other things, "old hyena" (*kaftar-e pir*), "vampire bat" (*khoffash-e khun asham*), "ominous owl" (*joghd-e shum*), "anti-Christ" (*dajjal*), "fire-breathing dragon" (*ezh-daha*), "Chinese female demon" (*efriteh-ye Machin*), and "*Zahhak*" (a king in Persian mythology who grew two snakes on his shoulders, which had to be fed with the brains of young people). The exilic popular press has dubbed Khomeini's regime "octopus" (*okhtapus*) and "the plague" (*ta'un*). Even Khomeini's own demonic characterization of the United States as "the great Satan" (*shaitan-e bozorg*) has been turned against him in the exile media.[37] Anthropology has shown us that liminal states, whether the Iranian revolutionary culture itself, which produced the "Great Satan" label originally, or the exilic polity that recycles it, require the invocation of existing beast-images or the creation of new theran-thropic and ornithanthropic monsters, whose real or imagined threat can serve to mobilize the entire society. Such monsterization of the United States by Khomeini, and of Khomeini and the ruling clerics in Iran by the exiles, is productive in the sense that it turns the sacred into the profane and at the same time theoretically serves to turn the chaos of revolution in the former case and the condition of exile in the latter case into a safe, symbolic communitas.

### The Garden

Art historians, literary critics, writers, and poets have explained the sig-nificance of garden imagery in Iranian arts and literature as an "antidote" to the "featureless, uninviting outer world" of the deserts and the plains (Ettinghausen 1979:xviii). The English word "paradise" is a transliteration of the Old Persian word *pairidaeza*, which referred to a walled garden (Moynihan 1979:1). In its idealized and aristocratic form, this garden consisted of an enclosed area in which geometrical plots of land bore sweet-smelling roses and flowers and rows of orderly trees, irrigated by rivulets of gurgling water fed from a centrally located pool containing colorful fish. Such gardens provided a private haven from both the violence of nature and the viciousness of society, and on hot summer evenings and cool early mornings became the centers of family life, where meals were taken and guests entertained. Even the homes of average people contained (and to some extent still do) some features of the garden described above. For Iranians, the idea of the garden has philosophical, religious, and psychological dimensions far transcending its material form. Literary critic Shahrokh Meskoob has produced a taxonomy of the garden: garden of childhood, garden of the soul, garden of the body, garden as homeland, garden of time, garden of imagination, garden of recollection, garden of nature, and "garden of gardens," that is, the garden of Eden (1991). In essence, the garden is that imaginary location from which humans originate and to which they must return. As an icon, the garden and its various representations encode a deep yearning for an abundant origin and a longing for a prosperous future yet to come. It is both nostalgic and utopian.[38]

The idealized garden represented in Persian miniatures, abstracted in carpets and tiles, framed and accessed through architectural designs, interpreted and reinterpreted in poetry and literature also finds its way into exilic literature and television. In its most elementary expression, the garden is represented on the sets of television programs by a verdant potted plant or a flamboyant bouquet of flowers that almost overshadows program hosts and guests. Persian classical music concerts and performances shown on television are also inexorably linked to the idea of the garden, symbolized by the presence of huge plants and flowers between performers.

To celebrate certain calendrical holidays, television programs are often taped inside luxurious homes containing abundant flowers and plants, in the lush gardens of these homes, or in well-groomed public parks.[39] Innumerable music videos show a lone singer, male or female, standing in a luxuriant garden, walking the paths, passing under overhanging tree branches, sitting on a bench or by a waterfall, all the while singing about life, love, homeland, and childhood—activating both memories of and desire to return to the source. Such a desire to return by the agency of the garden is strongly encoded in music videos, such as Homaira's *Mikham Beram Daryakenar* (I want to go to the seaside), that used footage of lush Iranian landscapes and gardens, particularly woods, rice paddies, and water lilies growing in the swamps in northern Iran. Homaira's singing image is surrounded by a wreath of flowers in bloom. This composite image is then keyed into images of verdant fields in Iran. All the while the singer's

Fig. 27. Symbolic garden: On the set of *Jam-e Jam*, March 1992.

voice intones such phrases as "no matter where I am, my heart is in Iran."
The topoi of flowers and garden act as agents of communitarianism across
waters and continents.[40]

Wilderness, sea, birds, and gardens act as icons, indexes, and symbols
of the natural order and of Iranian cosmology. In exile, each of these signs
heightens the experience of the other and of the senses, and each intensification in turn enlarges the grandeur of the other, leading to the development of what Gaston Bachelard has called "intimate immensity." The intimate intensity of individual exiles' feelings for their homeland is
expressed through their identification with the immensity and timelessness of these signs of nature. The final product of such imagining, however, is not so much any of these signs themselves as their signifieds, the
"consciousness of enlargement" (1969:184). The creation of such a sense
of expansion is psychologically redemptive and restorative because

> it brings calm and unity; it opens up unlimited space. It also
> teaches us to breathe with the air that rests on the horizon, far
> from the walls of the chimerical prisons that are the cause of our
> anguish. (Bachelard 1969:197)

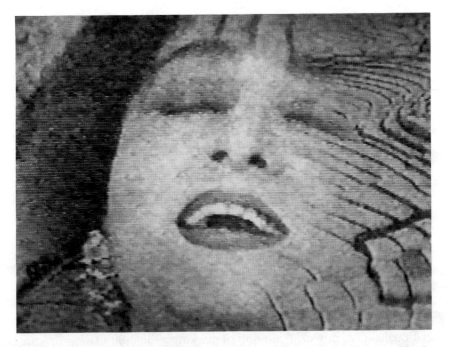

Fig. 28. Homeira singing in her video *I Want to Go to the Seaside*. Her image is merged into the rice paddies of northern Iran.

In this way, the walls of the "chimerical prison" of exile no longer matter; the exiles can leap over and soar free toward the homeland. Return is made metaphorically possible.

Since exile is processual, however, the contents of this encyclopedia of nature, too, must undergo changes through recoding, transgression, and transformation, thereby problematizing the return and its staging. This has occurred as a younger generation of pop singers and videographers, raised in exile, have began producing music videos that do not invoke Iranian wilderness, sea, birds, and gardens. Influenced by the dominant American music television channels and driven by their own individuating psychology, many of them are focusing more on interpersonal relationships here and now than on the relationship between here and there. These narratives are not only located in the present but also expressed in the present tense, as opposed to earlier music videos that were located in the past and stated in the past tense. This shift has also transformed the desire for return and the experience of intimate immensity. The younger generation is now less in touch with the timeless vastness of nature that spanned time and space for the older generation; instead, it is more open to the intimate intensity of everyday exilic affairs. In this way, immensity and symbiosis have began to give way to intimacy and individuation. The communal notion of the self, energized by the collective memory of the elsewhere and nostalgic return to it is being replaced by individuation and individual positioning here and now.

The signs of nature discussed here are agencies of a collective memory that evoke the homeland, encourage reexamination of the past, and enlarge life in exile. This is the opposite of the work of the fetishized images, which tend to repress the homeland and history and limit life's possibilities in the new society. Although each of these processes is restorative by itself, together they tend to incapacitate the exiles by holding them in an agonizing, agonistic space of ambivalence. One way to resolve this paradox is to construct a symbolic nation at a distance from exile; this will be discussed in the remainder of the chapter. Other ways of resolving the dilemma—through ambivalence, incoherence, doubling, mimicry, and hybridity—will be examined in the subsequent chapter.

## Symbolic Construction of a "Nation at a Distance"

Nationalism is a powerful method of marking exilic boundaries, promoting solidarity, and resolving the agonism of exile. It is not the opposite of exile, as Timothy Brennan asserts (1990:60); rather, as Edward Said has noted, nationalism is associated intrinsically with exile because "all nationalisms in their early stages posit as their goal the overcoming of some estrangement—from soil, from roots, from unity, from destiny" (1984: 50). Exile affirms belonging not just to a place but to what Bourdieu has called a "habitus," a community of language, customs, dispositions, and "structured structures predisposed to function as structuring structures" (1977:72). Indeed, national identification is always already combined with identifications of other kinds, whether it be language, ethnicity, race, class, politics, religion, or region. A number of these structures of structuration, such as ethnicity and race, emphasize descent and biology over culture and consent, but in exile not only descent but also consent relations are activated and problematized.[41] What is more, in exile, culture may eventually supersede the claims of biology as a marker of national consciousness.

To accomplish that, culture has to be placed at the service of constructing from a distance a nation in exile, if nationhood is understood to be, in Homi Bhabha's words, "a form of social and textual affiliation" (1990:292). Iranian media in Los Angeles, at least in their first decade since the revolution of 1978–79, attempted to construct such a social and textual affiliation among the exiles by emphasizing national and cultural similarities and by repressing or glossing over the exiles' fundamental differences, which stem from differences in ethnic origin, religious affiliation, class, region, language, politics, and time of departure. The contributions of exile-produced television programs to constructing *textual affiliation* are chiefly its fetishization of the homeland and its nostalgic narratives and chronotopes of return and reunion, which together create a kind of symbolic communitas. Television's contribution to the formation of *social affiliation* (in tandem with other components of the exilic popular culture) consists of helping Iranians to mark their cultural boundaries, process a hybrid individual subjectivity and syncretic cultural identity, create an exilic economy, and develop a national imaginary informed by nonbiological cultural constructs such as politics, language, and religion. The first of these—politics—has already been discussed; I will proceed to the second.

Throughout the 1980s and 1990s, exile media insisted on using a common language, Persian, which as a national language has historically wielded an enormous unifying power over the diverse peoples who lived on the Iranian plateau. As the literary historian Shahrokh Meskoob has noted, historically a collective memory expressed by means of a shared language and a common literature has been the chief guarantor of Iranian nationalism and culture. According to him, after Islam's conquest in the seventh century, Iranian nationalism became a "new tree" nourished by the water and climate of Islam but grown in the soil of its own ethnic collective memory, manifested through language (1989:27).

If this type of linguistic nationalism at home required control of the state over the official language, in exile it has necessitated control of the access to media in a civil society. The near-monopoly of media in Los Angeles held by royalist factions has been influential in ensuring linguistic nationalism in exile. Even though Iranian ethnoreligious and linguistic minorities are represented in higher proportions in Los Angeles than in Iran itself, almost all Iranian popular culture in exile is spoken and written in Persian. Television commentators, newscasters, and hosts (some of whom are Iranian minorities to whom Persian is a second language) made an effort to employ Persian in its most unsullied form. Some tried to prevent its "contamination" by two encroaching rival languages, Arabic and English.[42] Even after thirteen years, almost all of the commercials aired on Iranian television programs are spoken in Persian and little bilingualism is evident—although it is increasing.

Religion provided another socially constructed affiliation that aided both nationalism and identity formation in exile. The relationship between religion and nationalism, however, is complicated: on the one hand, religion and religious movements can aid nationalist surges, especially at the time that such surges are becoming mass movements.[43] On the other hand, when religious movements themselves achieve power they tend to decouple from nationalism and even work to thwart it; religion-in-power perceives nationalism as a formidable challenge to its monopolistic claim to the idea of the "nation." This is exactly what happened in postrevolutionary Iran. Upon achieving power, Ayatollah Khomeini denounced nationalism and proceeded to redefine and replace the secular concept of the nation (*mellat*), which had been popular, with the religious concept of the Islamic community (*ommat*). Even though Iranian exiles are heterogeneous in their religious beliefs and affiliations, they are highly secular and vehemently oppose theocracy. Soon after their arrival in the United States, a type of secular nationalism emerged among them that was virtually anti-Islamist, leading television programmers to ignore religion and Shi'ism or dismiss them as significant facts of Iranian politics.

Although both linguistic nationalism and anti-Islamist secularism helped form the textual and social affiliations necessary to construct a national imaginary in exile, there is a drawback to their use. Overinvestment in them demands that the concepts of nationalism and anti-Islamist secularism, like fetishes and their synecdoches, remain pure and unambiguous. This can lead to the national chauvinism so evident in the discourse of Iranian exile media that have insisted on an essentialist Iranian authenticity.

Nationalism without narration is impossible. If in Benedict Anderson's elitist formulation the national novel and newspaper shaped Western national consciousness, for Iranian exiles in America it is the popular culture they produce and consume, especially television, that circulates nationalist consciousness and narrative. Because exilic television's contribution to the formation of this consciousness and its narratives occurs at a distance, it works not only synchronically (to produce horizontal and spatial links among exile communities and those at home) but also diachronically (bridging the vertical and temporal gaps between those living in exile and those at home). The physical distance between Iran and the United States creates not only a difference of time zones (some 12 hours between Iran and the West Coast of the United States) but also a feeling that Islamist Iran is living in (or even reliving) a different historical epoch. Exile television bridges these dual gaps: the exiles, distanced spatially, are made synchronous temporally. Exile television can thus be considered an "artistic chronotope" in Bakhtin's definition—that is, a means by which temporal and spatial relationships are interconnected (1981:84).

But with what are they made synchronous? With an "invented tradition," in the sense employed by the historian E. J. Hobsbawm:

> "Invented tradition" is taken to mean a set of practices, normally governed by overtly or tacitly accepted rules and of a ritual or symbolic nature, which seek to inculcate certain values and norms of behavior by repetition [and] automatically [imply] continuity with the past. In fact, where possible, they normally attempt to establish continuity with a suitable historic past. (Hobsbawm and Ranger 1983:1)

The past that exilic television has found suitable as its reference point is chiefly the pre-Islamic past. Hobsbawm makes the point that when social patterns are weakened or destroyed, as in time of exile, the impulse to invent traditions increases.[44] He cites three types of traditions invented since the industrial revolution: those establishing or symbolizing social cohesion; those establishing or legitimizing institutions, status, and authority; and those establishing socialization, inculcation of beliefs, values, and behavior (p. 9). Over the years, the communitarian type of invented tradition symbolizing cohesion has tended to dominate, and it seems to dominate in exile as well. Its chief purposes seem to be to legitimize the past, to cement group solidarity in the present, and to guide political action in the future. That is why television and music videos place so much emphasis on the display of national emblems such as the flag and the map of the country.

Like all official histories/stories, the exilic ones are neither homogeneous nor fixed for long. Other histories/stories are generated and circulated in other exile media with which television develops sympathetic and dissonant resonances. What is more, while fetishization, nostalgic longing, and construction of a national imaginary in exile tend to stabilize individual subjectivity and group identity they also inscribe ambiguities, contradictions, and instabilities, which are examined in the next chapter. This conception of exile community as a culture that produces and consumes a variety of meanings and cultures contrasts sharply with functionalist and "integrative" traditions, such as that expounded by Durkheim, whose central conception of society was one that procured solidarity by subsuming differences.

# 6
# The Cultural Politics of Hybridity

## The Hybrid's Place

*I was invited by Tehran's University of the Arts to give a talk. The subject I chose was the way the arrival of Western cinema in the country at the turn of the century worked in tandem with other modernist reforms to overdetermine a kind of alienating identification among Iranians. Many film critics, journalists, writers, filmmakers, and university people were present. At the beginning, following the traditional procedure of courtesy, I apologized in advance for my somewhat rusty formal Persian, especially vis-à-vis appropriate equivalents for certain theoretical terms in psychoanalysis and cultural criticism. After the talk, there were polite questions from the audience, but there was little serious engagement. Clearly, something had gone wrong; I seemed to have failed to touch anyone. There was, of course, the possibility that my talk was uninteresting, that it was about a subject too far in the past, and that its foreign-accented theoretical language was too unfamiliar. It is also possible that the audience was disappointed not to hear, from a scholar living in the belly of the beast, something about the power and practices of the current American cinema—which despite official criticism is still admired in Iran. But I had a feeling that the trouble had to do partly with my speaking about something for which I was not culturally authorized—Iranian society and cinema. Having lived out of the*

166

*country for nearly two dozen years, having been absent during the turmoil of the revolution and the travail in its wake, I had become an outsider now, without the right to speak. I was authorized to speak about Iranian cinema abroad—something the person who introduced me lauded—but I could apparently not do so inside. A review of the talk that appeared in the film column of a sports magazine provided further clues: it poked fun at my statements of courtesy, took their self-effacing contents seriously as signs of actual shortcomings, and critiqued my self-reflexivity as a sign of condescension. The style of presentation I had thought would create a relaxing and friendly atmosphere had, alas, resulted in its opposite. Further, I seemed to have become an unreadable artifact: I was neither an authentic native nor a born-and-bred true foreigner, neither self nor other, neither here nor there, but an amphibolic person straddling both cultures who had produced partiality and hybrid positionality, not wholeness and stable positions. Like the turn-of-the-century Western cinema I had spoken about in my presentation, unknown to myself I had generated ambivalence and alienating identification. It was painful.*

*Life in the United States for hybrids is similar yet different. Here, hybrids often suffer from commodified de-fusion and diffusion, or from marginality and over-acceptance. To resist these, one has to be not only in a constant process of becoming but also incessantly defining, explaining, or justifying oneself, both to oneself and to others. This, too, is painful. Yet there are potential rewards: to be irritated and irritating, like the oyster and like the grain of sand in it, may produce pearls.*

## Fetishization and the Production of Instability

Hybridity and fetishism both involve split subjectivity—that is, the holding of two simultaneous psychical attitudes toward external reality. The former takes reality into consideration while the latter disavows it and replaces it with a "product of desire."[1] In fetishism, the product of desire is the fetish object itself; in hybridity, it is difference itself. Fetishization fixes on the fetish; hybridization fixes on nothing, on nonfixity, on the slippage between self and other, between home and host cultures. As Homi Bhabha states,

> Produced through the strategy of disavowal, the reference of discrimination is always to a process of splitting as the condition of subjection: a discrimination between the mother culture and its

bastards, the self and its doubles, where the trace of what is disavowed is not repressed but repeated as something *different*—a
mutation, a hybrid. (1986:172)

For the hybrid exilic identity to survive, the differentiation between the
self and "its bastard," the other, and between the host and the (m)other
culture must be restated continually and differentially. This process, along
with others already discussed, is perhaps at the heart of the aesthetics of
repetition and hesitation that mark all exiles.

Sattar's music video *Safarnameh* (Travelogue) inscribes such hesita-
tions.[2] He is seated next to a piano in a comfortable living room in the
United States, paging through a book (an album of photographs or a diary). As he sings and thumbs through the book, we see images of Iran: pigeon towers in verdant fields, tea groves, diggers of *qanats* (subterranean
water channels), tribal women, a shepherd boy and his flock of sheep. The
visuals invoke fetishized souvenirs of a past—indeed, of a primarily rural
Iran that is not in the background of urban emigrants from Iran—and the
lyrics speak of the hardship of the emigration journey and of its
metaphoric documentation in the diary: "My pen is my feet and my diary
is the long stretch of the road I have traveled." The contradiction between
the visuals, which emphasize unity with the homeland, and the lyrics,
which highlight separation, crystallizes in the last few lines, in which he
speaks of a tortured ambivalence:

> I am caught in the dead end of doubt and irresolution:
> Which of these two paths is mine?
> Help me, O love, so I may not perish in exile.

I have already demonstrated that the traces of what is disavowed are repressed through fetishization, nostalgic longing, and construction of an
imaginary nation in exile. Not all of that which is disavowed is totally or
hermetically repressed, however. There is excess and inevitably slippages
occur, and some disavowed knowledges escape to be repeated as *something different*—as ambivalence and instability. Fetishization and nationalism are both inherently ambivalent. In what follows I will focus on their
contribution to creating instability and ambivalence within the exilic
communitas.

As the critic George Steiner has aptly stated, it is not the literal past that
rules us; rather, "the image we carry of a lost coherence, of a center that
held, has authority greater than historical truth" (1971:8). Iranian exile television produced such a coherent image by fetishizing and stereotyping
Iran either in an ahistorical and secular past tense or in a tragic, tortured

present tense. But the historical truth, the fact of living in exile, intrudes. As long as the trauma that produced exile persists, so do the relative coherence and unity of the fetishes of the homeland and of the past. For Iranians in the United States, with the end of the hostage crisis (1981) and particularly with the cease-fire in the war with Iraq (1988), two major sources of trauma were removed, and with that the inherent ambiguities, instabilities, and dualities that accompany both fetishization and exile began to surface more fully.

A fetish is a synecdoche, a part for the whole. To be sure, this focus on fragments eases the pain of loss and separation, but it also impoverishes life in exile. It closes one off through fixation in the same moment that liminality opens one up to new possibilities. In the words of Ernest Becker, the fetish is a segment of the world which "has to bear the full load of life meaning" (1969:14). But this fragment cannot possibly fulfill forever the promise of satisfaction with which it is burdened.

In addition, the televisual fetish, like any other type of fetish, is unstable because it is paradoxically an index of what it is masking. The lack it masks then constantly threatens. Further, by incessantly circulating these representations of home, television programs not only acknowledge its continued existence but also end up elevating what they consider to be inferior and marginal—Islamist Iran. In exile, home colonizes the mind.

On the other hand, as a form of partial repression, fetishization constitutes the first step in forgetting the homeland—something that the exiles in the liminal period at least are loathe to do. Thus they alternate between belief and disbelief, avowal and disavowal, lack and plenitude, identification and repression, stability and instability. The marks of these tensions in exile-produced television are to be found in the hybrid magazine format, contradictory nested texts, highly segmented exilic flow, strategies of repetition and excess, and the dual subjectivity that I have discussed in previous chapters. They are also evident in the strategies of doubling, incoherence, and mimicry to which I turn below.

Any representation that contradicts the monolithic fetishized image of the homeland is likely to cause controversy in exile. Two cases will be briefly examined here. In 1990, UCLA Film and Television Archives organized an unprecedented festival of Iranian postrevolutionary cinema: 18 features and a number of shorts from Iran were shown.[3] The festival came under heavy attack by some exiles, particularly the royalist factions and a number of producers of exilic television programs and films, who condemned it for helping to whitewash the Islamist government in Iran by putting a humane face on its inhumane deeds. In flyers distributed prior to the festival and in demonstrations at the site of the event, they called for its boycott.[4] The films aroused intense emotions and were received with great enthusiasm by spectators who flocked to the theater in huge numbers (from as far away as New York City and Washington, D.C.) and at times waited in line for over eight hours to buy tickets. There were television producers who supported the festival, but these were a minority and some of them were also attacked by the opposing factions.[5] The vehemence with which the festival and its organizers (including myself) were criticized—even before the films were screened—suggests that the battle was perhaps not so much over politics as it was over maintenance of a restorative psychological barrier whose existence had come under question. It seemed that the films made in Iran were about to violate the barrier and unleash the threat heretofore kept in check—the threat of the homeland unfettered by the repressions and distortions of fetishization. The emotional reactions to the films, summarized in the following passage by a festival reviewer, show that the protesters' worst fears had come true. Exposure to films from the homeland had helped the audience break through the barrier and begin to think the unthinkable: the possibility of reconciliation and return.

> The atmosphere of the festival was emotionally charged; after several of the films, spectators would emerge moved, homesick, revitalized/demoralized, (dis)connected. Everywhere there was mention of a trip back home, a need to reattach. (Bloom 1990:95)

The vehemence of those opposing the festival and the cathartic enthusiasm of festivalgoers revealed that fetishization had served the political and economic interests of the community at the expense of other interests. Those who benefitted were torn by the conflicting needs to repress and fetishize and to reconnect and heal.

The second case is the inauguration in 1992 of *Aftab*, the first progovernment television show in exile, which began presenting a very different image of Iran. *Aftab*'s narrative and nonfictional segments gave the impression of a vibrant society alive with children, bazaars, parks, and bustling streets. The program created much controversy among Iranian broadcast media in Southern California, partly because it began attracting advertisers, potentially threatening the profit, even the livelihood, of some of the exile producers. The passionate and bitter reactions against the program, however, including calls for the boycott of businesses advertising on it, suggest that what was at stake was not solely political or economic interests but also the determination of who is authorized to represent Iran and of what that representation should consist. Until 1992, the anti-Islamist exiles had monopolized the televisual representations of Iran and of Iranian issues. *Aftab* posed a threat to that monopoly, particularly because, in its first few months, it attempted to stay away from directly political issues, limiting itself instead to presentation of "Iranian," not "Islamic" cultural values and products.

The UCLA film festival, *Aftab* television, the phone-in format of recent radio and television programs, the gradual acculturation, depoliticization, and democratization of Iranians in America, the softening of political hostility between the Iranian and American governments, and the recent trouble-free return trips to the homeland by exiles—all this contributed to the gradual crumbling of the barriers that fetishization had erected in the path of understanding the complexities of life both in Iran and in exile. This is not to say that fetishization is dead or that royalist dominance of televisual representation is over. They are both alive, but their dominance is not total and is no longer a given. Exile media, like all other media in the host's civil society, must compete for influence. In June 1992, *Sobh-e Ruz-e Jom'eh* for the first time featured a religious sermon (*rowzeh*) in commemoration of the death in Karbala of imam Hosain. Exile periodicals criticized the action and implicitly threatened its producer, but his program continued.[6] Like a mask or a chrysalis, fetishization can conceal a metamorphosis—one that may be shameful to the community. In this case fetishization had served to hide the metamorphosis of Iranians from exiles into ethnics, and of Islamic Iran from a one-dimensional monster into a complex organism. Both the festival and the emergence of *Aftab* exposed these disavowed transformations. As a result of such exposure and the instabilities of fetishization, discursive diversity is on the rise in Iranian television.

## Ambiguities in Constructing a Nation in Exile

Since nationalism is structurally ambivalent, the nationalist icons and the narratives in which they are embedded must also carry with them moments of disavowal and contestation, doubly so because exile itself is inherently ambivalent.[7] Citing Ernest Renan's formulation, Gellner asserts that "a shared amnesia, a collective forgetfulness, is . . . essential for the emergence of what we now consider to be a nation" (1987:6). The aesthetics and politics of national chauvinism and fetishization discussed in the previous chapter are based on partial repression of the reality of Iran and of the past; in that sense, they could be construed to be forms of amnesia engendered by exile. It is through this collective repressing/forgetting or deliberate misreading of the past that the exiles can symbolically create a sense of communal cohesion and exilic solidarity.

This collective identity, however, is not a prior condition; rather, it is a continually constituted and reconstructed discursive formation. Exile as a process of becoming necessarily entails not a fixed position or location, but positionality and locations. What this means is that the form of nationalism and national consciousness now evident surely will undergo modification in time. As Stuart Hall observes:

> Cultural identity is not a fixed essence at all, lying unchanged outside history and culture. It is not some universal and transcendental spirit inside us on which history has made no fundamental mark. It is not once-and-for-all. It is not a fixed origin to which we can make some final and absolute return. Of course, it is not a mere phantom, either. It is *something*—not a mere trick of the imagination. It has histories—and histories have their real, material and symbolic effects. The past continues to speak to us. But this is no longer a simple, factual "past," since our relation to it is, like the child's relation to the mother, always-already "after the break." It is always constructed through memory, fantasy, narrative and myth. Cultural identities are the points of identification, the unstable points of identification or suture, which are made within the discourses of history and culture. (1989:71–72)

To illustrate the changing and unstable points of personal and national identification in exile, let us return to reexamine in the light of the foregoing the two issues of linguistic nationalism fanned by monolingualism and secularism driven by anti-Khomeinism. In the first decade of Iranian exile television (1981–91), all programs were aired in Persian. In addition, the Persian used was of the official and formal variety sanctioned by the government in prerevolutionary Iran. The only forms of exilic television that admitted the vernacular language of the exiles (which has gradually become a hybrid language, mixing English and Persian) were talk shows (*Ma, Harf va Goft*) or phone-in programs (*Emshab ba Parviz, Sokhani ba Ravanshenas*) in which ordinary people (not professional announcers) spoke in a variety of accents and informal speech patterns. For years the only linguistic evidence of the exilic context of television programs was provided by the English-language texts on the screens that contained the addresses of Iranian businesses advertising their products and services. As exile wore on and the demands of acculturation and professionalism grew, however, experimentation with using English increased. In late 1991, Iranian producers and hosts of *You and the World of Medicine*, all medical doctors, began airing their program in two languages: three days a week in English and two days a week in Persian. This is a significant moment of acculturation of Iranians; what seems to have justified violation of the hitherto monolingual nationalism is not the propagation of Iranian culture but the demands of professionalism and expertise in a postindustrial society.

Likewise, their anti-Islamist position allowed television programs to rally Iranians—many of whom had fled their homeland from fear of religious and political persecution—to create an imaginary nation in exile. The twin ambivalence of exile and of nationalism, however, especially nationalism formed at a distance, served to gradually attenuate and destabilize the unifying anti-Islamist idea of an exilic nation. The case of the Islamic call to prayer (*azan*) illustrates this shifting terrain of nationalism and religion in exile media. In fact, let Nader Rafi'i, a television producer, explain the situation in his own words:

> Five years ago we had taped a beautiful *azan* for the month of Ramadan which we were going to air on *Iranian* television over the footage of the film *The Lovers' Wind*. We decided not to do so, however, because the political atmosphere [in Los Angeles] was not conducive to it. We now know that what Mr. Khomeini and his friends were saying then was somewhat different from Islam, and because of this realization the anti-Islamic prejudices have since lessened. Five years ago you could not offer your condolences on the air for the death of the prophet Mohammad. There was so much hatred of Khomeini that we could not show the picture of imam Ali. But now we can criticize and parody Khomeini and the Islamic government and right next to it we can broadcast the *azan*. (Interview with the author, 4/5/1989)

In Iran, both before and after the revolution, the national radio network marked noontime and nightfall by broadcasting a call to prayer, sung artfully and powerfully by famous muezzins. The call, heard repeatedly over the years in homes, in the bazaars and mosques, on the streets, in alleyways, in taxis, at work and in schools, appears to have assumed for many Iranians, regardless of their religion, ethnicity, politics, or class, the status of a metaphor for childhood, homeland, the past, and the national collective memory. Over a dozen years after an Islamist revolution drove many Iranians into exile, the issue of the call to prayer became a popular topic on *Seda-ye Iran* radio. In January 1992 a listener suggested on a live phone-in show that *Seda-ye Iran* begin to broadcast the call as did radio networks in Iran. During the next few days, many viewpoints were aired, including the surprising one from the religious minorities persecuted by the Islamist government who favored airing of the call to prayer. Baha'is, Jews, Zoroastrians, Assyrians, and Armenians as well as Muslims and nonreligious Iranians called to encourage the producers to air the call as an emblem of Iranian nationality and "national culture." As exile gradually was transformed for many into ethnicity, the tensions and ambivalences of the process and of nationalism itself began to force hitherto unthinkable reevaluations: the call to prayer started to lose its religious connotation as many exiles reinterpreted it as culture. That this debate was aired by a royalist radio show vehemently opposed to the Islamic government in Iran is also an indication of the types of accommodations at work in exilic popular culture. Nothing in exile remains pure, stable, and unsullied—even nationalism.

The discussion of the ambivalence of exilic nationalism cannot be complete without noting the contradictions that inevitably exist between the notions of the past and of history exiles have produced for themselves, and those imagined by the people living in the home country. Both are invented, but coming from different locations (in time and in space) they will continue to diverge. The exilic commonality with "home," then, is illusory. It must also be noted that the style of imagining is not homogeneous, that there are different versions of history: official versions and those held in popular memory. At home the official Islamist history is promulgated by mainline media; in Iranian exile in Los Angeles, a kind of exilic "official" royalist history is propagated by largely royalist producers and consumers.

Fetishization and construction of an imaginary nation in exile, like nostalgic longing and its cultural artifacts and processes, entail regressive practices even though they may be motivated by a realistic perception of the decline of the present time, of shock at the future to come, of deterritorialization and displacement, or by crises of identity. These practices are regressive because they seek not so much to preserve the past as to restore it through either fetishization of an idealized construction or by giving in to conspiracy theories.[8] Fetishization, nationalism, and nostalgia and their politics and aesthetics, like the "lie," help produce solidarity by concealing fundamental differences in descent relations and deep dissensions in consent relations in exile. Lacanian psychoanalysis tells us that in the mirror-phase, recognition of the self as the other is overlaid with misrecognition because the other is really not the self. Likewise, fetishized and nostalgically constructed Iran in which the exiles find themselves is not the real Iran, it is misrecognized as Iran, it is a lie of sorts. Anthony Cohen's observation about the lie seems apt for the work of fetishization, nostalgia, and symbolic construction of a nation in exile:

> The lie is one of the devices used to conceal from the outsider
> the reality of dissensus within a community. But the common
> ability of insiders to "read" a lie nudges them into consciousness
> of their co-membership and, by implication, of the outsider's ex-
> clusion. Moreover, the lie, quite apart from being honorific if
> well-perpetrated, may effectively mask the degree of internal con-
> flict and thereby help to preserve the sense of commonality. Ly-

ing is, par excellence, an example of behavior which has both
pragmatic and instrumental and symbolic efficacy. (1985:89)

Overinvestment in fetishization, nostalgia, and nationalism tends to produce certainty and absolute knowledge about the self, history, and the nation at the same time that exile produces doubt about them. To avoid giving in to the "politics of genocide" that this overinvestment can foster,[9]
the exiles must learn to distrust not just their own fetishes and lies but also
all those who claim to possess absolute forms of knowledge. As liminars,
they are in the enviable position of knowing (even if this knowledge is disavowed) that reality itself is provisional and artificial, that it can be constructed and de/reconstructed. As liminars, they also know, even if this
knowledge is disavowed, that they are "impure" and "partial."

The ambivalent strategies of self-deception that are pressed into the service of producing in exile psychic stability and communal purity and
wholeness are not hermetic. Through cracks in the fetishized and stereotyped televisual representations, we can glean either the threat of the splitting or the mongrelized fusion of the exile subject. Three instances of such
splitting and fusion are discussed below.

### Doppelgängers

One of the most graphic examples of splitting and doubling is the use of
doppelgängers of singers in music videos, which involves superimposing
two images of a singer (often the same size) on each other. Logos for a
number of programs also feature doubles or mirror images (e.g., *Jonbesh-e
Iran*). Such strategies of doubling were too frequently employed in the
early days of exile to be disregarded or to be attributed merely to a limited
repertoire of techniques. What is one to make of these double images that
are at the same time split images? Could one of them stand for the self at
home and the other for the one in exile? Is one threatening to encroach
upon or bleed into the other? Is one in the process of dissolution and the
other consolidation? Does one of them represent the familial and the
other the individuating self? Can they coexist, ambivalently? Is the doubling process itself indicative of a deep anxiety about the ambiguity and
indeterminacy of identity and one's status in exile?

A music video featuring the male singer Shahrokh sharpens these questions.[10] It shows two medium shots of Shahrokh, one behind the other.
The foreground image is realistic and shows him singing while the background image is a still, a computerized double or shadow of the foreground.

Lotte Eisner's classic study of the German Expressionist cinema reads
the double as representing the "dual soul" and the split identity of the

Fig. 29. Doppelgänger: Shahrokh and his double.

Germans (1973:109), and she considers the shadow as standing for the immanence of menacing, unseen forces, such as the unconscious (136). The Shahrokh video seems to play into both of these discourses.[11]

As well as being a double, the computerized image can also be taken to be a shadow, which in Jungian analysis would be the projection of the negative or the dark side of the individual personality or of the collective unconscious. According to Jung, recognition of the shadow is an "essential condition for any kind of self-knowledge, and it therefore, as a rule, meets with considerable resistance" (1958:7). Perhaps it is the resistance to recognition of the dark forces of liminality that accounts for the fixing of the image as a frozen shadow behind the singer.[12] By immobilizing the image, one symbolically keeps these forces in check. This and other music videos like it can be seen as both containing and expressing the split individual and collective subjectivity in exile.

### Incoherence

The instability of the unified self in exile is also signaled by the incoherent and fragmented style of some of the recent music videos. Michael Chanan in his study of Cuban cinema observed that one of the features of syncretism is an attitude of play, an essential aspect of which is a tolerance for conceptual chaos. Applying this notion to the Latin American cinema, he found that

> the films that seem the most exuberantly Latin American often
> display in their seeming formlessness—whether fiction or
> documentary—a much higher tolerance than European cinema
> for visual disorder, apparently haphazard bricolage and narrative
> or argumentative looseness. (1985:268)

The tolerance for conceptual chaos and visual disorder are not only features of the Cuban and Latin American cinemas but also perhaps of much of the Third World cinemas, which must grapple with very rapid and often disruptive tensions in their societies brought on by displacement, modernization, colonization, and liberation. That the displacement of exile might produce similar narratives and visuals is to be expected. The literary critic Ahmad Karimi-Hakkak compared the short stories of Gholamhosain Sa'edi both before and after his exile from Iran and found that his exilic works were characterized by "little regard for any sense of internal coherence" (1991:258). Iranian exilic television and music videos, likewise, display many instances of narrative chaos and visual incoherence either deliberately or inadvertently coded into the material. These videos violate the diegetic and narratological coherence of space, time, and causality cited by Bordwell et al. as characteristic of film realism and the classical Hollywood cinema style (1985b). Typically, in these videos, the image of an entertainer is fragmented into various altered forms: it is a frozen still; a portion of it is enlarged to reveal the dot structure of the TV screen; the image is slowed down or speeded up; and apparently unrelated spaces and locations are juxtaposed. Jamshid Alimorad's music video *Gol-e Morad* (Morad's flower) seems to be a documentary of a boat trip by two lovers to an island.[13] The discontinuity in time and space is created not by comparative cutting between here and there, exile and homeland—the video has no references to the homeland. Rather, discontinuity is generated by cutting between various seemingly unrelated locations on the journey to the island. Each shot showing the singer and his band, the two lovers, women dancers, and women wearing sunglasses is taken in a different location: on the mountains, at the sea, on the beach, in a casino, and in the boat. Cuts are not motivated by action, causality, or the chronology of the trip. Very few of the shots are in real time; most are processed and shown at slow, fast, stop-action, or very jerky speeds. Coherence of time, space, and narrative logic are gone. Ironically, however, the "incoherent" visuals are accompanied by a "cohering" ballad

whose oft-repeated refrain is "I am afraid." Afraid of love, of fragmentation, of incoherence, of dissolution, of exile? The coherence is illusory,
however, because the fear that created the coherence in the soundtrack
appears to have exploded the narrative and the visual track. This inscription of doubling is one of the characteristics of exile music videos.

## Discursive Strategies of Mimicry and Identity

The tensions attending either the splitting of the subject or its hybridized
fusion are expressed most complexly in strategies of mimicry. Exilic mimicry, like the colonial mimicry formulated by Bhabha, is

> the desire for a reformed, recognizable Other, as *a subject of
> difference that is almost the same, but not quite.* Which is to say
> that the discourse of mimicry is constructed around an *ambiva-
> lence*; in order to be effective, mimicry must continually produce
> its slippage, its excess, its difference. (1985:126)

In exile discourse, mimicry entails adopting certain features of the dominant other, behind the mask of which one may glean the gleam or hear
the heartbeat of the original self in the process of metamorphosis. But this
is not syncretism, because it is unstable and ambivalent. Mimicry also is
not merely imitation. It is that, to be sure, but it is imbued with ambivalence toward both that which is being imitated and that which is abandoned in the interest of imitation. This creates a slippage and opens up a
space for exiles to critique through parodic mimicry the host culture at the
same time that they idealize it and strive to assimilate. In this way, mimicry
creates an ambivalent cultural space and an inappropriate artifact that is
almost the same, but not quite. Of course, in this inappropriateness and
parody lies a critique also of the native culture. Two types of exilic
parodic texts will be examined here, music videos and tough-guy television serials.

### Music Videos

Music videos have inscribed more successfully and densely than other
forms of television these layers of ambivalence to produce texts that on
the surface seem puzzlingly contradictory. One long video, *Mafia*, by Jaklin, provides a critical (if moralist) catalog of life in the United States. It
posits that the country is imbued with the "Mafia ethics" of greed, violence, corruption, and crime and the social ills of injustice, homelessness,
addiction, degradation of women, and lax morality.[14] The lyrics and the
soundtrack tend either to develop ironic resonances with the images or

to contradict them. Over some of the critical images of the United States, we hear the ironic refrain of a popular American pop song: "Don't worry, be happy." In other places, while the host society is being savaged, the lyrics underscore the visuals, representing Iran as the ideal place for Iranians, to which the video urges them to return:

> America is a prison,
> It is worth nothing.
> I want to return to my homeland.
> My home is in Tehran
> In this ruinland,
> Iranians are only guests.
> Iranians say that we must return to our homeland.
> Your home is in Iran,
> My home is in Tehran.
> Woe upon America,
> Mercy upon America.
> Oh Iranians,
> It's time to leave this city of the Mafia.

The video not only taps into the discourse of the nostalgic return but also into the discourse of mimicry. Jaklin presents herself in two different personae, both borrowed ironically from the video's own catalog of negative images of America. In some sequences the image of the singer dressed as a Mafia don in a black suit, a black tie, and a fedora is superimposed over the image of a man firing a machine gun. In other sequences, she is dressed in a sexy sequined dress that shows off her body and her flowing hair while she plays a guitar and sings in front of her all-male band. By adopting the very negative images of the other at the same time that she critiques them, she is engaged in mimicry. She is playing with the other and creating slippage and excess.

Another long video (over 10 minutes), called *Pul* (Money), by the rock band Black Cats, critiques the intense interest of some Iranians and Americans in money by engaging in defamiliarization. This discourse examines the self indirectly, through criticism of an other (often disdained) that stands for the self. This is an ancient discourse. As Kaveh Safa has noted, a genre of literature developed in France in the sixteenth century whereby French writers, including Montesqieu in *Persian Letters*, used Iranians to criticize contemporary French society.[15] The *Money* video seems to belong to this genre. It uses wealthy Arab sheiks (disdained by many Iranian chauvinists) to criticize the infatuation with wealth of both Americans and Iranians (and Arabs) living in the United States. While the image track develops a parodic and exaggerated (if racist and sexist) narrative about Arab

Fig. 30. Mimic and amphibolic characters: Jaklin as Mafia don and *jahel* (tough guy), from the music video *Mafia*.

wealth and sexy women, the lyrics intone: "It doesn't matter to you who is asleep, who is awake, or whose head is upon the gallows; all your thoughts and imagination are concerned with dollars, rials [Iranian money], and dinars [Arabic money]." By mimicking the stereotypical image of the Iranian other (Arabs), the video defamiliarizes the stereotype and mobilizes it in the service of self-critique and critique of the host society.

This criticism is also encoded in the slippage that music videos produce between self and other. Recent sexist videos by male Iranian singers feature white leggy dark-haired Anglo female dancers who try to pass as Iranian, using their physical similarity to Iranian women as well as imitations of the Iranian dancing style. If the former qualities favor their inscription as Iranian women, the inexactness and exaggeration of their imitations give away their "inauthenticity."[16] The viewer is thus placed in an ambivalent position in deciphering the self from the other. In contradistinction, other music videos contain a kind of mimicry by Iranian singers based on the supposition that by adopting the performance style

Fig. 31. Becoming the other: Jaklin showing off her body in her *Mafia* video.

of mainstream American performers, they can pass as American.[17] Here again, exaggeration and inexactness reveal the lack of fit between self and other, and ultimately expose the incommensurability that marks the exiles.

Mimicry and its incommensurability can become economically fruitful and ideologically productive when the mimicked personae and the dissonant texts they inhabit are circulated via the commodified media of music videos, music concerts, and TV commercials in exile. By transferring the fondness of young Iranians from American pop icons (such as Michael Jackson) to themselves, Iranian performers are attempting to capitalize on the economic rewards of the transfer. In the process they consolidate in exile not only the commodification of themselves and their own images but also of their own fellow exiles as consumers. The economic diffusion of exilic music videos tends to defuse their subversive potentiality.

### Tough-Guy Serials

Iranian exilic television has produced other instances of mimicry, notably in two serials in the mid-1980s that were devoted to the exploits of the

Fig. 32. Parodizing the other: An Arab millionaire lines up coins on the back of a blond woman in a bikini, from the video *Money*.

Iranian tough guys called *jahels* or *lutis*. To contextualize these discursive tough guys, it is necessary to explain their place in Iranian history and society.

In the Iranian performing arts, *taqlid* (literally "imitation, mimicry") refers to the nonreligious comic theater that developed in the eighteenth century. A chief plot element in these plays was the placement of protagonists called *lutis* in situations that required them to parody the regional dialects and behavior of the various Iranian peoples (Shahriari 1986:80). *Lutis* (usually translated as "tough guys") were figures important in history who entertained people and, as mercenary tough guys, enforced traditional values, Islamic moral codes, and the rule of the local power elite.

Gradually, a *siah* (literally "black") character was added to the mimic theater (now called *ruhowzi*). He wore blackface, and his origin can be traced back to the black African slaves kept by the rich and the royalty of Iran.[18] In the *taqlid* and *ruhowzi* theaters, the blackface character would continually mimic and subvert the authority of his Persian master and the culture he represented by pretending not to be sufficiently familiar with them. He would establish this parodic distance by intentional inattention to his master, deliberate misunderstanding of his words, broad or absurd imitation of his language and behavior, excessive courtesy and obsequiousness, and direct criticism of him and of his way of life. These performers were ambivalent mimics, and the source of their ambivalence was not only national and racial slippage but also sexual ambiguity. They were white Iranians in blackface, and they were androgynous figures who at times performed as women.[19] Once a year, the blackface character of traditional Persian theater also appeared as Haji Firuz, to entertain the public during the New Year celebrations.

Iranian contact with the West since the mid-nineteenth century engendered several other ambivalent social types who seem to fulfill the mimic functions described here. These include *fokoli* (one who wears a celluloid collar), *farangi ma'ab* (literally, foreign-mannered), *Zhigolo* and *Zhigolet* (Westernized dandies), and *gharbzadeh* (literally, Westernstruck). These types imitated the outward markers of the West (dress, makeup, hairstyle, body language, speech) but burlesqued—hence potentially subversive. On the one hand, in imitating the West they devalued their own native customs, and on the other hand, in the surplus and satire of their imitation, they criticized the Western way of life. This ambivalence and excess made them indecipherable in Iran, however, because mimic characters were producing hybridity and shifting signifiers, not universal stable subjects. The excess, as a criticism of native and foreign cultures, was either misread or left unread. As a result, these figures were scorned both for debasing the authority and purity of native traditions and for unproblematical copycatting of the West.

Of various other Iranian mimic figures only the blackface character and the tough guy have been successfully transplanted into exile. The former appears as Haji Firuz on television, on the cover of periodicals, and at parties usually during the month of March, the Iranian New Year month. He also appears with particular regularity in TV commercials around this time of the year to sell products from groceries to cars.[20]

The tough-guy type and ideology are more complex and significant to Iranian history and culture, and their transplantation does not create the kinds of dissonance that the blackface character produced. These types were so popular in the prerevolutionary Iranian cinema that they formed a genre of *jaheli* or *luti* films (Naficy 1992a). In the tough-guy characters two contradictory tendencies commingle. In the movies, they act as both pious Robin Hoods and villainous middlemen. It is their villainous aspect that allows these amphibolic figures to take up the new through mimicry. They syncretically adopt features of Western dress at the same time that they mimic them by overexaggeration. It seems the height of excess and inappropriateness, for example, for a tough, burly, mustachioed man who gets into brawls and knife-fights to wear delicate see-through nylon socks (as was popular with them in 1970s Iran). Their syncretism also produces other contradictions: while the tough guys champion their kin and defend the poor of their neighborhood, as villainous middlemen they work on behalf of the clerics and the local power elite. In addition, they profess, and often practice, piety and spirituality at the same time that they frequent worldly establishments such as cabarets, bars, and nightclubs and engage in such unethical activities as gambling, drinking, and even pimping—much of which was coded as being Western. By flaunting what was perceived to be Western, they flouted both the native self and the Western other.

Before the revolution, the *jaheli* film genre encoded these contradictions and ambiguities and a few films highlighted them further by staging tough-guy exploits in a foreign context, usually a major city in the West.[21] Immediately after the revolution, a public theater in Los Angeles treated Iranian exiles to some twenty tough-guy films made prior to the revolution. Exile cinema did not produce any tough-guy films, but exile television did attempt to revive the genre by broadcasting two local tough-guy serials in Los Angeles: *Balatar az Khandeh* (Beyond laughter) and *Gharibehha* (Strangers).[22] Parody imbues the discourse of these serials. Even the title of *Balatar az Khandeh* is parodic because it mimics the Persian title of the American TV series *Mission Impossible*, which was popular in Iran in the 1970s (it was called *Balatar az Khatar*, meaning "Beyond danger"). The parody, of course, surpasses titling and goes to the heart of the *Mission Impossible* series, in many of whose episodes the American crime-fighting team is sent abroad to thwart dictators and other assorted Third World bad guys. In all cases, the team triumphs thanks to superior American technology, know-how, righteousness, and laws. The team and the ideology for which it strove were not only never questioned but also ruled the discourse of the series and became the basis for judging the various Third World countries into which it made its forays. Certainty (in response to the uncertainties of the Vietnam War) was encoded into the fabric of the series.

In *Beyond Laughter*, on the other hand, a group of displaced Iranian tough guys attempt to recreate in exile their former lifestyle and narrative traditions. In both *Beyond Laughter* and the *Strangers* serial, the tough guys do not determine their exilic context, as do the American team their Third World diegeses. In fact, they are wholly out of context and inappropriate and, as a result, in these shows it is ambivalence that is encoded not certainty. The tough guys' black suits, black fedora hats, their thick mustaches and their special gait and posturing are all out of place in the streets of Los Angeles, as they pass shop windows with English lettering and walls with gang graffiti on them. In such a context, their traditional concern with meting out personal justice through acts of revenge can be appropriated by being recoded as invoking the American revenge genre (typified by Charles Bronson movies). What cannot be recoded, however, is the inappropriateness of the sight of tough guys running around Los Angeles streets with drawn machetes and gigantic knives.[23] Further, their penchant for mysticism, generosity toward cohorts, ruthless violence against their adversaries, kindness toward their women, kin, and children, and exaggerated emotionality appear old-fashioned, unfit, even "primitive" in the context of life in America. Decontextualized, these characters are defamiliarized and rendered for the time being inappropriate and inappropriatable. Hence the apparent demise of the tough-guy serials in exile. However, it is safe to say that they will not disappear entirely from exilic narratives because producers and viewers (particularly the older generation) continue to admire as authentically Iranian the tough guys' positive qualities, and draw a certain amount of self-validation from watching them enacted. As Manuchehr Bibian, producer of *Jam-e Jam* TV, which aired *Beyond Laughter*, told me in an interview:

> *Lutis* [tough guys] are representatives of Iranian culture and tradition. The Islamic regime is destroying all that. But by doing this series, we help preserve that culture and tradition. (2/25/1985)

Additionally, the act of viewing these tough guys in exile itself links the elder members of the audience to their own personal past through remembering (often with fondness and recognition) the tough-guy exploits prior to the revolution in Iran both in real life and on the screens. Since the tough-guy genre is filled with culturally specific formulas, it requires the active complicity of viewers for reconstruction of the text—a process that validates the audience as culturally astute, something the older generation cannot claim vis-à-vis the host culture. In this sense, then, both producers and viewers, uprooted from home, become guardians of popular memory, since together they construct in exile what Teshome Gabriel has called "an ongoing consensus of cultural confirmation through the affirmation of shared memory" (1989a:62).

The tough-guy characters have occasionally surfaced in pop concerts and music videos of the younger Iranians in exile in a way that appears to recuperate their parodic excess syncretically in the service of entertainment, transgression of traditional gender roles, and consumerism. *Del Beh Del* (Heart to heart), a music video by Morteza, shows him on stage singing

Fig. 33. Amphibolic characters in transition: Bahman Mofid, playing the part of a *luti*, chases a rival in the streets of Los Angeles, from the serial *Beyond Laughter*.

and dancing with three female dancers who are dressed like tough guys, in black suit, shawl, and fedora hat (but no mustache!).[24] One of the dancers appears to be an Iranian woman who herself is imitating the dancing style of the male tough guys while the other two are imitating the imitator. This doubling is clearly coded as parodic and playful. (Likewise, in the *Mafia* video, Jaklin's outfit as a Mafia don is very similar to that of the Iranian tough guys.)

These videos point out the potential for amphibolic (ambiguous, double-sided) figures to permit transgression of previously fixed boundaries of gender—in this case women mimicking men. Such gender-crossing mimicry is part of a larger destabilization. Iranian women in exile have been able to free themselves more than the men from the clutches of traditional patriarchy, and their mimicking of the men is an indication of this instability and newfound freedom. These videos also demonstrate a basic principle of syncretism: that without parallels or points of similarity in both lending and borrowing cultures, syncretic absorption and

Fig. 34. Amphibolic characters in transition: "Tough guy" style of dancing by women, from the music video *Heart to Heart*, by Morteza.

borrowing cannot take place. The dissonance between the Iranian blackface character and the racist production of blackface in America made the Iranian Haji Firuz an unabsorbable foreign body. On the other hand, the parallels in the ideology, everyday practices, and physical appearance between American Mafia figures and Iranian tough-guy characters provide a rich terrain for the development of further syncretic practices, figures, and narratives. We should expect to see more of the tough guys.

Iranian mimic surplus is evident not only in music videos and television serials but also in the gaudy furnishing popular with Iranian upper classes (both in Iran and in exile). The ostentation of the fancy French and Italian furniture and giant crystal chandeliers seems out of place when one visits apartments, condos, and homes of well-to-do Iranians in Southern California. As a rule Iranians in Los Angeles are very fashion-conscious, but in this and in the clothes they wear they reveal an element of excess, of exaggeration, of lack of fit that gives away the syncretic tensions underlying the practice.[25]

## The Politics of Hybridity and Mimicry

Fetishization, nostalgic longing, construction of an imaginary nation at a distance, ambivalence, hybridity, duality, incoherence, and mimicry are both *signs* of the tensions of exile and *strategies* of resistance and syncretic acculturation. As signs they reveal the unconscious and inadvertent defense mechanisms at work; as strategies they bespeak conscious and deliberate defensive tactics. In these various strategies of exilic deterritorialization and syncretic reterritorialization one can begin to get a sense of the slipzone of exile as a space of agonism and difference systematically denied by those who seek authority and certainty in the authenticity of origins. Total interpellation is illusory because the subject is *not* always already positioned, and difference provides potential slippages in which the subject may recognize the illusion. Whether recognition by itself is sufficient as political praxis is a subject to which I will turn in a moment. In exile, however, cultural dissonance turns that potential slippage into reality by forcing the subject to constantly face not only the vision and voice of the interpellating authority ("Hey, you there!" in Althusserian discourse) but also his own "inauthenticity" and lack of fit. This exposes the constructedness of all ideologies, and it is due to this exposure that even the politically conservative exile television, which appeals so much to Iranian origin (*asliat*) and authenticity (*esalat*), has not been able to escape from the ambivalence of exilic hybridity. As a result of their inability to hermetically contain the "authenticity of origins," these programs have gradually produced, unknown to themselves, a kind of syncretic, adaptive politics and culture that can raise questions about both the dominant and the native cultures. If these represent the liberatory promises of exilic ambivalence and hybridity, there are also certain drawbacks to them, which I will explore in the remainder of this chapter.

If syncretism involves creating a third culture and hybridity involves ambivalent positionalities, then the liminality of exile belongs more to hybridity, but it continually seeks to resolve itself into syncretism. Hybridity can be incapacitating because its practitioner hovers between several sets of subjectivities, among them those of home/host and exile/host cultures. The power relationship between the dominant host and the subordinate exile cultures is not one in which the host by mere injection of dominant ideology interpellates or assimilates the exiles, nor is it one involving suppression of the exiles and their native traditions into invisibility and silence. Rather, it is a relationship that produces psychological and ideological ambivalences which, when unresolved into syncretism, can lead to the various defensive hybrid strategies of disavowal that have been described here. While these strategies can be read as "resis-

tance," their effectivity appears to be limited to individual and textual domains, and in the end they serve only to perpetuate the domination of the
host society's political systems.

Syncretism is a process of collective acculturation in traumatic intercultural encounters such as slavery and exile. Hybridity seems to be a special
case of syncretism, less motivated by trauma and limited to the individual
or to small groups. In addition, syncretism is more stable and long-lasting
than hybridity, since it receives social sanction and currency, and it is
passed on from generation to generation (with some changes). Hybridity,
on the other hand, can remain an idiosyncratic form of adaptation whose
influence may fail to reach across time. The difference that such hybrids
as Mirza Malkum Khan in Iran, Salman Rushdie in England, and Carlos
Fuentes in Mexico have produced can make them potent political
reformers and visionary intellectuals and artists. But difference can be
read differently—in fact misread—and used against them by proponents
of purity and authenticity, leading to their isolation or incarceration. The
violent response to the hybridity and difference Salman Rushdie's exile
novel *The Satanic Verses* produced indicates that Iranian authorities did
not read them as Rushdie had encoded them. They (mis)read them as critiquing only Islamic history and theology and not also Indian and Western
popular cultures. This case demonstrates that hybridity may indeed produce a critique of the status quo, but just as surely, it will generate "aber-
rant" (mis)readings. When such readings are followed by violence,
whether individual or state-sponsored, the risk becomes too great indeed.
The production of such texts in exile is particularly problematic since as
liminal figures, exile artists run the risk of being left totally unprotected.
Alternatively, the protection they receive may be withdrawn depending
on expediency and the shifting polities of the home and host governments.[26] In the isolation of individual hybridity, one is without agency,
a lone figure floating in the tumultuous rivers of history.[27]

The criticism of hybridity need not be based only on its potential to be
misread; there are legitimate negative consequences to it. The critical analysis that the influential writer and social critic Jalal Al-e Ahmad initiated
in the 1960s against Westernized Third World and Iranian intellectuals
may be cited here as an example of criticism based on such negative consequences. In his polemical monograph *Gharbzadegi* (Westernstruckness), Al-e Ahmad rearticulated an earlier discourse about Westernization
that likened it to a disease that infests and destroys a susceptible native organism from inside (1961:27). Two decades before Homi Bhabha's writings, Al-e Ahmad suggested that the chief causes of this susceptibility are
ambivalence, mimicry, and hybridity—without talking about them in exactly these terms. Despite his lack of theoretical rigor and his overvehe-

mence, Al-e Ahmad's identification of the Third World intellectual as the "ambivalent one" is astute and his critique of such intellectuals speaks directly to the negative dimensions of ambivalence suppressed in Bhabha's writings. His argument spoken through Bhabha's discourse is this: Westernstruck intellectuals only imitate the West, they do not mimic it. There is no parodic distance in their imitation, only pure identification. This total identification with the other serves to create doubt, even shame, about the self and indigenous cultures. At the same time, since the object of identification is usually the superficial trappings of the West and not its deep values, philosophy, or technology, Westernstruck individuals are forced into an alienating form of ambivalence about both native and Western cultures, as a result of which they know neither of them well nor do they fully belong to either. The ambivalent ones, therefore, become floating signifiers in search of signifieds. Al-e Ahmad provides a veritable catalog of the ills that he suggests such a state of rootless unbelonging produces. According to him, a Westernstruck individual is a "featherweight floating on the waves of events" (1961:92), "an ass in lion's skin" (92), a "shiftless character," "unscrupulous" (93), "only a spectator," "without belief or conviction," "indifferent (94), "inauthentic," "dissembling," "fearful," "insecure" (95), "effeminate," "overdressed," and "a faithful consumer of Western industrial goods" (96). The preponderance of terms that speak of doubling, ambivalence, and mimicry is uncanny. But unlike Bhabha, who validates many of these as *strategies* of resistance and subversiveness, Al-e Ahmad considers them *essences* that structure in dominance, impotence, and subservience. He, like many other social critics, advocated a revivalist return to native roots—thereby helping to lay the intellectual foundations for the Islamist revolution that would materialize three decades later.

Mimicry is not an essence, but it can be a strategy of resistance only if it carries a critical or parodic "spin." Otherwise, it will remain only a form of noncritical and nonliberatory imitation, identification, and idealization. Mimicry will be examined here briefly first at the level of the text and then as social practice. As I have shown, Iranian music videos and television serials do inscribe a parodic, critical spin in their mimicry, but the spin appears to be misread or left unread by audiences, particularly the intellectuals who damn them for being banal and imitative. The dominant host culture, too, ignores the parodic minority texts or, if any attention is paid to them, it is the classic one of recuperation by exoticization. The texts' potential for liberation is thus thwarted. This creates major problems for postcolonial discourses of mimicry and hybridity, which seem to foreground textual agency at the expense of (or at least in place of) political, social, and moral agency. The case of Iranian music videos and TV programs in exile shows that even the production of ironic texts does not automatically translate into textual agency because, at the reception end, the texts are not necessarily decoded in the way they were encoded. Unless the resistances and ambivalences are read as such, they remain absent, for all intents and purposes as though they were never inscribed.

At the level of social practice, the mimic in Bhabha's discourse is "almost the same but not quite," he/she is "less than whole but multiple." As a "partial" and an "inappropriate" object, the mimic is both "resemblance" and "menace," threatening and undermining the authority of the dominant power, which demands not partiality but wholeness, absolute difference. The foregoing analysis of Iranian television and music videos showed that such partial and inappropriate objects are indeed produced in *discourse*, but whether such is necessarily the case in *history* is open to debate. This is because at the same time that partiality and inappropriateness undermine the authority of both the native culture and that of the dominant host, they steal away the exiles' chief weapon from them also, which is the establishment of collective difference between themselves and the host society. As a result, their identities are destabilized and political action problematized. To invoke Vivek Dhareshwar's question in another context, if the exiles and the host culture have "different semiotic histories, how can they have the same regulative psychobiography?" (1989:26). If differences are elided by continual slippage, then political action, which must rely on some element of certainty, becomes impossible. Thus instead of being liberated, this partial or fractured presence potentially can get caught in a state of paralysis, what the philosopher Daryush Shayegan calls a "purgatory state" (1977:88–91). These are almost exactly the words that the exiled psychiatrist Gholamhosain Sa'edi used a decade later to describe the incapacitating state of his own exile, as being a "purgatory located between two cultures, between life and death" (1986:8–9). This celibate state is "neither this nor that," the obverse of Rushdie's celebratory description of a mongrelized and hybridized culture as "a bit of this and a bit of that" (1990:52). Politically, there seems to be little difference between "neither this nor that" and the denial of both "this" *and* "that," resulting in political opportunism or philosophical nihilism, whereby belief is transformed entirely into doubt and certainty into mere wishfulness. When the dissolution of differences or the incessant multiplication of differences become utopian dreams, what we may end up with is a reality suffused with indifference and with what Baudrillard has called "weightlessness":

> In the end, this is what the universal cultural problematic of deconstruction is all about. Without a center, without a transcen-

dent context, how do you value difference? Thanks to the hegemony of the West, indifference has become a universal fact. In
the future, power will belong to those peoples with no origins
and no authenticity. It will belong to those who, like America
from the beginning, can achieve "deterritorialization" and
weightlessness and figure out how to exploit the situation to the
full extent. (1989:53)

In the crosscultural discourse of exile, "neither this nor that" can be read
to mean "neither here (host culture) nor there (home culture)," hence the
description of exile as purgatory and liminality. The exiles cannot fully
practice the art of weightlessness because, although they are in a liminal
state, they are still too attached to soil, roots, history, and descent relations. In addition, exile heightens the desire for constructing difference,
for creating weight. The quest intensifies for authenticity, authentication,
differentiation, and construction of some kind of originary history and national imaginary. Indeed, one of the contributions of the exiles to the
dominant host culture in America is their injection of history, memory,
distance, and context into a society that is fast losing these and is engaged
in a paroxysm of celebration of the loss. The contradiction of living
differentially in an indifferent culture and epoch creates agonistic and
phantasmagoric hybrids. Parviz Kardan of *Shahr-e Farang* in an interview
with me mobilized humorous Iranian proverbs to talk about the irrecon-
cilability of exilic hybridity: "We Iranians in exile are neither donkeys nor
asses, we are mules. We live a camel-cow-leopard life, all mixed up." Such
fabulous chimeras cannot live indifferently, weightlessly.

Hybridity's emphasis as social practice on highly contextualized strategies of distancing and doubling and of individual subject positioning fore-
stalls its ability to engage in sustained social and collective struggles. It
confines the struggle to the personal and to local and cellular resistance.
It is this that partly accounts for the gradual, but inexorable, acculturation
of both Iranian television and the exiles themselves—their production of
hybrid texts and cultures notwithstanding. Exilic popular culture and television are instrumental in the survival of uprooted Iranians. They constructed a cohesive semiotic and discursive space for exilic communitas
and an exilic economy, but their commercially driven nature served ultimately to recuperate their resistive and counterhegemonic spin, turning
them chiefly into social agencies of assimilation.

This is because the resistance that Iranian exilic media produced, like
that formulated by much of film and television and cultural studies critics,
was limited to cultural resistance. Such a mode of resistance, Mas'ud
Zavarzadeh tells us, is "more an idealistic, ahistorical force than a social

and materialistic entity. It is, in fact, an ideological device used to relegitimate the autonomous subject of free enterprise" (1991:55). What the exiles—and other (in)appropriate others—need to prevent their total appropriation and relegitimization, in the words of JanMohammed and Lloyd, is political struggle, not ironic distance (1990:16). One way to live differentially—to produce difference—without creating psychic dissonance and social weightlessness is to live not individually but socially according to the norms of culture(s) or group(s) with whom one identifies.

Living in the (post)modern world of exiles necessitates the formation of a symphony of synchronic affiliations, whereby individuals could claim belonging to multiple collectivities simultaneously. What sustained for a dozen years the Iranians in Los Angeles and even helped them to flourish as a community—without being forced to live in a single physical enclave—was their ability to weave their individual exilic existence into the larger fabric of synchronic collective affiliations created by hybrid cultures and their economy. Television programs tended to encourage formation of a collective identity more than individual subjectivity. Such communal linkages and collective identities may act as a series of anchors to slow the destabilizing effects of the small exiles from which one suffers in the Great Exile. As Edward Said notes, exile can be construed to be redemptive, an "experience that must be endured so as to restore identity, or even life itself, to fuller, more meaningful status" (1984:53). Exile is filled with predicaments, however: isolated and displaced, the exiles resort to various ambivalent and repressive strategies to gain control and leverage over the flux of liminality. This produces resistance against both acculturation and commitment, and fans the fire of exilic purgatory. But as Said states, to live as if "everything around you were temporary and perhaps trivial is to fall prey to petulant cynicism as well as to querulous lovelessness" (54). It is to avoid such a life that the exiles have striven to create new sets of group affiliations, seen at celebratory occasions (weddings, parties, concerts, nightclubs) and in salons, ephemeral associations, and political factions.

Perhaps the greatest liability of postmodern indifference is not that it takes away from the hybridized exiles the power of positive action, but that it denies them the empowerment that *negation* offers. Negation and self-denial are great sources of affirmation and self-validation—whether they be fasting, various kinds of religious *jihads* with the inner self or an external enemy, Gandhi's "negative resistance," the ecological strategy of voluntary simplicity, or the "negative dialectic" of the Frankfurt School. Social change and utopian imaginings are possible only through defining the established order as the other and by negating it (Marcuse 1968). To avoid co-optation, opposition must be defined not in terms of or in reaction to that which the dominant has formulated, but in contradiction to it and proactively against it. The problem with hybridity is that it is formulated to be forever reactive, not proactive. Such utopia-driven negative dialectic is not possible when one is caught in unresolvable irresolutions of ambivalence, indifference, and weightlessness. As Gitlin states, "Our political and aesthetic project at the fin de millennium is to continue the search, to refuse to be smug about living in a weightless culture" (1989: 53). Multiple positioning, multiple beliefs, and polyidentity may well be marks of postmodern subjectivit(ies) and exilic hybridity, but they should not be valorized to the point of reification. Their positive political ramifications do not seem to be as numerous as the multiplicity of positions putatively available! What is more, overreliance on them may turn living in exile into a series of opportunistic compromises, shifting positionalities, and veiling strategies, which make life hermeneutically rewarding—as befits postmodernism's obsession with the production and processing of information and identities—but raise troubling questions about hybridity's ethical and moral agency. Where does "ambivalence" and "sly civility" as resistance end and wiliness and opportunism begin? How does one distinguish in discourse as well as in practice between doubling and duplicity? To what extent do these strategies keep us at the level of synchrony and prevent us from entering diachrony? When ambivalence rules, difference turns into indifference and resistance into its opposite, into complicity. In such a situation, what will happen to beliefs and political actions, which must be based on the foundation of some type of certainty and solidarity? The ideologies of hybridity and multiplicity and the ensuing indeterminacy flatten out distinctions, indeed remove contradictions, thereby allowing (in)difference to become tolerable, and marketable as a commodity. This, then, lends credence to the ever-renewable metaphor of the United States as a "melting pot" society in which all differences, hierarchies, and inequalities are obliterated. (This obliteration is largely discursive, however, because social differences and class inequalities have in fact escalated. Under recent administrations, discursive plurality has veiled increasing social polarity.)

What is more, even discursive plurality itself has a limit. The absence of a fixed point of origin or what Derrida has called "the transcendental signified" might make the play of signification and the slippage between self and other, signifier and signified, appear to be endless. But such is not the case. To prove that there is no "transcendental or privileged signified and that the domain or play of signification henceforth has no limit, one must reject even the concept of the word 'sign' itself—which is precisely what cannot be done" (1978,81).

The strategic use of essentialism, negation, and Manicheanism therefore would stand us in good stead, and would help to clear the mind about who is speaking and who is listening, who is doing what to whom, and which action must be taken to what end. Gayatri Spivak speaks of the "strategic use of positivist essentialism" as a viable political action that will place its practitioners

> in line with the Marx who locates fetishization, the ideological determination of the "concrete," and spins the narrative of the development of the money-form; with the Nietzsche who offers us genealogy in place of historiography, the Foucault who plots the construction of a "counter-memory," the Barthes of semiotropy and the Derrida of "affirmative deconstruction." This would allow them to use the critical force of anti-humanism, in other words, even as they share its constitutive paradox: that the essentializing moment, the object of their criticism, is irreducible. (1987:205)[28]

Ambivalence, mimicry, and hybridity are not permanent and static things or states. They are only strategies, and for them to be productive as modes of resistance, they must be dynamic and capable of change in response to changing exigencies. Liminality is not a steady or a permanent state. The exiles must finally get on with the process of living, which moves them gradually—but not inexorably nor permanently nor totally nor unidirectionally—out of liminality and into ethnicity. With the crossing of cultural and psychic thresholds, the exiles emerge potentially less ambivalent toward the dominant culture and less intensely focused on the home culture. They might then have the necessary psychic as well as social confidence to have "a bit of this and a bit of that," to create a third syncretic culture without being totally unattached and weightless hybrids. The split subject may become partially whole again as a syncretic being. Ayatollah Khomeini's death decree on Rushdie that forced him into seclusion also forced the author, whose fascinating works and life have championed hybridity and mongrelization, to face the vulnerability and the harrowing political ramifications of these ideologies and practices. Confronting what he calls the "Actually Existing Islam," he found that it was necessary for him to "cross the threshold, go inside the room and *then* fight for your humanized, historicized, secularized way of being a Muslim" (1991).

Strategic essentialism is equivalent to crossing the threshold of liminality and "entering the room" of the host culture, in order to move out of irony and into struggle to become an instrumental part of social formation of the host society. As some recent immigrant communities, such as Koreans, found out in the aftermath of the 1992 Los Angeles unrest, eco-

nomic success must be translated into historicized political representation, otherwise the community will remain weightlessly vulnerable.
Iranians, too, have gradually become cognizant of the potential liabilities
of their liminal and politically weightless status and they have begun to
get involved in the politics of the United States. Exilic television programs
not only reflect through their news coverage but also facilitate through
their organizing news functions the entry of the Iranian exiles into the
host society's politics. In 1992 an Iranian-American ran for a Senate seat
in Maryland and Iranian television in Los Angeles interviewed him exten-
sively and promoted him heavily. Since 1990, exile media in general have
covered and facilitated the involvement of various Iranian groups in Los
Angeles with the Republican and Democratic candidates for state and national offices. Exilic television has thus become part of the politics of
agency not only vis-à-vis the homeland but also the host society. If it has
been unsuccessful in effecting from a distance any change in the politics
of the homeland, it is expected to play a more effective role in U.S. politics. In this, it will complement its other roles, discussed throughout this
study, as an agent of acculturation and assimilation.

This turn toward involvement in political agency in the host society has
potentially far-reaching consequences, as it can help the exiles become
aware of their social status in America as an ethnic minority, not just an
exilic community, as hyphenated Iranian-Americans and not just Iranians.
This awareness requires that they, in the words of Stuart Hall, "struggle
to come into representation" (1988:27). This struggle, however, requires
a rethinking of traditional notions of ethnicity. Traditionally, racial and
ethnic designations have been ascribed or adopted usually on the basis of
biology or origin. To come into representation means to disarticulate old
designations and the meanings invested in them in order to articulate new
meanings to new designations. This changes the status of terms such as
"Negro," "Black," "African-American," and "people of color" from biological givens to politically constructed categories, which "cannot be
grounded in a set of fixed trans-cultural or transcendental racial categories
and which therefore [have] no guarantees in Nature" (28). As designations
become more cultural and political than biological, they become also
more of a sign of identity for which one must struggle in a continual politics of alliance and disalliance. This means the end of the innocent notion
of the essential ethnic subject and entry into the politics of minority discourse in the sense proposed by JanMohammed and Lloyd. For them
minority discourse, in the singular, does not mean focusing on the specificity of each minority culture but rather articulating the relationship
among them by describing and defining the common denominators that
link them (1990:1). To "become minor" in this context means to move

out of liminality. It does not mean, however, subscribing to ethnic or racial essentialism or to originary nationalism; rather, it implies engagement in strategic essentialism and alliance politics so as to articulate a collective political position vis-à-vis the dominant forces of the host society. In this syncretic notion of unity in difference lies the recognition of the specific experiences, cultures, and identities of each diasporic or exiled group at the same time that there is an acknowledgment of their shared experiences and common positionalities as marginalized peoples. As Hall states,

> What is involved is the splitting of the notion of ethnicity between, on the one hand the dominant notion which connects it to nation and to "race" and, on the other hand what I think is the beginning of a positive conception of the ethnicity of the margins, of the periphery. That is to say, a recognition that we all speak from a particular place, out of a particular history, out of a particular experience, a particular culture, without being contained by that position as "ethnic artists" or film-makers. We are all, in that sense, *ethnically* located and our ethnic identities are crucial to our subjective sense of who we are. But this is also a recognition that this is not an ethnicity which is doomed to survive, as Englishness was, only by marginalising, dispossessing, displacing and forgetting other ethnicities. (29)

Engagement in this politics of representation and minority discourse is the central and urgent task ahead. In the meantime, exile television's strategies of doubling and ambivalence create not a problem of location but a discourse about locations. As such, the exiles are engaged in what we might call a "discourse of synchronicity" in that they are both here and there and they determine their own process of becoming here in the light of what is perceived to be there. In this simultaneous, synchronous zone many established binary categories such as self/other, inside/outside, high/low, and here/there collapse or are continually problematized. To invoke my own biography:

> The "elsewhere" . . . is dissolved both in fact and in fantasy. The "elsewhere" is now "here." Me, myself, I, he, others(s)—all of me—are here at once, no distance separates us. But, look, a switch is taking place! Another "elsewhere," another Other, is now looming large. I am speaking of home, against which I must begin to define myself anew. (Naficy 1989c:51)

Of course, from a position in exile, the home(s) against which one continues to redefine oneself is no longer a place but a construct, no more than a wish or a desire. And like all constructs this one is potentially a lie, and like all desires this one is charged with displacements and distortions. There is thus a continual process of unveiling and veiling and unveiling again: as soon as you feel confident that finally you have gotten a fix on "self," "other," "home," "here," or "there," a slippage occurs, something shifts and removes the shield, uneasily revealing the raw bones of incommensurability underneath. In exile, one is in the process of ceaseless exchange, of becoming.

Table 1. Persian-Language Periodicals published in Los Angeles, 1980–92

| Title | Type | Affiliation/tendency | Frequency |
|-------|------|---------------------|-----------|
| *A'ineh* | Satirical | | Weekly |
| *Andisheh* | Cultural | Kanun-e Andisheh | Periodic |
| *Aqaz-e No\** | Political | Leftist | Irregular |
| *Arya* | Political | Royalist | Periodic |
| *Asa* | Political | Royalist | Periodic |
| *Asqar Aqa* | Satirical | | Periodic |
| *Asr-e Emruz\** | News | | Daily |
| *Atash-e Moqaddas\** | Political | Royalist | Periodic |
| *Atoor* | Religio-ethnic | Assyrian | Monthly |
| *Ayandegan* | News | Royalist | Weekly |
| *Baray-e Azadi* | Eclectic | | |
| *Barresi-ye Ketab\** | Literary | | Quarterly |
| *Bazar\** | Advertisements | | Weekly |
| *Chemsandaz\** | Religio-ethnic | Jewish | Periodic |
| *Daad\** | Legal | | Monthly |
| *Donia-ye Yahud\** | Religio-ethnic | Jewish | Monthly |
| *Elements* | Architecture | Geltaftan Foundation | Quarterly |
| *Elm va Erfan* | Religious | Islamic mysticism | Periodic |
| *Farman-e Panjom* | Religio-ethnic | Jewish | Periodic |
| *Fogholadeh\** | Eclectic | | Weekly |
| *Forugh\** | Women | | Quarterly |
| *Hafteh Nameh* | Eclectic | | Weekly |
| *Iran Life* | Eclectic | | Monthly |
| *Iran News\** | Eclectic | Royalist | Weekly |
| *Iran Post* | Eclectic | | Weekly |
| *Iran-e Emruz* | Eclectic | Royalist | |
| *Iran Report* | Eclectic | Royalist | Weekly |
| *Iran Tribune* | Eclectic | | Weekly |
| *Iranian Recycler* | Advertisements | | Weekly |
| *Jahan-e Pezeshgi\** | Medical | | Quarterly |
| *Jahan-e Varzesh* | Sports | | Weekly |
| *Jam-e Jam* | Eclectic | Jam-e Jam TV | Weekly |
| *Javanan\** | Eclectic | | Weekly |
| *Jebheh-ye Hamgam* | Political | Iranian Coalition Front | Monthly |
| *Jebheh-ye Jam* | Political | Mellion Front | Bimonthly |
| *Jelveh\** | Political | | Monthly |
| *Jonbesh-e Irani-ye Banitorah* | Religio-ethnic | | Jewish |
| *Jong* | Literary | | Bimonthly |
| *Kabobnameh* | Eclectic | Kabobi Restaurant | Periodic |
| *Kajnazar* | Religio-ethnic | Armenian | Monthly |
| *Kargar-e Emruz* | Political | Leftist | Periodic |
| *Ketab-e Nima* | Literary | Kanun-e Farhangi-ye Nima | Periodic |
| *Khabarnameh-ye Zanan* | Women | Kanun-e Nashr-e Khabarnameh-ye Zanan | Monthly |
| *Khandaniha\** | Political | Royalist | Periodic |
| *Khaneh va Zamin* | Real estate | | |

| | | | |
|---|---|---|---|
| *Koja Miravi* | Political | Royalist | Weekly |
| *Kurosh-e Bozorg\** | Eclectic | Royalist | Bimonthly |
| *Mellat-e Bidar* | Literary | Royalist | Monthly |
| *Mowj* | Political | | Periodic |
| *Nasl-e Now* | Eclectic | | Monthly |
| *Negareh* | | | One issue |
| *Niazmandiha\** | Advertisements | | Weekly |
| *Omid* | Literary | Radio-Televizion-e Omid | Periodic |
| *Pardis* | Political | Royalist | Weekly |
| *Pars* | Economical | | Monthly |
| *Payk-e Aramesh* | | | |
| *Payam-e Ashena\** | Eclectic | | Monthly |
| *Payam-e Azadi* | Political | Royalist | Bimonthly |
| *Payam-e Iran\** | Political | Nehzat-e Moqavemat-e Melli | Bimonthly |
| *Payman* | Religio-ethnic | Jewish | Monthly |
| *Payvand* | Eclectic | | Monthly |
| *Payvand Nameh* | Eclectic | Markaz-e Farhangi va Ejtema'i-ye Iranian | Monthly |
| *Payk-e Ketab\** | Literary | Sherkat-e Ketab | Periodic |
| *Pol* | | | |
| *Qalam dar Khedmat-e Jahad* | Political | Mojahedins from Afghanistan | Monthly |
| *Rah-e Zendegi\** | Women | | Weekly |
| *Rahavard\** | Literary | | Quarterly |
| *Rayegan* | Eclectic | | Weekly |
| *Sarnevesht\** | Parapsycho-logical | | Monthly |
| *Seda-ye Shahr* | Literary | Leftist | Quarterly |
| *Shahr-e Farang* | Eclectic | | Periodic |
| *Shakhsar* | Religio-ethnic | Baha'is | Monthly |
| *Shofar\** | Religio-ethnic | Jewish | Monthly |
| *Simorgh\** | Literary | Leftist | Monthly |
| *Sobh-e Iran\** | News | | Daily |
| *Sosialism* | Political | Leftist | Monthly |
| *Sowgand* | Eclectic | | Weekly |
| *Sufi\** | Religion | Islamic mysticism | |
| *Tamasha\** | Eclectic | | Bimonthly |
| *Tamasha 64* | Entertainment | | Monthly |
| *Tamasha Bazaar\** | Advertisements | | Weekly |
| *Towfigh-e Ejbari\** | Satirical | | Bimonthly |
| *Touka\** | Children | | Monthly |
| *Vauli-Vaul* | Physical fitness | | Periodic |
| *Zamaneh\** | Literary | | Monthly |
| *Zan\** | Women | | Periodic |

*Note:* All periodicals marked with an asterisk are currently in publication. The rest have ceased. No figures on their circulation are available.
*Source:* Compiled by the author.

Table 2. Regularly scheduled radio programs aired in Los Angeles, 1980–92

| Name of Program | Type | Language | Frequency | Program Length (hours) |
|---|---|---|---|---|
| *Happy Harry* | Eclectic | Armenian | 5 nights | 1.00 |
| *Iran* | Eclectic | Persian | Daily | 1.00 |
| *Iranian** | Eclectic | Persian | Continuous | 24.00 |
| *Nayiri* | Ethnic | Armenian | 5 nights | 1.00 |
| *Omid-e Iran* | Eclectic | Persian | 6 nights | 3.00 |
| *Payam* | Eclectic | Persian | Weekly | 1.00 |
| *Payam-e Enqelab-e Eslami* (supporter of Islamic Republic) | Political | Persian | Weekly | 0.50 |
| *Purang* | Eclectic | Persian | Weekly | 1.00 |
| *Rah-e Shab* | Eclectic | Persian | Weekly | 8.00 |
| *Rangarang* | Youth | Persian | Weekly | 2.00 |
| *Seda-ye Afghanistan*[1] (supporter of Afghani Mojahedins) | Ethnic | Dari Persian | Weekly | 1.00 |
| *Seda-ye Arameneh* | Ethnic | Armenian | Sat/Sunday | 3.00 |
| *Seda-ye Azadi* (supporter of Sazman-e Mojahedin-e Khalq) | Political | Persian | Weekly | 1.00 |
| *Seda-ye Hezb-e Komonist* (supporter of Iranian Communist Party) | Political | Persian | | |
| *Seda-ye Iran-Javid* (Royalist) | Political | Persian | Weekly | 0.50 |
| *Seda-ye Iran** (Royalist) | Eclectic | Persian | Continuous | 24.00 |
| *Seda-ye Nehzat* (Royalist, supporter of Bakhtiar faction) | Political | Persian | Saturday | 1.00 |
| *You're on the Air** (produced by Islamic Information service) | Religious | English | Weekly | 0.30[1] |

[1]*You're on the Air* is not aimed specifically at Iranians but at all Muslims living in Southern California. It is a live program focusing on current topics and featuring a call-in segment. *Seda-ye Afghanistan* is produced by and for the Afghan exiles but since its language is understandable to Iranians, it is included here.

*Note:* Programs marked with an asterisk are still on the air.

*Source:* Compiled by the author.

Table 3. Organizations sponsoring "newscasts" by telephone in Los Angeles

| Sponsoring Organization | Affiliation |
| --- | --- |
| Anjoman-e Daneshjuyan-e Irani dar Jonub-e Kalifornia | Fada'ian-e Khalq—Majority faction and the Tudeh Party |
| Anjoman-e Daneshjuyan-e Mosalman-e Emrika va Kanada* | Sazman-e Mojahedin-e Khalq |
| Sazman-e Daneshjuyan-e Irani dar Jonub-e Kalifornia | Confederation of Iranian students (CIS), Fada'ian Khalq—Minority faction |
| Anjoman-e Eslami-ye Daneshjuyan dar Emrika va Kanada* | Islamic Republic of Iran |

*Note:* Extant services are marked with an asterisk.
*Source:* Compiled by the author.

**Table 4. Feature fiction films made by Iranians in exile**

| Title | Director | Year | Country of Production |
|---|---|---|---|
| Blueface | Shirin Bazleh | 1992 | USA |
| Cat in a Cage | Tony Zarindast | 1985 | USA |
| Checkpoint (*Sarhad*) | Parviz Sayyad | 1987 | USA |
| Destination Unknown | Sohrab Shahid-Saless | 1983 | Germany |
| Escape | Tony Zarindast | ? | USA |
| Face of the Enemy | Hassan Ildari | 1989 | USA |
| Far From Home | S. Shahid-Saless | 1975 | Germany |
| Final Incident (*Hadeseh*) | Kayvon Derakhshanian | 1992 | USA |
| The Guests of Hotel Astoria | Reza Allamehzadeh | 1989 | USA/Holland |
| The Guns and the Fury | Tony Zarindast | ? | USA |
| Heaven Can Help | Tony Zarindast | 1989 | USA |
| House Beyond the Sand | Tony Zarindast | ? | USA |
| Kill Allex Kill | Tony Zarindast | ? | USA |
| A Little Stiff | Caveh Zahedi & Greg Watkins | 1992 | USA |
| The Mission (*Ferestadeh*) | Parviz Sayyad | 1983 | USA |
| Nightsongs | Marva Nabili | 1984 | USA |
| The Nuclear Baby | Jalal Fatemi | 1990 | USA |
| Raha | Farrokh Majidi | 1990 | Denmark |
| Revolt | Jim Shaibani | 1985 | USA |
| The State of Crisis (*L'etat de Crise*) | Mamad Haghighat | 1984 | France |
| The Suitors (*Khastgaran*) | Ghasem Ebrahimian | 1989 | USA |
| Le Tablier de ma Mere | Arbi Avanesian | 1980 | France |
| Terror in Beverly Hills | Moshe Bibian | 1989 | USA |
| The Time of Maturity | S. Shahid-Saless | 1976 | Germany |
| Treasure of the Lost Desert | Tony Zarindast | ? | USA |
| Utopia | S. Shahid-Saless | 1982 | Germany |
| Veiled Threat | Cyrus Nowrasteh | 1988 | USA |

*Source:* Compiled by the author.

**Table 5. Types of Iranian associations and examples**

| Type of Association | Examples |
| --- | --- |
| Professional | Iranian Medical Association, Iranian Nurses Association |
| Business | Coalition of Iranian Entrepreneurs |
| Religious | California Zoroastrian Center, Iranian Jewish Federation, Iranian Armenian Center, Baha'i Center, Muslim Student Association, Assyrian Cultural Center |
| Ethnic | Azarbaijan Association, various Kurdish, Jewish, and Armenian groups |
| Regional | Esfahan Club, Gilanian Society |
| Political | National Resistance Front, Organization of Peoples Guerrillas |
| Women | Women's Cultural Society |
| Student | At least one Iranian student association on each major university campus in Southern California |
| Alumni | Graduates from high schools (Alborz), graduates from universities (Shiraz) |
| Literary and cultural services | Nima Cultural Center, Kia Foundation Iranian Assistance Foundation, Iranian Refugee Relief Organization, Rotary Club |

*Source:* Compiled by the author.

Table 6. Societies and social functions they have sponsored at UCLA, 1980–90

| Sponsoring Societies and Groups | Description and Types of Function |
| --- | --- |
| UCLA Near Eastern Studies Center | Seminars on the Shahnameh, philosophy, culture, politics, economics, sociology; film screenings |
| Anjoman-e Farhangi-ye Nima | Frequent seminars on national identity, culture, role of intellectuals, cinema, women, language, literature; film screenings |
| Kanun-e Andisheh | Periodic seminars on culture, art, poetry, cinema |
| Radio Omid-e Iran | Occasional lectures, seminars on culture, art, literature |
| UCLA Student Association | Art exhibits, film screenings, dances, picnics |
| UCLA Iran Education & Research Group | Frequent lectures, seminars on culture, literature, cinema, history, politics, sociology, language; film screenings |
| Kanun-e Farhangi Siyasi-e Iranian | Bimonthly lectures on history, politics, culture, Marxism, philosophy, feminism |
| Anjoman-e Farhangi-e Zanan | Periodic seminars on feminism, gender identity, literature, politics; art exhibits |
| Komiteh-ye Demokratik-e Zanan-e Iran | Art exhibit, seminars |
| Kanun-e Hambastegi-ye Zanan-e Irani | Lectures about women |
| Komiteh-ye Defa' az Hoquq-e Demokratik-e Zanan (pro-Fada'ian-e Khalq) | Lectures on feminism and politics |
| Anjoman-e Defa' az Hoquq-e Demokratik-e Zanan-e Iran | Seminars on feminism and women's literature, poetry, psychology, politics; film screenings |
| Tashakol-e Mostaqqal-e Zanan dar Jonub-e Kalifornia | Seminars on feminism, politics |
| Anjoman-e Azadi-e Zan | Seminars on feminism, politics |
| Anjoman-e Eslami-ye Daneshjuyan dar Emrika va Kanada (pro-Islamic Rep.) | Weekly meetings; seminars on Iranian politics, women, Islam, prayer, screening of documentaries & feature films from Iran |
| Anjoman-e Daneshjuyan-e Irani (supporter of Majority Fada'ian) | Occasional meetings; seminars on politics; film screenings |
| Havadaran-e Cherikha-ye Fada'i Khalq | Occasional meetings; seminars on politics; film screenings |
| Anjoman-e Daneshjuyan-e Mosalman (supporter of Mojahedin-e Khalq) | Weekly meetings, lectures, videos of activities and speeches by Mojahedin leaders, musical performances |
| Hezb-e Komonist-e Iran | Occasional lectures, seminars on politics, Kurdish uprising, war with Iraq; musical performances, film screenings |
| Iranian Association of America | Occasional seminars on Persian culture, literature |

| | |
|---|---|
| Sazman-e Havadaran-e Hezb-e Tudeh-ye Iran | Occasional lectures; plays; slide-tapes |
| Hezb-e Demokrat-e Kordestan | Occasional seminars, lectures, shows, & films |
| Komite-ye Bainolmelali-ye Defa' az Hoquq-e Demokratik-e Mardom-e Iran | Occasional lectures, film screenings, musical performances |

*Source:* Compiled by the author.

Table 7. Program profile, regularly scheduled Iranian TV programs in
Los Angeles, 1981–92

| Title (Persian/English) | Length (minutes) | Year (first aired) | Frequency | Broadcast Channel (call letter and number) |
|---|---|---|---|---|
| *Bet Naharin* (Assyria)* | 60 | 1974 | Weekly | Cablecast |
| *Iranian** | 60 | 1981 | Weekly | KSCI (18) |
| *Jam-e Jam* (Bowl of Jamshid) | 60 | 1981 | Weekly | KSCI (18) |
| *Sima-ye Ashna* (Familiar face)*[1] | 30 | 1982 | Daily | KSCI (18) |
| *Melli/National* | 60 | 1982 | Weekly | KSCI (18) |
| *Mikhak-e Noqreb'i* (Silver carnation) | 60 | 1983 | Weekly | KSCI (18) |
| *Mehr-e Iran* (Iran's love) | 60 | 1983 | Weekly | KSCI (18) |
| *Jonbesh-e Iran* (Iran's uprising)* | 60 | 1983 | Weekly | KSCI (18) |
| *Ebrouni: Armenian TV Times* | 60 | 1983 | ? | KSCI (18) |
| *Parsian* (Persian) | 60 | 1984 | Weekly | KSCI (18) |
| *Sima-ye Azadi* (Face of freedom)* | 60 | 1986 | Weekly | KSCI (18) |
| *Iranian Music TV* | 60 | 1986 | Weekly | KSCI (18) |
| *Jom'-eh* (Friday) | 60 | 1986 | Weekly | KSCI (18) |
| *Mellat* (Nation) | 60 | 1986 | Weekly | KSCI (18) |
| *Iran** | 30 | 1987 | Daily | Cablecast (KCLA) |
| *Pars** | 60 | 1987 | Weekly | KSCI (18) |
| *Melli-e Pars* (Pars National) | 60 | 1987 | Weekly | KSCI (18) |
| *Midnight Show** | 30 | 1987 | Weekly | KSCI (18) |
| *Cheshmak* (Wink) | 30 | 1987 | Weekly | KSCI (18) |
| *Dabestan-e Iran* (Iran's school) | 30 | 1987 | Weekly | KSCI (18) |
| *Negah* (Look) | 30 | 1988 | Weekly | KSCI (18) |
| *Negah* (Look)* | 30 | 1988 | Weekly | Cablecast (KCLA) |
| *Jong-e Bamdadi* (Morning magazine)* | 30 | 1988 | Daily | KSCI (18) |
| *Omid-e Iran* (Iran's hope) | 30 | 1988 | Daily | KSCI (18) |
| *Jahan Nama* (World show) | 30 | 1988 | Weekly | KSCI (18) |
| *Arya in L.A.* (Aryan in L.A.) | 30 | 1988 | Weekly | KSCI (18) |
| *Didar* (Visit) | 60 | 1988 | Weekly | KSCI (18) |
| *Sobh-e Ruz-e Jom'eh* (Friday A.M.)* | 30 | 1988 | Weekly | KSCI (18) |
| *Iranian P.M.* | 30 | 1989 | Weekly | KSCI (18) |
| *Tamasha* (Spectacle) | 30 | 1989 | Weekly | KSCI (18) |
| *Iran va Jahan* (Iran & the world)* | 30 | 1989 | Weekly | KSCI (18) |

| | | | | |
|---|---|---|---|---|
| *Ma* (Us) | 60 | 1989 | Weekly | KSCI (18) |
| *Foghóladeh* (Extra) | 30 | 1989 | Weekly | KSCI (18) |
| *Assurian* (Assyrian) | 60 | 1989 | Weekly | Cablecast |
| *Zendegi-ye Behtar* (Better life) | 30 | 1989 | Weekly | KSCI (18) |
| *Khorus-e Bimahal* (Untimely crow) | 30 | 1989 | Weekly | KSCI (18) |
| *Qod Qod-e Morgh* (Hen's cackle) | 30 | 1989 | Weekly | KSCI (18) |
| *Khub O' Bad O' Zesht* (Good, bad, and ugly) | 30 | 1989 | Weekly | KSCI (18) |
| *Shahr-e Farang* (Peep show)* | 60 | 1989 | Weekly | Cablecast (KCLA) |
| *Tapesh* (Pulse) | 30 | 1990 | Weekly | Cablecast |
| *Sima va Nava-ye Iran* (Vision and voice of Iran) | 30 | 1990 | Weekly | Cablecast |
| *Chemshandaz* (Perspective) | 30 | 1990 | Weekly | Cablecast |
| *Assyrian Weekly Magazine* | — | | Weekly | Cablecast |
| *Assyrian American Association* | — | | Weekly | Cablecast |
| *Assyrian American Civic TV** | | | Weekly | Cablecast |
| *Emshab ba Parviz* (Tonight with Parviz)* | 30 | 1991 | Nightly | KSCI (18) |
| *Apadana* | 30 | 1991 | Weekly | KSCI (18) |
| *Pezeshg-e Khub-e Khanevadeh* (Family's good doctor)* | 30 | 1991 | Weekly | KSCI (18) |
| *Cheshmandaz* (Perspective)* | 30 | 1991 | Biweekly | KSCI (18) |
| *Shoma* (You) | 30 | 1991 | Weekly | Cablecast |
| *Javanan va Nowjavanan* (Youth & teenagers) | 30 | 1991 | Weekly | KSCI (18) |
| *Irangeles* | 30 | 1991 | Weekly | Cablecast |
| *Studio Karnaval* (Carnival studio) | 30 | 1991 | Weekly | Cablecast |
| *Tasvir va Tamasha* (Picture and spectacle) | 30 | 1992 | Weekly | Cablecast |
| *Mardom va Jahan-e Pezeshgi* (People & the world of medicine)* | 30 | 1992 | Biweekly | KSCI (18) |
| *You & the World of Medicine** | 30 | 1992 | Triweekly | KSCI (18) |
| *Mozhdeh* (Glad tidings)* | 30 | 1992 | Weekly | Cablecast/ Public access |
| *Aftab* (Sunshine)* | 120 | 1992 | Weekly | KRCA (62) |
| *Diyar* (Country)* | 60 | 1992 | Weekly | Cablecast (KCLA) |
| *Melli* (National)* | 60 | 1992 | Weekly | Cablecast (KCLA) |

| | | | | |
|---|---|---|---|---|
| *Harf va Goft* | 30 | 1992 | Biweekly | KSCI (18) |
| (Words and talk)* | | | | |
| *Sokhani ba Ravanshenas* | 30 | 1992 | Weekly | KSCI (18) |
| (Talk with psychologist)* | | | | |

[1]*Sima-ye Ashna* began as a 60-minute show on Sunday afternoons. In 1983 it moved to weekday mornings. In that slot, it was first one hour long but soon *Jong-e Bamdadi* rented the second half of the program. The first half was periodically leased to *Cheshmandaz*.
*Note:* All programs marked with an asterisk are currently on the air.
*Source:* Compiled by the author.

Table 8. Broadcast schedule and program types: Iranian programs in Los Angeles KSCI Channel 18 and cable TV channels, May 1992

| Broadcast Time | Days of the Week | | | | | | |
| --- | --- | --- | --- | --- | --- | --- | --- |
| | Monday | Tuesday | Wednesday | Thursday | Friday | Saturday | Sunday |
| 07:30 | *Sima-ye Ashna* (news/ features) (30 min) | *Chesh-mandaz* (news/ comments) (30 min) | *Sima-ye Ashna* (news/ features) (30 min) | *Chesh-mandaz* (news/ comments) (30 min) | *Sima-ye Ashna* (news/ features) (30 min) | – | – |
| 08:00 | *Jong-e Bamdadi* (National/international news/commentary) (30 min) | *Jong-e Bamdadi* (30 min) | *Jong-e Bamdadi* (30 min) | *Jong-e Bamdadi* (30 min) | *Jong-e Bamdadi* (30 min) | – | – |
| 08:30 | *Pezeshg-e Khub* (medical) (30 min) | *Mardom va J. Pezeshgi* (medical) (30 min) | – | *Mardom va J. Pezeshgi* (medical) (30 min) | *Sobh-e Ruz-e Jom'eh* (talk/ads) (30 min) | – | – |
| 09:30 | *You & World of Medicine* (medical) (30 min) | – | *You & World of Medicine* (medical) (30 min) | | *You & World of Medicine* (medical) (30 min) | – | – |
| 11:00 | – | – | – | – | – | – | *Iranian* (news/ comments) (60 min) |
| 12:00 | – | – | – | – | – | – | *Jonbesh-e Iran* (comments/ variety) (60 min) |
| 13:00 | – | – | – | – | – | – | *Jam-e Jam* (variety/ news) (60 min) |
| 14:00 | – | – | – | – | – | – | *Aftab* (variety/ films) (120 min) |
| 15:00 | – | – | – | – | – | – | *Assyrian Civic TV* (ethnic) (60 min) |
| 20:30 | *Iran* (variety) (60 min) | – | – | – | – | – | *Melli* (variety) (60 min) |

| Time | | | | | | | |
|---|---|---|---|---|---|---|---|
| 21:00 | | *Iran* (variety/entertainment/local news) (60 min) | *Iran* (60 min) | *Iran* | *Iran* (60 min) | *Iran* (60 min) | – |
| 21:30 | *Iran va Jahan* (variety) (60 min) | – | – | – | – | – | *Negah* (serial/culture) (30 min) |
| 22:00 | – | – | – | – | *Shahr-e Farang* (variety) (60 min) | – | *Diyar* (music) (60 min) |
| 22:30 | – | *Mozhdeh* (religious) (30 min) | – | – | – | – | – |
| 24:00 | *Sokhani ba Ravan-shenas* (call-in show) (30 min) | *Harf va Goft* (talk show) (30 min) | *Emshab ba Parviz* (call-in show) (30 min) | *Harf va Goft* (talk show) (30 min) | *Emshab ba Parviz* (call-in show) (30 min) | *Sima-ye Azadi* (comments) (60 min) | *Midnight Show* (talk show) (30 min) |
| 00:30 | – | – | – | – | *Pars* (variety) (30 min) | – | – |
| 01:00 | – | – | – | – | *Agahi-ye Behtar* (advertisement) (30 min) | – | – |

*Note:* The table gives four pieces of information for each program: title, time and day of broadcast, type and format, and length in minutes.

*Source:* Compiled by the author.

**Table 9.** Iranian TV programs currently in tape syndication, May 1992

| Syndicated Programs | Countries | Cities |
|---|---|---|
| *Iran* | USA | Los Angeles, New York, San Francisco, San Jose, Washington, D.C. |
| *Iranian* | USA | Los Angeles, Miami, San Diego, Portland, Washington, D.C. |
| | Germany | Berlin |
| | Iran | |
| *Jam-e Jam* | USA | Baltimore, Fresno, Los Angeles, Norfolk, San Diego, San Francisco, San Jose, Santa Barbara, Washington, D.C. |
| | Canada | Montreal |
| | Germany | Berlin |
| *Jonbesh-e Iran* | USA | Los Angeles, San Diego, San Francisco, San Jose, Washington, D.C. |
| | Germany | Berlin, Frankfurt, Hamburg |
| | Persian Gulf countries | |
| | Iran | |
| *Midnight Show* | USA | Austin, Baltimore, Los Angeles, Dallas, Norfolk, San Antonio, San Diego, San Francisco, San Jose, Washington, D.C. |
| | Canada | |
| *Negah* | USA | Los Angeles, San Francisco, Washington, D.C. |
| *Shahr-e Farang* | USA | Norfolk, San Francisco, San Jose, Seattle, Washington, D.C. |

*Source:* Compiled by the author from information drawn from *Iranian Directory Yellow Pages*, 1991.

Table 10. Estimated revenues from advertisements for current programs

| Title | Frequency per Week | Length in Minutes | Unit Price | Total per Week |
|---|---|---|---|---|
| *Aftab* | 1 | 120 | $5,400 | $5,400[1] |
| *Assyrian American Civic TV* | 1 | no ads | | |
| *Bet Naharin* | 1 | no ads | | |
| *Chemshandaz* | 1 | 30 | 2,700 | 2,700 |
| *Diyar* | 1 | 60 | 5,400 | 5,400 |
| *Emshab ba Parviz* | 2 | 30 | 2,700 | 5,400 |
| *Harf va Goft* | 2 | 30 | 2,700 | 5,400 |
| *Iran* | 5 | 30 | 2,700 | 13,500 |
| *Iranian* | 1 | 60 | 5,400 | 5,400 |
| *Iran va Jahan* | 1 | 60 | 5,400 | |
| *Jam-e Jam* | 1 | 60 | 5,400 | 5,400 |
| *Jonbesh-e Iran* | 1 | 60 | 5,400 | 5,400 |
| *Jong-e Bamdadi* | 5 | 30 | 2,700 | 13,500 |
| *Mardom va Jahan-e Pezeshgi* | 2 | 30 | 2,700 | 5,400 |
| *Melli* | 1 | 60 | 5,400 | 5,400 |
| *Midnight Show* | 1 | 30 | 2,700 | 2,700 |
| *Mozhdeh* | 1 | no ads | | |
| *Negah* | 1 | 30 | 2,700 | 2,700 |
| *Pars* | 1 | 60 | 5,400 | 5,400 |
| *Pezeshg-e Khub-e Khanevadeh* | 1 | 30 | 2,700 | 2,700 |
| *Shahr-e Farang* | 1 | 60 | 5,400 | 5,400 |
| *Sima-ye Ashna* | 5 | 30 | 2,700 | 13,500 |
| *Sima-ye Azadi* | 1 | no ads | | |
| *Sobh-e Ruz-e Jom'eh* | 1 | 30 | 2,700 | 2,700 |
| *Sokhani ba Ravanshenas* | 1 | 30 | 2,700 | 2,700 |
| *You & the World of Medicine* | 2 | 30 | 2,700 | 5,400 |
| Total per Week | | | | $121,500 |
| Total per Month | | | | $486,000 |
| Total per Year | | | | $5,832,000 |

[1]Because *Aftab* is a new program, it has far fewer ads than do others. I have assumed that the two-hour program contains ads equaling those of a one-hour show.
*Note:* For convenience, I have assumed that each thirty-second and sixty-second ad generates for a producer an average of $135 and $270, respectively. Half-hour programs are assumed to contain a minimum of 10 minutes of ads and hour-long shows a minimum of 20 minutes.
*Source:* Compiled by the author.

Table 11. KSCI-TV's airtime rate schedule (effective 1992): cost in dollars per hour/half hour

| Time Period | Weekday | Weekend |
| --- | --- | --- |
| 7 A.M. to 4 P.M. | 1,500/750 | 3,000/1,500 |
| 4 P.M. to 6 P.M. | 2,000/1,000 | 3,400/1,700 |
| 6 P.M. to 7 P.M. | 2,800/1,400 | 3,600/1,800 |
| 7 P.M. to 11 P.M. | 4,000/2,000 | 4,400/2,200 |
| 11 P.M. to 12 A.M. | 2,000/1,000 | 2,200/1,100 |
| 12 A.M. to 1 A.M. | 1,500/750 | 2,000/1,000 |
| 1 A.M. to 7 A.M. | 1,000/500 | 1,200/600 |

Source: KSCI-TV, 1992.

Table 12. Estimated cost of renting airtime for current Iranian programs

| Program Titles | Dollars per Week |
|---|---|
| *Aftab* | $1,200 |
| *Assyrian American Civic TV* | 300 |
| *Bet Naharin* | 300 |
| *Chemshandaz* | 2,000 |
| *Diyar* | 3,000 |
| *Emshab ba Parviz* | 2,000 |
| *Harf va Goft* | 2,000 |
| *Iran* | 15,000 |
| *Iranian* | 3,000 |
| *Iran va Jahan* | 3,000 |
| *Jam-e Jam* | 3,000 |
| *Jonbesh-e Iran* | 3,000 |
| *Jong-e Bamdadi* | 3,750 |
| *Mardom va Jahan-e Pezeshgi* | 1,500 |
| *Melli* | 3,000 |
| *Midnight Show* | 1,100 |
| *Mozhdeh* | 1,000 |
| *Negah* | 1,500 |
| *Pars* | 2,000 |
| *Pezeshg-e Khub-e Khanevadeh* | 750 |
| *Shahr-e Farang* | 3,000 |
| *Sima-ye Ashna* | 3,750 |
| *Sima-ye Azadi* | 2,200 |
| *Sobh-e Ruz-e Jom'eh* | 750 |
| *Sokhani ba Ravanshenas* | 1,000 |
| *You & the World of Medicine* | 1,500 |
| Total | $    64,600 |
| | $3,359,200 |

*Note:* The table includes all programs that are broadcast over the air and over cable. The figures for the cost of renting airtime for KSCI-TV are based on the rate card schedule listed in Table 11. For cable companies, there is much variation, and I have used as an average Century Cable's figures of $300 and $600 for renting half-hour and hour-long airtime, respectively.

*Source:* Compiled by the author based on information obtained from broadcasting stations and cable companies.

Table 13. Producers' profile: Iranian TV programs in Los Angeles, 1981–82

| Program Title | Religio-ethnic Affiliation | Media Background |
|---|---|---|
| *Aftab* (Sunshine)* | Muslim | |
| *Apadana* | Muslim | TV reporter/Iran |
| *Arya in L.A.* (Aryan in L.A.) | Muslim | Radio announcer/ Iran |
| *Assurian* (Assyrian) | Assyrian Christian | Singer |
| *Assyrian American Assn.* | Assyrian Christian | |
| *Assyrian Ame'n Civic** | Assyrian Christian | President, Assyrian Club |
| *Assyrian Weekly Magazine* | Assyrian Christian | Singer |
| *Bet Naharin* (Assyria)* | Assyrian Christian[1] | Politician |
| *Chemshandaz* (Perspective) | Muslim | Theater actor/Iran |
| *Cheshmak* (Wink) | Baha'i | TV production/U.S. |
| *Cheshmandaz* (Perspective)* | Muslim | TV network executive |
| *Dabestan-e Iran* (Iran's school) | Muslim | Business/Iran |
| *Didar* (Visit) | Baha'i | Radio producer/ Iran |
| *Diyar* (Country)* | Armenian Christian | Announcer/Iran |
| | Armenian Christian | |
| *Ebrouni: Armenian TV Times* | Armenian Christian | |
| *Emshab ba Parviz* (Tonight with Parviz)* | Muslim/Turk | TV production/U.S. |
| *Fogholadeh* (Extra) | Armenian Christian | Printer/U.S. |
| *Harf va Goft* (Words and talk)* | Muslim | Network executive/ Iran |
| *Iran** | Muslim | Sports announcer/ Iran |
| *Iran va Jahan* (Iran & the world)* | Jewish | News Commentator/Israel |
| *Irangeles* | Muslim | Athlete |
| *Iranian** | Muslim | Ad agency/Iran |
| *Iranian Music TV* | Muslim | TV technician/Iran |
| *Iranian P.M.* | Muslim | Ad agency/Iran |
| *Jahan Nama* (World show) | Jewish | News commentator/Israel |
| *Jam-e Jam 2* (Bowl of Jamshid 2) | Jewish | Music producer/ Iran |
| *Jam-e Jam* (Cup of Jamshid)* | Jewish | Music producer/ Iran |
| *Javanan va Nowjavanan* (Youth and teenagers) | Muslim | Theater actor/Iran |
| *Jom'-eh* (Friday) | Muslim | Film actor/Iran |

| | | |
|---|---|---|
| *Jonbesh-e Iran* (Iran's uprising)* | Muslim | Film actor/Iran |
| *Jong-e Bamdadi* (Morning magazine)* | Baha'i | TV news anchor/ Iran |
| *Khorus-e Bimahal* (Untimely crow) | Muslim | Talent agent/Iran |
| *Khub O' Bad O' Zesht* (Good, bad, and ugly) | Armenian Christian | TV actor/Iran |
| *Ma* (Us) | Muslim | Radio announcer |
| *Mardom va Jahan-e Pezeshgi* (People and world of medicine)* | | Physician/U.S. |
| *Mehr-e Iran* (Iran's love) | Baha'i | TV production/U.S. |
| *Mellat* (Nation) | Muslim | Production mgr./ Iran |
| *Melli-e Pars* (Pars National) | Muslim | Accountant/Iran |
| *Melli* (National)* | Muslim | Accountant/Iran |
| *Midnight Show*\* | Muslim | TV production/U.S. |
| *Mikhak-e Noqreh'i* (Silver carnation) | Muslim | TV engineer/Iran |
| *Mozhdeh* (Glad tidings)* | Protestant Christian | |
| *Negah* (Look)* | Muslim | Actor/director/Iran |
| *Negah* (Look) | Armenian Christian | TV production/Iran |
| *Omid-e Iran* (Iran's hope) | Muslim | TV executive/Iran |
| *Pars*\* | Muslim | TV engineer/Iran |
| *Parsian* (Persian) | Muslim | Actor/director/Iran |
| *Pezeshg-e Khub-e Khanevadeh* (Family's good doctor)* | Muslim | Ad agency/Iran |
| *Qod Qod-e Morgh* (Hen's cackle) | Muslim | Radio production |
| *Shahr-e Farang* (Peep show)* | Muslim | TV prod/actor/Iran |
| *Shoma* (You) | Muslim | |
| *Sima va Nava-ye Iran* (Vision and voice of Iran) | Muslim | Film actor/Iran |
| *Sima-ye Ashna* (Familiar face)* | Muslim | TV production/U.S. |
| *Sima-ye Azadi* (Face of freedom)* | Muslim | |
| *Sobh-e Ruz-e Jom'eh* (Friday morning)* | Muslim | Ad agency/Iran |

| | | |
|---|---|---|
| *Sokhani ba Ravanshenas* (Talk with a psychologist)* | | Psychologist |
| *Studio Karnaval* (Carnival studio) | Muslim | Journalist/Iran |
| *Tamasha* (Spectacle) | Baha'i | TV production/U.S. |
| *Tapesh* (Pulse) | Muslim | TV production |
| *Tasvir va Tamasha* (Picture & spectacle) | Armenian | Sports announcer/ Iran |
| *You & the World of Medicine** | | Physician |
| *Zendegi-ye Behtar* (Better life) | Muslim | Ad agency/Iran |

[1]Of the Assyrian programs, *Assyria* is run by Iraqi and Arab Assyrians. All others are run by Iranian Assyrians.

*Note:* Programs marked with an asterisk are currently on the air.

*Source:* Compiled by the author.

Table 14. Frequency of viewing of Iranian internal religio-ethnic TV audiences (in %)

|                            | Armenians | Baha'is | Jews | Muslims |
|----------------------------|-----------|---------|------|---------|
| Iranian Exile TV Programs  |           |         |      |         |
| Often                      | 48.7      | 39.1    | 48.9 | 32.5    |
| Not often                  | 51.3      | 60.9    | 51.1 | 67.5    |
| American TV Programs       |           |         |      |         |
| Often                      | 78.0      | 55.2    | 66.4 | 66.0    |
| Not often                  | 22.1      | 44.8    | 33.5 | 34.0    |
| Armenian Exile TV Programs |           |         |      |         |
| Often                      | 63.8      |         |      |         |
| Not often                  | 36.2      | –       | –    | –       |

*Source:* UCLA Study of Iranians in Los Angeles.

Table 15. Viewing patterns of Iranian religio-ethnic audiences for videos by language (in %)

|  | Armenians | Baha'is | Jews | Muslims |
|---|---|---|---|---|
| Persian | 3.1 | 14.9 | 37.4 | 12.7 |
| English | 80.3 | 71.6 | 46.5 | 73.9 |
| Persian/English | 16.5 | 13.5 | 16.1 | 13.3 |

*Source:* UCLA Study of Iranians in Los Angeles.

Table 16. Iranian Armenian audience by age, education, and income

| | Videos | | | Persian TV Programs | | American Television | | Armenian TV | |
|---|---|---|---|---|---|---|---|---|---|
| | Persian | English | Persian/ English | Often | Not Often | Often | Not Often | Often | Not Often |
| *Age* | | | | | | | | | |
| 25–40 | 25.0 | 25.5 | 28.6 | 17.0 | 28.3 | 22.4 | 23.2 | 30.0 | 18.7 |
| 41–60 | 75.0 | 51.0 | 33.3 | 34.1 | 46.3 | 42.8 | 34.8 | 47.1 | 36.6 |
| 61 + | 0.0 | 23.5 | 38.1 | 48.9 | 25.3 | 34.8 | 41.9 | 22.9 | 44.7 |
| *Education* | | | | | | | | | |
| High school or less | 75.0 | 49.0 | 45.0 | 66.3 | 50.5 | 59.7 | 51.2 | 64.5 | 47.1 |
| AA/BA degree | 25.0 | 27.5 | 50.0 | 19.3 | 29.5 | 23.7 | 29.3 | 22.7 | 27.9 |
| MA degree | 0.0 | 23.5 | 5.0 | 14.4 | 20.0 | 16.6 | 19.5 | 12.8 | 25.0 |
| *Income* | | | | | | | | | |
| 24K–45K | 100.0 | 66.7 | 65.0 | 77.9 | 64.6 | 71.3 | 70.7 | 76.1 | 62.3 |
| 46K–75K | 0.0 | 22.2 | 15.0 | 15.1 | 20.8 | 18.9 | 14.6 | 15.9 | 21.7 |
| 76K + | 0.0 | 11.1 | 20.0 | 7.0 | 14.6 | 9.8 | 14.7 | 8.0 | 16.0 |

*Source:* UCLA Study of Iranians in Los Angeles.

Table 17. Iranian Baha'i audience by age, education, and income

| | Videos | | | Persian TV Programs | | American TV Programs | |
|---|---|---|---|---|---|---|---|
| | Persian | English | Persian/ English | Often | Not Often | Often | Not Often |
| *Age* | | | | | | | |
| 25–40 | 0.0 | 32.69 | 20.0 | 14.71 | 28.85 | 18.75 | 28.95 |
| 41–60 | 18.18 | 57.69 | 6.0 | 41.18 | 59.62 | 56.25 | 47.37 |
| 60 + | 81.82 | 9.62 | 20.0 | 44.12 | 11.54 | 25.0 | 23.68 |
| *Education* | | | | | | | |
| High school or less | 70.0 | 19.2 | 30.0 | 45.5 | 15.4 | 37.0 | 15.38 |
| AA/BA degree | 20.0 | 34.6 | 30.0 | 33.3 | 25.0 | 37.0 | 17.95 |
| MA degree | 10.0 | 46.2 | 40.0 | 21.2 | 59.6 | 26.0 | 66.67 |
| *Income* | | | | | | | |
| 24K-45K | 72.1 | 41.50 | 57.14 | 65.63 | 39.22 | 47.83 | 51.35 |
| 46K-75K | 18.1 | 37.50 | 28.57 | 25.0 | 35.29 | 30.43 | 32.43 |
| 76K + | 9.8 | 21.0 | 14.29 | 9.38 | 25.49 | 21.74 | 16.22 |

*Source:* UCLA Study of Iranians in Los Angeles.

Table 18. Iranian Jewish audience by age, education, and income

| | Videos | | | Persian TV Programs | | American TV Programs | |
|---|---|---|---|---|---|---|---|
| | Persian | English | Persian/ English | Often | Not Often | Often | Not Often |
| *Age* | | | | | | | |
| 25–40 | 8.62 | 23.61 | 16.0 | 7.61 | 25.0 | 16.80 | 15.87 |
| 41–60 | 43.10 | 55.56 | 32.0 | 39.13 | 54.17 | 46.40 | 47.62 |
| 60 + | 48.28 | 20.83 | 52.0 | 53.26 | 20.83 | 36.80 | 36.51 |
| *Education* | | | | | | | |
| High school or less | 60.4 | 23.61 | 34.8 | 54.1 | 23.2 | 39.2 | 35.0 |
| AA/BA degree | 20.8 | 34.72 | 34.8 | 21.2 | 36.8 | 30.8 | 26.7 |
| MA degree | 18.8 | 41.67 | 30.4 | 24.7 | 40.0 | 30.0 | 38.3 |
| *Income* | | | | | | | |
| 24K-45K | 71.11 | 35.0 | 65.0 | 62.50 | 44.74 | 56.44 | 46.81 |
| 46K-75K | 17.78 | 28.33 | 25.0 | 20.83 | 27.63 | 24.75 | 23.40 |
| 76K + | 11.11 | 36.67 | 10.0 | 16.67 | 27.63 | 18.81 | 29.79 |

*Source:* UCLA Study of Iranians in Los Angeles.

Table 19. Iranian Muslim audience by age, education, and income

| | Videos | | | Persian TV Programs | | American TV Programs | |
| | Persian | English | Persian/English | Often | Not Often | Often | Not Often |
|---|---|---|---|---|---|---|---|
| *Age* | | | | | | | |
| 25–40 | 33.33 | 38.52 | 27.27 | 29.23 | 40.0 | 34.09 | 41.18 |
| 41–60 | 52.38 | 54.92 | 40.91 | 50.77 | 53.33 | 52.27 | 52.94 |
| 60 + | 14.29 | 6.56 | 31.82 | 20.0 | 6.67 | 13.64 | 5.88 |
| *Education* | | | | | | | |
| High school or less | 10.0 | 7.44 | 18.18 | 14.3 | 9.0 | 8.5 | 14.71 |
| AA/BA degree | 45.0 | 45.45 | 45.45 | 38.1 | 49.3 | 51.1 | 36.76 |
| MA degree | 45.0 | 47.11 | 36.36 | 47.6 | 41.7 | 40.4 | 48.53 |
| *Income* | | | | | | | |
| 24K-45K | 83.33 | 50.43 | 61.90 | 68.85 | 58.27 | 58.54 | 66.15 |
| 46K-75K | 5.56 | 27.83 | 23.81 | 13.11 | 25.98 | 23.58 | 20.0 |
| 76K + | 11.11 | 21.74 | 14.29 | 18.03 | 15.75 | 17.89 | 13.85 |

*Source:* UCLA Study of Iranians in Los Angeles.

Table 20. Iranian internal ethnic audiences for Persian language video
and television (by age)

| Religion/ethnicity by Age | Video (%) | Television (%) |
| --- | --- | --- |
| *25–40 Years* | | |
| Armenians | 25 | 17 |
| Baha'is | 0 | 15 |
| Jews | 9 | 8 |
| Muslims | 33 | 29 |
| *41–60 Years* | | |
| Armenians | 75 | 34 |
| Baha'is | 18 | 41 |
| Jews | 43 | 39 |
| Muslims | 52 | 51 |
| *60 Years and Over* | | |
| Armenians | 0 | 49 |
| Baha'is | 82 | 44 |
| Jews | 48 | 53 |
| Muslims | 14 | 28 |

*Source:* UCLA Study of Iranians in Los Angeles.

**Table 21. KSCI-TV's "ethnic schedule" of programs (by language), 3/17/1992**

| Airtime | Mon. | Tue. | Wed. | Thu. | Fri. | Sat. | Sun. | Time |
|---|---|---|---|---|---|---|---|---|
| 5:00 | Inspirational and program length advertisements | | | | | Program length ads | | 5:00 |
| 5:30 | | | | | | | | 5:30 |
| 6:00 | | | | | | | Japanese | 6:00 |
| 6:30 | | | Filipino News | | | Cambodian | Korean | 6:30 |
| 7:00 | | Japanese | | | | | | 7:00 |
| 7:30 | | | | | | | | 7:30 |
| 8:00 | | | | | | | | 8:00 |
| 8:30 | | Persian | | | | | | 8:30 |
| 9:00 | | | | | | Vietnamese | | 9:00 |
| 9:30 | | | | | Vietnamese | | Armenian | 9:30 |
| 10:00 | | | | | | | | 10:00 |
| 10:30 | | | Information | | | Armenian | | 10:30 |
| 11:00 | | | | | | | | 11:00 |
| 11:30 | | | Chinese | | | Hindi | Persian | 11:30 |
| 12:00 | | | | | | | | 12:00 |
| 12:30 | | | | | | Chinese | | 12:30 |
| 13:00 | | | | | | | | 13:00 |
| 13:30 | | Chinese | | | | Information | | 13:30 |
| 14:00 | | | | | | | | 14:00 |
| 14:30 | | | | | | | | 14:30 |
| 15:00 | | Japanese | | | | | Chinese | 15:00 |
| 15:30 | | | | | | Arabic | | 15:30 |
| 16:00 | | Program length advertisement | | | German | | | 16:00 |
| 16:30 | | | | | Russian | | Hebrew | 16:30 |
| 17:00 | Japanese | | | | | | | 17:00 |
| 17:30 | | | Filipino News | | | Armenian | Italian | 17:30 |
| 18:00 | | | Vietnamese News | | | | Hungarian | 18:00 |
| 18:30 | | | French News | | | | | 18:30 |
| 19:00 | | | Chinese/Chinese news | | | Korean | Japanese | 19:00 |
| 19:30 | | | | | | | | 19:30 |
| 20:00 | | | | | | | | 20:00 |
| 20:30 | | | | | | | | 20:30 |
| 21:00 | | | | | | | | 21:00 |
| 21:30 | ads | | | | | | | 21:30 |
| 22:00 | | | | | | Japanese | | 22:00 |
| 22:30 | | Korean | | | | | | 22:30 |
| 23:00 | Japanese | | | | | | Chinese | 23:00 |
| 23:30 | | | | | | | | 23:30 |
| 24:00 | ads | | | | | | Armenian | 24:00 |
| 0:30 | | Persian | | | | Persian | Persian | 0:30 |
| 1:00 | | | | | Persian | | | 1:00 |
| 1:30 | | Program length advertisement | | | | | | 1:30 |
| 2:00 | | | | | | Program length ads | | 2:00 |
| 2:30 | | | | | | | | 2:30 |
| 3:00 | | Inspirational | | | | | | 3:00 |
| 3:30 | | | | | | | Inspirational | 3:30 |
| 4:00 | | | | | | | | 4:00 |

*Source:* KSCI-TV.

# Notes

## 1. Exile Discourse

1. Among the dislocated people are refugees, whose number worldwide remained at a steady level of approximately 10 million from 1980 to 1985 but increased drastically to 14.4 million by 1989 (Gallagher 1986:141, Smolowe 1989:26).

2. The shift in migration pattern from European to non-European is reflected in Cheng and Evans's figures, which show that in the period between 1949 and 1951 (early phase of the Cold War), only 11.2 percent of immigrants into the United States were from underdeveloped, non-European countries, while in the years between 1977 and 1979 (after the war in southeast Asia), the percentage increased to 81.3 (1988:2).

3. For example, from 1956 to 1960, only 7.79 percent of all immigrants to the U.S. were professionals, a figure that increased to 41% by 1971 (Cheng and Evans 1988:2).

4. The unrest in South Central Los Angeles in April 1992, which pitted African-Americans and Chicanos against Korean-Americans, Asian-Americans, and other recent immigrants, demonstrated that conformist metaphors and ideologies are not adequate because they gloss over differences. A metaphor such as "cats in a bag," highlighting differences, may be more appropriate now (Mindel and Habenstein 1976:2). The problem with all of these metaphors, however, is that they are assimilationist: one set encodes assimilation as digestion, the other inscribes it as domestication.

5. The term is Patrick Geddes's (Geddes 1915). U.S. Census Bureau figures show that the foreign-born population of the United States rose dramatically, from 6.2 percent in 1980 to 7.9 percent in 1990 of all residents. Most of these immigrants live in large urban centers (Jackson 1992:A2).

6. See, for example, the works of Wallerstein (1974) and Amin (1974).

7. Much fear and anxiety is being expressed about this situation. On the one hand, some Los Angeles "natives" feel that too many immigrants are pouring into the city and, on the

other hand, some newcomers feel they are being trapped permanently in an underclass position. See Kotkin 1989.

8. See the following: The special issue of *Los Angeles Times Sunday Calendar* called "The Big Mix" (2/5/1989); a special issue of the *Los Angeles Times Magazine* called "New Prosperity, New Power" (11/6/1988); Kotkin; John Mitchell; Ruben Martinez; and Nancy Gibbs. *Time* magazine also did a special issue (11/18/1991) called "California: The Endangered Dream."

9. See, for example, a pocket-size, glossy magazine *The Book / Los Angeles*, one of whose 1989 issues (1:3) on "Culture Shock" contained the following breathless editorial, quoted in its entirety: "I guess L.A.'s the ultimate culture shock! Experience the whole world in one city, under one sun. From a homeless Australian filmmaker to an exhibitionist Japanese fashion designer . . . a multinational Afro band to an American subway freak artist . . . Gaultier and Montana to the Pope (?) as seen on Melrose. . . . This is L.A., distinctive, authentic, forward. A wide open place that welcomes the most unique, the offbeat and the eccentric. A land where reality is only a perception. And dreams . . . the absolute standard."

10. Many Iranian entrepreneurs had owned businesses in Iran. A high proportion of them are college graduates and professionals. Statistical comparison between American and Iranian populations in Los Angeles demonstrates the situation. In 1980, 66.5 percent of Americans age 25 or older were high school graduates and 16.2 percent were college graduates, while these percentages were much higher among entrepreneurial Vietnamese, Israelis, Chinese, Indians, and Koreans (Light 1988:62) and Iranians (Bozorgmehr and Sabagh 1988). The phenomenon of leap frogging has occurred among Asian immigrants as well (Light 1983:322–23).

11. The factors that permit leapfrogging also, however, create grave problems for many immigrants, especially for those from the Middle East. Although these immigrants can benefit from their professionalism and education and their claim to the "white skin privilege," they must put up with the vagaries of a system of racial and ethnic classification that refuses to recognize them as an official minority. As a result, they are caught in a zone of unofficial statuslessness, neither white nor a minority. As "whites but not quite" they can compete neither with the "truly whites" nor with the "official minorities" who benefit from entitlement to loans, grants, financial aid, fellowships, and employment opportunities that are designed to redress historical prejudices and injustices.

12. For a sampling of articles on videos imported from home countries and sold or rented by ethnic stores in Southern California, see the following: On Japanese videos, Aoki 1989a; on Filipino videos, Terry Atkinson and Paul Vargas 1989; on Chinese videos, Valle 1989; on Mexican videos, Barrios 1989a; on Indian videos, Vanderknyff 1989; on Middle Eastern videos, Atkinson and Sims 1989; on French videos, Barrios 1989b; on Korean videos, Aoki 1989b; on British videos, Bernstein 1992; and on Vietnamese videos, Smith 1989. On the piracy issue of videos, see Watanabe 1990; and Atkinson and Sims 1989.

13. I have borrowed the term "slipzone" from Alexander (1987:44) in another context.

14. I have developed the concept of haggling in opposition to hailing elsewhere. See Naficy 1989c.

15. See Edward Said's development of exilic privilege in his analysis of Erich Auerbach's monumental *Mimesis*, written in exile in Turkey (1983a:7).

16. For an analysis of Sa'edi's last plays and short stories in exile, see Safa 1990 and Karimi-Hakkak 1991, respectively.

17. One of the modalities of exilic dystopia is for intellectuals to consider exile as a pathology. Fassih calls exile a "coma" (1985), Amirshahi (1987) and Karimi-Hakkak (1991: 259) consider it "paralysis" and "indecision," Mirzadeh (1988:57) calls it "absolute dizzi-

ness," Sa'edi (1983) labels it "gradual death." Albert Camus in his novel *The Plague* (1972) explored the effects of the plague upon the afflicted town in terms of deprivation and exile of a most profound nature.

18. For Farrahi's last writings and for various accounts of and views about his controversial action, see the following Persian-language journals devoted to Farrahi's self-immolation: *Ketab-e Nima* 1 (Winter 1987); *Rayegan* (11/25/1987); *Jahan-e Now* (October 1987). Also see Kelly 1987 and Beckland 1987.

19. For further readings on the work of the Karbala paradigm in grieving, see Fischer 1980:21; Fischer and Abedi 1990:167; and Good et al. 1985:387.

20. Among Iranians, grief and sadness are exhibited during private rituals organized to mourn the death of loved ones or in the course of public sermons and religious ceremonies designed to recount and commemorate the martyrdom of Shi'i imams, especially the tragic and brutal slaying of imam Hosain and his followers in the plains of Karbala (in the year 61 A.H. in Iraq) by the Ummayid Caliphate. This particular event is commemorated annually in Iran in a ten-day grand ritual involving processions, self-flagellation with chains, chest-beating, self-wounding with swords, and the dramatic recreations, called *ta'ziyeh*, of the massacre and martyrdom (Thaiss 1973; Chelkowski 1979; Beeman 1982; Pettys 1982). The events in Karbala have achieved the status of a paradigm for Iranian Shi'ism because, as Fischer notes, they provide both "models for living and a mnemonic for thinking about how to live" and "a way of clearly demarcating Shi'ite understanding from Sunni understanding of Islam and Islamic history" (1980:21). The "paradigmatic cluster of emotions" of which Good et al. speak has to do with guilt and repentance over failure to defend the imam and his followers (the oppressed), righteous anger at Yazid and other Ummayid caliphs (the oppressors), and total fusion and identification with the martyrs (1985:387). In Iran, the Karbala paradigm and its clusters of emotions have been mobilized and the concomitant *ta'ziyeh* drama and processions have been staged from time to time in moments of social crisis, and have been very effective in bringing about political change and removing corrupt and unjust rules—the most recent example being the anti-Shah revolution of 1978–79 (Chelkowski 1985; Fischer 1980).

21. Perhaps the first example of a mourning performance (*rowzeh*) on exile television occurred in June 1992 on *Sobh-e Ruz-e Jom'eh*. It is during such performances that the Karbala paradigm is invoked.

22. For more explanation of the various conceptions of emigres in this paragraph see the following sources: for "openly marginal" see Park 1928 and Stonequist 1937; for "secretly marginal" see Riesman 1951; for "dually marginal" see Ansari 1988; for "stranger" see Simmel 1950; for "culture traveller" see Furnham and Bochner 1986; for "refugee" see Goodwin-Gill 1983; for "sojourner" see Siu 1952; for "homeless" see Sa'edi 1983 and Kho'i 1987; and for "diaspora" see Safran (1991).

23. For more on syncretism, see Spicer 1968:21–22, Redfield et al. 1936:14, and Winick 1956:520.

24. Studies of religious syncretism from the Arctic to the New Guinean tribes of Markham Valley have shown that often underneath the syncretic practices borrowed from Christianity or side by side with them there flourishes in psychic life, emotional orientation, and fundamental attitudes the pre-Christian native values and beliefs. For example, Christian missionaries complained in the late 1800s that although Indians had been baptized and regularly said their prayers and confessed, very often they retained "within their hearts pagan ideas and maxims which will often be the norm of their daily action" (Whitehead 1981:106).

25. That syncretism is a means used by oppressed people to ensure the survival of their beliefs and way of life is clear from situations where external threats engendering syncretism

have been removed. In such situations, often the result is a flourishing of the previous non-syncretized beliefs and practices. For examples see Lanternari 1965:252.

26. Haji Firuz character was transformed and adopted as a stereotypical figure called "black" (*siah*) in a type of traditional theater called *ruhowzi*. The black is a figure of tremendous power who mimics, makes fun of, critiques, and subverts all authorities. See Baiza'i 1965, Haery 1982, and the last chapter of this book.

27. This figure, which was very popular, came under attack for being racist and offensive to African-Americans just one year before the revolution. See *Iran Times*, 3/17/1989:17B.

28. *Haftsin* refers to the seven food items beginning with the letter "S" in Persian that are displayed as part of the Iranian New Year celebrations; *sizdahbedar* is the thirteenth day of the new year, the day Iranians celebrate by going on collective picnics to the countryside and parks.

29. Asim Roy, too, has demonstrated that Islamic syncretism has been a "necessary stage in the progress of Islamization" in Bengal, where Bengali cultural mediators bent on disseminating Islam in a "more locally familiar and meaningful form" introduced syncretic elements from the Bengali indigenous myths, cosmology, and literature (1983:251).

30. This is particularly true of the folk versions of the *Shahnameh* in which, for example, archetypal mythical characters that pre-date Islam (such as the hero Rostam) meet and engage in combat with historical Shi'i figures (such as imam Ali). In such a combat narrative neither of the two mythical or historical figures loses (though Rostam is physically beaten by Ali). Both Ferdowsi's *Shahnameh* and the folk versions of the *Shahnameh* are filled with cultural syncretism of this sort in which Islam and Iranian culture meet and mix.

31. For an illustrated and celebratory account of this event, see *National Geographic* 133:3 (March 1968):301–20.

32. For a critical account from an eyewitness to the 2,500th anniversary celebrations, see George Ball 1982:434–36.

33. A significant feature of this shift of paradigm is a shift in the source of the blame. While in the early part of this century the source of social ills was often considered to be an internally generated ill (backwardness), the new Islamist paradigm assigned it to an externally generated corrupting influence (the West). For a comparison of the rhetorical visions of the Shah and Khomeini, see Helsey and Trebing 1983.

34. For these statistics, see Mofid 1987:19, Beckland 1987:27, Beauchamp 1988:60–66, *Time* (6/18/1983:22), *Javanan* 10/21/1988:30, *Kayhan-e Hava'i* 8/30/89:2, Perry 1992:H11.

35. According to Bozorgmehr and Sabagh (1988:29), the personal income of Iranian non-students is very high, their mean 1979 income of $17,537 is nearly double that of all recent immigrants and approximately 60 percent higher than that of native-born Americans. The educational achievement of Iranians is "remarkable," write Bozorgmehr and Sabagh (1988:25), with approximately 23 percent of them holding a graduate university degree, as compared to 12.5 percent for the foreign-born and 7.5 percent for natives. The percentage of nonstudent Iranians who are self-employed (22) is much higher than that of the natives (6.9) or other high-achieving recent immigrants such as Koreans (12.2) (Bozorgmehr and Sabagh 1988:26). A higher percentage of Iranians are independent professionals (27.3) compared to the much lower levels both for natives (12.3) and all recent immigrants (10.8) (1988:26).

36. *Forbes* magazine ran a piece entitled "Welcome to Tehran, Calif." (Beauchamp 1988) and the *Los Angeles Times*'s feature was called "A New Persian Empire" (John Mitchell 1989).

37. The breakdown of self-employment among Iranian ethnics is as follows: Most Jewish Iranians are in wholesale and retail trade, particularly apparel and jewelry; Armenians tend to concentrate in finance, insurance, real estate, and repair services; Muslims and Baha'is are mostly in construction and manufacturing of durable goods and health and legal services.

Iranians from all ethnic groups are highly visible in the construction sector of the economy (Bozorgmehr, Sabagh, and Der-Martirosian 1991:13).

38. "Fugitive" is a term that the Islamic government generally applied to the exiles immediately after the revolution. This term also covers young draft dodgers, who escaped the country in droves during the eight-year war with Iraq. "Self-exiled" is also another term of condemnation used by the detractors of those who left Iran, implying that their exile was voluntary and their hardship in a foreign country does not deserve sympathy.

39. For a book on Iranian exiles in Los Angeles that uses these terms, see Moslehi 1984.

40. That these changing definitions are not local but are part of larger shifts in the traditional definitions and paradigms of belonging is indicated by the policies of the Islamic government in Iran vis-à-vis its citizens abroad. In the early 1990s the government appeared to have changed its definition of what constitutes an Iranian, from a single to a dual citizen.

41. On the dynamics of internal ethnicity among Iranian and Middle Eastern television programs, see Naficy 1993a.

## 2. Iranian Exilic Popular Culture

1. In some ways this symbolic community resembles the maroon communities formed by rebel African slaves in the Americas. The culture that runaway maroons formed was essentially syncretic in that they retained aspects of their indigenous African values and practices while enlivening them with new adaptations. Even those African slaves who remained on plantations developed their own separate "slave culture," which gave them a measure of autonomy and self-confidence (Blassingame 1972:41). The resulting culture could be traced reliably neither to specific original African culture nor to that of the slavemasters (Price 1979:29). Syncretic institutions such as maroon communities in the United States and *candombles* and *quilombos* formed by African slaves in Brazil were sustained for years, resulting in creation of what Bastide has called "encysted communities," that is, community niches within which uprooted people, deprived of previous social ties, recreate new ties and a new communion (1985:283).

2. This is also true of the early press in the history of American journalism, when "the ideology of partisanship was in perfect synchronization with the aims of publishers and editors that sought political office and financial reward for their party loyalty" (Ruttenbeck 1991:130).

3. For an elaboration of a similar development in the eighteenth-century British press, see Hall 1986c:32–33.

4. For more on the conflict between exile television programs and periodicals, see chapter 3, on exile television.

5. In an interview in Ali Reza Maibodi, a program director of *Seda-ye Iran*, told me that 3,000 of these special receivers had been sold. This number has increased severalfold since then.

6. On these transnational broadcasts, see Sreberny-Mohammadi 1985:129–32, Tehranian 1979:11, Tehranian 1982:43, and *Kayhan Hava'i*, 12/6/1989:15. Computer bulletin boards that cross national boundaries, including those operated by Iranians, are part of the transnationalization of exilic cultures.

7. The following list contains the titles of all the fictional feature films produced in Iran prior to the revolution and shown in Los Angeles commercial cinemas during the 1980s: *Ajal-e Mo'allaq, Alafha-ye Harz, Ali Baba, Aludeh, Aqa-ye Halu, Aramesh dar Hozur-e Digaran, Asrar-e Ganj-e Darreh-ye Jenni, Baba Shamal, Bandari, Bar Faraz-e Asemanha, Bedeh Dar Rah-e Khoda, Biganeh, Biqarar, Bita, Bonbast, Bot, Charkh va Falak, Chesh-*

*meb, Dalahu, Dar Emtedad-e Shab, Dash Akol, Dashneh, Doroshgehchi, Ehsas-e Dagh, Em-shab Dokhtari Mimirad, Farar az Taleh, Faryad-e Zir-e Ab, Faseleh, Ganj-e Qarun, Gav, Gavaznha, Gharibeh va Meh, Ghazal, Gholam Zhandarm, Haft Shahr-e Eshq, Hamkelas, Hamsafar, Hasan Kachal, Hasan Siah, Hashtomin Ruz-e Hafteh, Hasrat, Havas, In Goruh-e Mahkumin, Javanmard, Jenjal-e Arusi, Kajkolah Khan, Kalaq, Kandu, Khak-e Sar Behmohr, Khakestari, Khaneh Kharab, Khashm-e Oqabha, Khastegar, Khaterkhah, Khoda Qovvat, Khodahafez Tehran, Khorus, Khoshgel-e Mahalleh, Khoshgeltarin Zan-e Alam, Ki Dasteh Gol Beh Ab Dadeh?, Kineh, Laili va Majnun, Mah-e Asal, Malek-e Duzakh, Mamal-e Emrika'i, Man ham Geryeh Kardam, Mard-e bi Setareh, Mard-e Sharqi, Zan-e Farangi, Marg dar Baran, Marsiyeh, Mehman, Mi'adgah-e Khashm, Mo'jezeh-ye Eshq, Mogholha, Mohallel, Mosalkh, Moshgel-e Aqa-ye E'temad, Mowj-e Tufan, Mozzafar, Naqs-e Fanni, Nazanin, O.K. Mister, Panjereh, Pashneh Tala, Pol, Qafas, Qaisar, Qalandar, Qasr-e Zarrin, Ragbar, Ranandeh-ye Ejbari, Raqqaseh, Reza Motori, Salomeh, Samad Art-ist Mishavad, Samad beh Madreseh Miravad, Samad dar Rah-e Ezhdaha, Samad Darbeh-dar Mishavad, Samad Khoshbakht Mishavad, Samad va Qalicheh-ye Hazrat-e Solaiman, Samad va Sami Laila va Lili, Saraydar, Say-eh ha-ye Boland-e Bad, Sazesh, Sehta Bezan-bahador, Shab-e Ghariban, Shab-e Yalda, Shahrashub, Shazdeh Ehtejab, Showhar-e Ker-ayeh'i, Showhar-e Pastorizeh, Showharjunam Asheq Shodeh, Sutehdelan, Tabi'at-e Bijan, Takhtehkhab-e Seh Nafareh, Taksi-ye Eshq, Tangsir, Tavalodat Mobarak, Topoli, Towqi, Tufan-e Nuh, Usta Karim Nokaretim, Yaqut-e Seh Cheshm, Yek Del va Do Delbar, Yek Esfa-hani dar New York, Yek Esfahani dar Sarzamin-e Hitler, Yeki Khosh Seda va Yeki Khosh Dast, Zabih, Zanburak, Zir-e Bazarcheh.*

8. The new-wave films shown in exile include the following: *Aramesh dar Hozur-e Digaran, Asrar-e Ganj-e Darreh-ye Jenni, Bonbast, Cheshmeh, Dash Akol, Gav, Ghazal, Khak-e Sar Behmohr, Marsiyeh, Mogholha, O.K. Mister, Ragbar, Saraydar, Shazdeh Ehtejab, Sutehdelan, Tabi'at-e Bijan, Tangsir, Topoli.* Since 1980, many documentary, ani-mated, and short-subject films made in Iran or in exile have also been shown in Los Angeles, usually by political and cultural groups. For details on the new-wave films and the Iranian feature film industry prior to the revolution, see Akrami 1991; Gaffary 1991; Issari 1989; and Naficy 1979, 1981.

9. On anti-Iranianism of mainstream American popular culture, see Naficy 1989a.

10. For details on the Iranian postrevolution cinema, see Naficy 1987, 1990a, 1992b.

11. For synopsis of all the films about Iran, see Naficy 1990c.

12. Savak was the Shah's security agency—the secret police.

13. For an analysis of theater productions in exile, see Naficy 1993b.

14. Contemporary feminists in their research and writings have emphasized the impor-tant role that women's networks have played in empowering women. For a survey and a critique of these writings concerning Middle Eastern women, see Waltz 1990. For their sig-nificance for women's labor among Iranians in Los Angeles, see Dallalfar 1989.

15. In the 1960s and early 1970s, when most Iranians in the United States were students, intellectual and political debate took the form of doctrinaire leftist political parties such as the Confederation of Iranian Students, an authoritarian organization with branches on many campuses. For a history of the Confederation, see Matin Asghari 1991.

16. Pars Video, Caltext, and Taraneh are the major record companies and music video producers.

17. See "Seda-ye Amrika va Tabligh bara-ye Motrebha-ye Irani," *Kayhan-e Hava'i* (1/8/1992), p. 4.

18. For a valuable ethnographic and theoretical analysis of the dialectics of identity and authenticity as played out in the Iranian exilic culture, see Fischer and Abedi 1990:253–332.

## 3. Structure and Political Economy of Exilic Television

1. The breakdown of these programs by languages on KSCI-TV is as follows (hours/week, week of May 17, 1992): Arabic 3.0, Armenian 5.0, Cambodian 1.5, Mandarin 9.5, French 2.5, Tagalog/English 5.0, Deutsche .50, Hungarian .50, Hindi/English 1.0, Persian 15.5, Italian .50, Japanese 14.5, Hebrew 1.0, Korean 22.5, Russian 1.0, and Vietnamese 5.0. [SOURCE: compiled by the author from KSCI-TV data.] On the concept of "diaspora television," see Naficy 1993a.

2. For example, 50 percent of the programs carried by Univision Television Network—the leader in Spanish-language programming in the United States, which reaches some 60 percent of Spanish-speaking audience—is produced in the United States, with the balance imported chiefly from Mexico and Venezuela (Puig 1992:D1). These programs, which are often modeled after proven U.S. or Latin American shows, neither adequately address problems of acculturation nor issues of diversity and specificity of various Latin American, Central American, and Chicano populations living in the United States. Instead, they appear, on the one hand, to reinforce the assimilation and Americanization of Latino populations (Valle 1988) and, on the other hand, the "cubanization" of Spanish-language programming.

3. In addition to these regularly scheduled programs, KSCI-TV has aired occasional specials produced by Iranian emigres. Some, such as *Iranian Jewish Senior Center Program* (aired in February 1986) or *Iranian Refugee Telethon* (aired in March 1988), promoted the welfare of the Iranian community in exile. Others celebrated various national or religious occasions, such as Iranian New Year, Passover, Christmas, and Winter Solstice.

4. This is borne out by Bozorgmehr and Sabagh's study, which shows that since 1980 the "major mode of legal status attainment among Iranians" has been to "enter as nonimmigrants and subsequently change their status to immigrants." As a result, the number of Iranians who have become naturalized citizens increased at least twofold between 1984 and 1986 (1988:11). Ironically, naturalization, instead of suppressing nationalism, may be enhancing it—perhaps temporarily.

5. On the state of television broadcasting in postrevolutionary Iran, which is structurally similar to NIRT, see Sreberny-Mohammadi and Mohammadi 1991a.

6. For an analysis of the use of broadcasting in a number of Third World countries, including Iran, see Katz and Wedell 1977.

7. These so-called godfathers of production are Ali Limonadi (Studio Cinegraphics, producer of *Iranian*), Manuchehr Bibian (Jam-e Jam Productions, producer of *Jam-e Jam*), Hamid Shabkhiz (producer of *Iran* ), and Parviz Qarib Afshar (who uses the KSCI-TV facilities and produces *Sima-ye Ashna* and *Emshab ba Parviz*).

8. Author's interview with Rosemary Fincher, KSCI-TV station manager, 2/16/1988.

9. The description, profile, and program offerings of the International Channel Network are based on materials supplied to me in May 1992 by the network.

10. Interview with Iraj Gorgin, producer of the *Omid* programs, 4/23/1988, Los Angeles.

11. For examples of such criticism in exile periodicals, see *Iran News* (8/7/1987, p. 23), which claimed that hour-long television programs contained between 48 and 52 minutes of ads; *Payam-e Iran* (27 Esfand, 1367/1988, p. 6), which contended that hour-long TV programs contained 40 minutes of ads; *Rayegan* (1/22/1988, p. 35), which wrote that the hour-long *Jam-e Jam* program contained 45 minutes of ads. For additional criticism, see "Barresi-ye Televizionha-ye Yekshanbeh," *Rayegan* (5/13/1988, p. 22). Farhang Farrahi, "Chera Goruhi Javanan-e Porshur-e Vatanparast E'tesab-e Ghaza Konand Amma Yek Televizion Bekhahad az an Natayej-e Khosusi Khod ra Begirad?," *Rayegan* (4/8/1988, p. 5. "4 So'al az 4 Televizion," *Kabobnameh* (Ordibehesht 1361/1982):8. "Goft va Shonudi ba Tagi Mokhtar," *Par* 27 (Farvardin 1367/1988):20–23.

12. The exact figures for advertising rates are unwritten, fluctuate over time and with individuals, and are held as proprietary information by competing producers, so they cannot be independently verified. I have chosen to stay with the figures cited the most by the majority of producers (between $3 and $6 per second).

13. In interviews with me in 1989, Bibian of *Jam-e Jam* gave $4,500 as his monthly gross and Rafi'i of *Midnight Show* stated that his monthly net income was $3,500.

14. Limonadi of *Iranian*, who owns his own studio, stated in an interview with me that he makes approximately $3,500 per month from renting his facilities to other producers.

15. For example, Gorgin was in debt when his program, *Omid*, went off the air; Ehsan of *Didar* lost some $40,000 before closing down; and Bibian of *Jam-e Jam* lost over $100,000 in the first two years of his program. These figures are based on my interviews with the producers.

16. "Mojahedin" is the abbreviated name for *Sazman-e Mojahedin-e Khalq-e Iran* (Organization of Fighters for Iranian People), a guerrilla organization that engaged in armed struggle against the Shah in the 1970s and, after a period of cooperation with the nascent Islamic government, turned to armed struggle against it in 1981. The headquarters of the organization at present is in Iraq, from where a number of incursions against the Iranian forces have been made. The organization produces and airs a regularly scheduled TV show in Iraq, *Sima-ye Moqavemat*, which is beamed to Western Iran. This is in addition to *Sima-ye Azadi*, which it airs in the United States. For more on the organization, see Abrahamian 1989.

17. For more details of this case, see Naficy 1990b:177–81.

18. This physical move by the organization fit the U.S. foreign policy at the time. This policy heavily favored Iraq against Iran and it must have finally established the Mojahedin's opposition to the Islamic government in Iran.

19. In contradistinction to the anti-Khomeini Iranian exiles, the anti-Castro Cuban exiles have received much direct help from the U.S. government because the politics of the latter either coincide or are dictated by the U.S. government. Radio Marti has been beaming anti-Castro programming from the U.S. mainland for quite some time and in 1990 the U.S. government began TV Marti with the same purpose.

20. Author's interview with Caren Garces, then community relations chief, 2/16/1988.

21. In my interviews with various television producers and ad agencies, I was told that leaders of monarchist political factions, such as Shapur Bakhtiar, Ali Amini, Ahmad Madani, and Reza Pahlavi, have regularly paid for their own "news" interviews inserted in Iranian TV newscasts.

22. For Iranians this duality of private (*andarun*) versus public (*birun*) resonates strongly with two other dyads: intimacy (*samimiat*) versus cleverness (*zarangi*) and interior *(baten)* versus exterior (*zaher*).

23. Critics point to the excessive and single-minded commercialization of programs. See the "exilic economy" section for examples of such criticism.

24. For example, Manuchehr Buzarjomehri, the producer of *Melli* in the early 1980s, was arrested and apparently convicted on charges of possession and sale of narcotics.

25. A few telethon organizers, who also produce television programs, have been accused of having diverted to their own personal ends the funds they have collected under the guise of social service. In April 1989, Jamshid Kaveh, producer of *Arya*, ran a series of investigative reports in which he charged that Feraidun Farrokhzad, host of a telethon aired on November 20, 1988, and designed to help Iranian children captured by Iraq, had allegedly diverted to his own personal uses the $28,500 raised by the telethon. On the debate caused by the telethon and by *Arya*'s reports, see *Iran News* (11/25/1988, p. 29); *Rayegan* (4/28/1989, pp. 32–33); and *Javanan* (11/3/1989, pp. 36–37). Such charges and countercharges of misrepresentation and malfeasance are complicated and hard to sort out.

26. For example, KSCI-TV terminated *Parsian* on the grounds of the personal attacks of its producer (Parviz Sayyad) on an organizer of an Iranian beauty pageant (Faranak Qahhari). Likewise, *Iran* was canceled apparently because of its violation of U.S. election laws.

27. In denying the charges to me in an interview (Los Angeles, 5/1/1989), Ehsan counter-charged that attacks by Jamshid Kaveh, producer of *Arya*, were part of an organized effort by Shapour Bakhtiar's political faction to discredit her, thinking that she was supported by Ashraf Pahlavi's political faction. Although the Bakhtiar and Pahlavi factions are both monarchist, they differ in some respects and generally have been antagonistic to each other.

28. The periodical *Iran News* called distrust a "canker" that has invaded the exile community (11/25/1988, p. 29). Likewise, while lauding *Arya* TV's investigative efforts, *Khandaniha* bemoaned the possibility that such reporting could frighten away philanthropists (Bahman 1367/1988, p. 6).

29. For a critique of this action, see "Sokhani az Nasher," *Asr-e Emruz* (4/13/1992, p. 2).

30. For a recent study on how U.S. news media more often than not followed the cues of foreign policy makers rather than using independent judgment in their reporting on Iran under the Shah, see Dorman and Farhang 1987.

31. See "Vahshat-e Saltanattalaban az Pakhsh-e Barnamehha-ye Sima-ye Jomhuri-ye Eslami-e Iran dar Los Angjeles," *Kayhan Hava'i* (5/20/1992, p. 2).

32. Author's interviews with Parviz Qarib Afshar and Iraj Gorgin, producers of the two respective programs, Los Angeles, May 1992.

33. According to KSCI-TV's figures, the Iranian audience in 1987 ranked fourth in terms of number of households, after Filipinos, Japanese, and Koreans. These figures, however, seem to be based more on statistical probability of the population than on an actual survey of audiences.

34. Author's interviews with Manuchehr Bibian and Ali Limonadi, producers respectively, of *Jam-e Jam* and *Iranian*. Also see Table 9.

35. The producer of *Didar*, Homa Ehsan, gave a prize for the best name for her Persian cat and Hamid Shabkhiz of *Iran* gave a prize to the caller who named the largest Iranian city. If the contests seem insignificant, the viewers responses are valuable for feedback-starved producers, especially if one takes seriously Shabkhiz's claim, in an interview with me, that on average he would receive between 100 and 125 calls after each show containing a contest. In an interview (5/10/1992), Parviz Qarib Afshar of *Sima-ye Ashna*, which is aired nationally via satellite, stated that he received 1,400 calls nationwide when he gave out a 900 telephone number.

36. The material in this section of the book is based on data from the study of Iranians in Los Angeles conducted by Georges Sabagh, Ivan Light, Mehdi Bozorgmehr, and Claudia Der-Martirosian. All interpretations here are mine.

37. Although 29 percent of the Armenian heads of household surveyed were female, control for gender showed no difference. Hence gender was eliminated from consideration.

38. This is true particularly of Armenian and Assyrian subgroups.

## 4. The Exilic Television Genre and Its Textual Politics and Signifying Practices

1. This has left two remaining universalist projects confronting each other: Western liberal democracy and resurgent Islam.

2. For relevant comments on the notion of boundary-marking rituals, see Turner 1967; Carpenter 1973; Myerhoff 1978; Cohen 1985.

3. There are also some similarities among the various ethnic texts, particularly among those produced in diaspora, in terms of program formats, use of music, iconographic strate-

gies, and subject positioning. This includes particularly Iranian, Armenian, Arabic, and some Israeli-Jewish shows. For elaboration, see Naficy 1993a.

4. For more on syntagmatic and paradigmatic intertextuality, see Naficy 1989b.

5. For over ten years, *60 Minutes* has been the most successful example of the magazine format, staying among the top ten shows throughout the 1980s and 1990s. However, a book (Rose 1985) which devoted nineteen chapters to various television genres failed to deal with the magazine as a genre.

6. For an early but thorough analysis of the television news magazine, see Swallow 1966.

7. On the importance of the news anchor, see Matusow 1983.

8. On the installation of the television set after World War II within the American home and family environment, see Spigel 1992.

9. In fact, all television texts and the schedule itself are suffused with self-reflexive strategies and self-referential promotions. On these topics, see White 1986, Naficy 1989b.

10. Early American cinema did develop a "variety format," consisting of a number of shorts in different genres, that is intriguingly similar to the televisual magazine format. For more on this, see Hansen 1991:29-30.

11. A number of the shows listed here can be classified under several categories.

12. These include *Khaneh Bedush* (Homeless), *Mard-e Aval* (Top man), *Daqayeq-e Akhar* (Final minutes), *Parvaz* (Flight), and *Nameh'i beh Vatan* (A letter to the homeland).

13. In 1981, KSCI-TV ran a series of programs produced by the Baha'i Center in Illinois. For details, see Naficy 1984:116.

14. In the Islamist discourse in Iran, for example, actors cannot be considered to be neutral bearers of personas and parts since they, too, are social subjects. This produces a paradox that throws into question the art of acting itself. For example, a high-ranking clerical leader, Hojjatollah Javad Mohaddesi, states that an actor's life off-screen and his roles on-screen should not conflict with one another. He went on to advise that "clean" roles should not be assigned to "corrupt" individuals because this would cause an unacceptable contradiction within the actor himself as well as in the minds of the audience. For him a contaminated mouth dirties the truth it utters (1989:155). After the revolution, this notion was used to purge the motion picture industry of movie stars who were thought to have led immoral lifestyles or who had acted in movies depicting immorality (Naficy 1987, 1992b).

15. David Bordwell makes a similar point based on a different theoretical approach (1985a:30).

16. I am not sure whether hierarchical relations encoded in the system of ritual courtesy are inflected in shot composition in cinema and television, but if Iranian miniature paintings are any indication, there is reason to expect that. In many miniatures, the most important object is not necessarily placed closest to the viewer or in the direct line of sight, as in a quattrocento perspective. Persons with a higher rank are usually distinguished from others in the same scene by their larger size, their central and at times higher location within the diegesis, the intense and vivid colors and particularly detailed craftsmanship with which they are portrayed, their emblems of power and wealth, such as hats, turbans, jewelry, and fine clothing, and their being the object of the gaze of others in the scene. Social status is signaled not by the position of the figure in the picture vis-à-vis the viewer outside the frame but by the diegetic position of the figure in relation to others in the scene. This implies also that these paintings do not construct their spectator as a unified, unifying, individuated self for whom vision must be organized and space narrativized; rather, he or she is construed to be a social individual who will read the signs of social hierarchy encoded in the painting as part of the spectatorial activity.

17. In his analysis of a sequence of John Ford's *Stagecoach*, Nick Browne (1975) shows

that the spectator's conception of the social order can trigger an emotional identification with the diegetic characters that is contrary to that which the textual practice of the film itself encourages. In the sequence he analyzed, we see Dallas (a prostitute) from the point of view of others who disdain her; however, we identify not with them but with her, because our sympathy is enlisted on account of her social position as an underdog and a social outcast.

18. As social productions of knowledge, film and television texts inscribe these schemas. A major source of drama in cinema, therefore, can be said to reside in the film's violation and restoration of rules encoded in these schemas. It seems the case also that the absence of certain film genres in a culture may be explained by the unacceptable violation of cultural schemas that these genres produce. One reason for the underdevelopment of the horror genre in Iranian cinema, for example, may be sought in this genre's violation of the etiquette of formal relationships between strangers dictated by the system of ritual courtesy, which requires control of emotions and display of ritual politeness. This system authorizes, even encourages, the display of certain emotions such as sadness but it prohibits behaviors such as frightening someone, rage, and graphic violence against women and children—which are the staples of the horror genre. One of the recent horror films made in Iran is *Telesm* (The spell, 1986), directed by Dariush Farhang. But even this film, which is aware of the Gothic generic conventions, underplays the elements that terrify audiences.

19. This might account for the apparent "chaos" in the mise-en-scène and editing of many Iranian films and TV programs, which tend not to conform to the Western codes of organizing the vision for a unitary subject position—a characteristic that one can observe also in the so-called "primitive" cinema of the teens. On the mode of (re)presentation in the primitive cinema and spectatorial activity, see Hansen 1991; and Mayne 1990:157–83.

20. Hamid Shabkhiz of *Iran* regularly uses the former form (*shoma azizan*) and Hushang Purang of *Sobh-e Ruz-e Jom'eh* used the latter (*nazenin, hamvatan, yeganeh, salam bar toe*) in his program on 6/27/1992. Compare these phrases with those which the hosts of mainstream American shows use to see the difference in the way the relationship between host/show and viewer is established. A typical phrase is "I'll be right back after these messages," which makes no reference to the audience at all.

21. Author's interview with Ali Limonadi, producer of *Iranian*, 2/4/1989.

22. On the centrality of the systems of ritual courtesy, sincerity, and inner purity (*safa-ye baten*) in the constitution of an "essential Iranian subjectivity," see Beeman 1986, Bateson et al. 1977, Bateson 1979, and Naficy 1990c.

23. Since sincerity is so highly valued among Iranians and it is, in truth, so difficult to achieve, simulation of sincerity on television has great practical value. Here I am merely pointing out a cultural nuance, not casting doubt on the newsman's sincerity.

24. Robert Ray uses the term "implied contract" to talk about the expectation that Classical Hollywood Cinema has over the years cultivated in the spectators of giving them the optimum vantage point on what is occurring on the screen (1985:33).

25. In an Islamist reading of this hierarchical spectator positioning, Sayyed Mortaza Avini goes so far as to suggest that the relationship between the spectator and the projected film is one in which the former worships and accepts the guardianship (*velayat*) of the latter (1989:110).

26. As I have formulated elsewhere, veiling and unveiling practices are also mobilized in the reception of films in Iranian cinema in such a way as to inscribe the spectator in the text (Naficy 1991a).

27. According to Bozorgmehr and Sabagh, half of Iran-born population in their study was between 20 and 35 years old, a high proportion of which was single persons, particularly males (1988:21).

28. Author's interview with program producer, Ali Limonadi, Los Angeles, 2/4/1989.

29. In addition to *Iranian*, *Didar* seems to have been the only program that featured a regular section in English designed, according to its producer Homa Ehsan, for both American spouses of Iranians and Iranian youngsters. Based on the telephone calls she received, this was a successful segment but it was discontinued (interview 5/1/1989).

30. These functions are similar in some measure to what Fiske and Hartley have called television's "bardic function." According to them this includes the following six functions: implicating dominant values, celebrating the culture and its representatives, assuring the culture of its adequacy, exposing its inadequacies, convincing viewers that their identity is guaranteed by the culture, and transmitting a sense of cultural security (1978:88).

31. For a detailed treatise on the Simorgh and its multiple meanings, see Schmidt 1980.

32. The music video, *Ma Hameh Irooni Hastim*, was aired on *Tamasha* on 1/2/1989.

33. The first two were produced and directed by Mas'ud Assadollahi and aired by *Negah*, the latter was produced by Shohreh Aqdashlu and aired on *Sima va Nava-ye Iran*. According to their producers, these serials were highly successful.

34. On the compulsion to repeat, see Freud 1961 and Laplanche and Pontalis 1973: 78–80.

35. On the efficacy of repetition in television soap operas, see Allen 1985; on its circulation within the economy of televisual texts in general, see Newcomb 1988.

36. Satirical serials and series include *Jan Nesar; Nan, Eshq va Ta'ahod; Haft Negah, Daqayeq-e Akhar; Los Anjeles, Shahr-e Fereshtehha; Zir-e Aseman-e Kabud; Mosafer-e Zaman; LA TV; Samad Aqa; Alghorbat; Ma'muriat-e Alefba; Balatar az Khandeh*. Soap-opera serials include *Parvaz; Ro'ya-ye Emrika'i; Payvand; Faseleh; Shayad Behtar Bud; Panahandeh*. These series and serials are shown by various Iranian programs in brief installments of five to ten minutes' duration, lasting several months.

37. Jaklin's video, *Mafia*, and Black Cat's video, *Pul*, are good examples.

38. Author's interview with Caren Garces, then handling client services for KSCI-TV, 2/16/1988.

39. Ali Limonadi, producer of *Iranian*, stated in an interview with me that KSCI-TV forbids Iranian programs to express support for Iranian political factions, although many of them have done exactly that in a disguised form. Further, according to him, the station urged programmers in the aftermath of the hostage crisis to refrain from "politicizing" their programs for fear of backlash from citizens.

40. For example, KSCI-TV has had to teach Iranian producers about the U.S. copyright laws governing use of proprietary photos, clippings from newspapers, and film footage. This educational process is necessary for programmers who come from countries not signatory to the international copyright conventions and in whom the ideology of the copyright is not deeply rooted—as is the case with Iranians.

41. Among these professional routines is punctuality. According to Iraj Gorgin, producer of *Omid* TV, one episode of his program arrived a little past the deadline, to which the station responded by not airing the program, containing many paid-for advertisements.

## 5. Fetishization, Nostalgic Longing, and the Exilic National Imaginary

1. Television as a fetish does involve such an unequal power and knowledge relationship. The panoptic regime of television, made up of the advertising-driven schedule, audience measurement systems, programming strategies, and the ceaseless flows of programs that do not depend on the presence or control of viewers all contribute to establishing an essentially unequal power relation between the TV set and the viewer.

2. Freud himself refers to war as a source of traumatic neurosis (1977:274).

3. In their detailed textual analysis of over 30 years of news about Iran printed in major U.S. periodicals, Dorman and Farhang concluded that "the press, far from fulfilling the watchdog role assigned it in democratic theory or popular imagination, is deferential rather than adversative in the foreign policy arena" (1987:2).

4. For an elaboration on the dynamics of "here" and "there," in crosscultural discourses, see Geertz 1988.

5. Such imagined communities can be found in many parts of the world. For example, two films, *Ori* (1989) and *Quilombo* (1984), document and recreate respectively the rise and fall and the continued imaginary existence of Quilombo de Palmares in Brazil.

6. The video was aired by *Iran* (on 3/7/1988) and *Jonbesh-e Iran* (on 2/5/1989).

7. The debate about the flag abroad was in the context of the postrevolutionary politics of semiotics and representation in Iran which led to creation of a new national flag. For a detailed analysis of the current flag of the Islamic Republic, see Fischer and Abedi 1990: 341–46.

8. *Shir va Shamshir* was aired by *Jahan Nama* TV on 3/28/1988.

9. For example, the following show titles: *Iranian, Jam-e Jam* (The cup of Jamshid), *Mehr-e Iran* (Iran's love), *Melli* (National), *Jonbesh-e Melli* (National movement), *Parsian* (Persian), *Mellat* (The nation), *Iran, Pars, Omid-e Iran* (Hope of Iran), *Arya in L.A.*

10. Such as *Sima-ye Ashna* (Familiar face), *Didar* (Visit), *Ma* (Us), *Cheshmak* (Wink), *Negah* (Look), *Mikhak-e Noqreh'i* (Silver carnation). For a full list of show titles in Persian and their English equivalents, see Table 7.

11. One practical reason for this intense focus on and extensive circulation of certain images from inside Iran is the limitation of access to the country by outside photographers and journalists. Interestingly, the images of Iran that are available are almost always of public events (war, demonstrations) and public places (cemeteries, streets, parliament) open to outsiders. Rarely are there images of the interior spaces of homes and of the private lives of Iranians. So what ends up as fetish in exile are these exterior images, which uncannily come to represent, if not the interior of homes, at least the interior spaces of the country. This doubling and reversal is a function of exile, according to which the outside becomes the inside and vice versa.

12. *Mona's Execution* was aired by *Cheshmak* on 12/14/1987.

13. On the body as text, see Kroker and Cook 1986:25, and de Certeau 1986:159–67.

14. In the first decade of the Islamic government, two criteria according to which members of the first few Cabinets were selected were imprisonment or torture for their political and religious beliefs by the Shah's government.

15. See "Nehzatha-ye Borun Marzi," *Iran Times* (3/15/1991):10.

16. It must be noted that the discourse on the tortured body is dialogic in that the Islamic government itself has contributed to it. For example, in 1984 and 1986 the Tehran prosecutor general published two volumes of a book in which it reproduced in compulsive details the capture and torture to death of three high ranking pasdaran (Revolutionary Guards) by the Mojahedin in Iran. The books contained copies of the handwritten confessions of the Mojahedin torturers who had been captured by government authorities. They also contained gruesome photos of tortured and mutilated bodies of the victims (Dadsetani-ye Enqelab-e Eslami-ye Tehran 1984, 1986).

17. The music video *Sorud-e Hambastegi* was widely shown by various TV shows in January 1988, including by *Negah* on 1/31/1988.

18. Nostalgia is not just restorative; it can also be retrogressive, as I will show in the next chapter.

19. Shihabuddin Yahya Suhrawardi, the founder of the theosophical-philosophical illuminationist school in the twelfth century, in his treatise "A Tale of Occidental Exile," also

provides a discourse on these themes (1982).

20. The vein of the discourse of mysticism as spelled out by Rumi has been productively explored by artists in exile. For example, an entire issue (no. 3, 1989) of *Seda-ye Shahr*, the audio magazine, was devoted to Rumi's poetry; the musical compositions of avant-garde performance artist Susan Daihim, who lives in New York, are much influenced by him, as are the sculptural works of Shirazeh Hushiari, who works in London (for an interview with Hushiari, see Morgan 1989). The short, poetic film *Nafir* (Plaintive song, 1982), made by Jahanshah Ardalan, takes its title and its poetic sensibilities from Rumi's "Song of the Reed," quoted here. Nahid Rachlin's exile novel *Foreigner*, defying Freud, Lacan, and Rumi, stages not only the return of an Iranian emigre woman to her motherland but also her reunion with her long-lost biological mother.

21. Rachlin's novel *Foreigner* suffers precisely from her unproblematical staging of such a complete and total reunion.

22. This is also true of maroon societies founded by black African slaves in Brazil, as Bastide notes: "Maroonage involved more a nostalgia for Africa than an exact reconstitution of it . . . for new geographical, demographic, and political conditions obtained and these had to be dealt with" (1979:199).

23. The most thorough theorization of the phenomenology of cinematic experience in English is provided by Vivian Sobchack (1992). Also see a special issue of *Quarterly Review of Film and Video* (12:3, 1990) devoted to "Phenomenology in Film and Television," edited by Frank P. Tomasulo.

24. On the concept of the chronotope, see Bakhtin 1981.

25. Katherine S. Kovacs in a fascinating article (1991) demonstrates the link in Spanish cinema between certain recurring landscapes and the formation of the Spanish national cinema style.

26. *Sarzamin-e Man* was aired by *Jam-e Jam* on 11/27/1988. The lyrics for this video appear in a book called *Alaleh*, by H. Mirafshar, Los Angeles, 1988.

27. For an illuminating analysis of the topos of England as an island, see Beer 1990.

28. The 1924 film *Grass*, made by Merian C. Cooper, Ernest B. Schoedsack, and Margueritte Harrison, has provided another enduring topos for Iranian national consciousness, i.e., that of nomadism. It is significant that some of the major chronotopes of nationhood for Iranians are first (and in some ways best) expressed by foreigners to Iranian culture. Distance is necessary for self-reflexivity and metadiscourse, something Iranians have shown little of until recently.

29. The music video *Parandush* was aired by *Cheshmak* on 1/31/1989.

30. The Persian expression *darya del* (sea-hearted) refers to an individual who is magnanimous (openhanded) or courageous (lionhearted). This video seems not to refer to this expression but to the homology between a heart beating for a loved one and a tumultuous sea separating the exiles from their homeland. The exile heart is a pulsating sea, pounding on both shores.

31. The music video *Ashena* was aired by *Negah* in 1988.

32. This type of union with the sea as enacted in music videos is highly suggestive of the earliest infant-mother relationship, once called, appropriate to this context, the "oceanic feeling." Nowadays this union is called symbiosis. On oceanic feeling, see Masson 1980.

33. "Road movies" based on a trip over rough mountains, from Tehran to the Caspian Sea, were sufficiently prevalent in prerevolutionary cinema that they could be said to form a cinematic genre. They signified, among other things, escape from urban centers to natural surroundings; escape from the confinement of city life to carefree time by the sea; escape from authoritarian family, religion, and governmental structures to the relatively structureless freedoms of northern Iran. As a result, many of these movies, such as *Hamsafar* (Fellow-

traveller, 1975), were vehicles for budding love relationships, impossible to nurture in the constricting environment of one's own hometown. Even the postrevolutionary cinema has produced its own version of this genre, exemplified by *Arus* (Bride, 1991), which generated the highest box-office revenues in the history of Iranian cinema.

34. The exile-produced short film *Chand Jomleh-ye Sadeh* (A few simple sentences), directed by Reza Allamehzadeh, utilizes a wounded pigeon as a central symbol for a boy in exile.

35. A good cinematic example is the film *Dash Akol* (1969) directed by Mas'ud Kimia'i and based on a short story by Sadeq Hedayat. In the film, a caged lovebird symbolizes many things, among them the love the *luti* (tough guy) Dash Akol feels for his ward, Marjan, his sense of being imprisoned by that love, and his feeling of having become confined as a result of accepting the obligation of guardianship. The caged bird may also symbolize Marjan, who is confined by both patriarchy and religious tradition. For more details, see Naficy 1985, 1992a.

36. This episode was aired on October 14, 1991.

37. For an analysis of the evolution and significance of the concept of the Great Satan, see Beeman 1983.

38. Although the pleasure and the security of the gardens are available only a few months of the year due to seasonal changes, the idea of the garden has been planted so deeply in the Iranian consciousness that it has became necessary to create a "portable" and year-round substitute—namely, colorful and intricately designed carpets, which could be used by all social strata. Michael Hillman describes their significance and multiple uses: "Nowhere in the world are oriental carpets more important in daily life than in Iran. Persian carpets are woven on migrations, in villages, towns, and cities, and in fields, yards, private homes, and large factories throughout Iran. They are used by nomads as floorcoverings in tents. They are underfoot during daily ritual Moslem prayers. They are found everywhere, in hovels and palaces, in dingy slum rooms, in high-rise apartments and villas, in government offices and hotels" (1984:9).

39. These calendrical events include Noruz (Persian New Year, which falls on the spring equinox), *sizdah bedar* (the thirteenth day after the New Year), and *mehregan* (the beginning of the fall season).

40. Another evidence for this contention is the emergence of flower-delivering businesses in the United States that allow Iranian exiles to send flowers to loved ones in Iran by simply placing a phone call.

41. Iranian interethnic communities, particularly Assyrians, have produced their own ethnoreligious television programs (see Table 13) and their own nationalistic music videos, such as the 20-minute *Avarah* (In exile, 1992), produced and directed by Beni Atoori. Kurdish Iranians, particularly those fighting the Islamic regime in Iran produced a number of propaganda and documentary videos of their struggle. For details of these, see Naficy 1984:25, 78–80.

42. The morning daily newspaper, *Sobh-e Iran*, is a pioneer in the effort to purify the Persian language by using "authentic," pre-Islamic Persian words. Since many of these words are rather obscure and unfamiliar even to the educated readers, however, the daily is forced to provide their current equivalents as well.

43. As Cottam (1979) has demonstrated, major political changes in twentieth-century Iran, including the revolution of 1979, were ushered in by an alliance of religious activists and liberal secularists.

44. This sense of nationalism at a distance is constructed by invoking other moments of nationalist surges in Iranian history, particularly the constitutional revolution of 1906 and occasionally the short-lived premiership of Mohammad Mosaddeq in the early 1950s.

## 6. The Cultural Politics of Hybridity

1. For more on split subjectivity, see Laplanche and Pontalis 1973:427–29.

2. The music video *Safarnameh* was aired by *Parsian* on 9/22/1984.

3. For what was shown, see Naficy 1990a and the festival catalog, *A Decade of Iranian Cinema: 1980–1990*, written by the present author and published by the UCLA Film and Television Archives.

4. The following producers and filmmakers living in Los Angeles, not all of whom are royalist, opposed the festival and called for its boycott. TV producers: Shohreh Aqdashlu (*Sima va Nava-ye Iran* TV), Parviz Kardan (*Shahr-e Farang* TV), Parviz Sayyad (*Parsian* TV), and Hushang Towzi (various TV serials). A few of these did eventually attend some of the screenings. Filmmakers: Mary Apik, Hushang Baharlu, Shahrokh Golestan, Marva Nabili, and Barbod Taheri.

5. These producers include Iraj Gorgin (*Omid* radio and TV), Parviz Qarib Afshar (*Sima-ye Ashna*), Mas'ud Assadollahi (*Negah*), and Ali Limonadi (*Iranian*).

6. For example, the editor of *Sobh-e Iran* newspaper ominously warned the program producer (Hushang Purang) that showing Islamic sermons on TV was "not advisable" and urged him and others interested in sermons to "go back to Iran" (6/29/1992, p. 2).

7. On the ambivalence of nationalism, see Nairn 1981 and Bhabha 1990.

8. Historian Abbas Amanat has noted that disillusionment with the outcome of the 1979 revolution led certain strata of the Iranian society "to seek answers in the action of foreign powers, the course of change in modern Iran, and the evolution of religion. In this process a certain amount of confusion is inevitable, whether by resorting to conspiratorial theories, or taking refuge in a nostalgic picture of the Pahlavi era, or seeking relief in an idealized religion of pre-Islamic Iran, or making an escapist retreat to some mystical version of the reality" (1989:18).

9. Witness the Nazi savagery in the name of a nostalgic return to an idealized racial construction. Witness also the more recent "high crimes and misdemeanors," to deploy the phrase used in presidential impeachment proceedings, which were committed by the U.S. government in the Persian Gulf war, partly justified by a nostalgic return to earlier primal scenes two centuries apart: the American war of independence against the British and the American war against Vietnam. The nostalgia for the success of the former and fear of the repetition of defeat in the latter energized the drive to pulverize the Iraqi economic and industrial infrastructures, allowing the president and the mainline media to declare the "Vietnam syndrome" dead. Recall President Bush's oft-repeated remark: This fight is for the independence of Kuwait, it is not another Vietnam war. True enough, but was the war not justified as an attempt partially to restore the nostalgic image of an undefeated United States?

10. The interplay between Shahrokh and his shadow in this video is highly reminiscent of the most celebrated modernist Iranian novel, *The Blind Owl* (1957), by Sadeq Hedayat, published in exile in 1935. In it the narrator tells his story of dislocation and disillusionment to his own shadow stretched across the wall of his room. Likewise, in a recent poem published by Mortaza Miraftabi in exile, "Sayeh'am Gom Shodeh" (My shadow is lost), the poet seems to posit that in Iran he and his shadow were united; however, now in exile, his shadow is lost—perhaps because it has returned to the poet's homeland—leaving him shadowless (split) (*Simorgh* 1:7, December 1989, 39).

11. Michael Beard discusses the various doubles that appear in Hedayat's *The Blind Owl* through Otto Rank's discourse (1990).

12. Jung makes a comment about the shadow that is appropriate in the context of ethnicity and exile. He states that the shadow might be not only the dark forces within the individual but also the archetypal "ethnic self." In a racist discourse, he then posits the African

Arabs to be the archetypal shadows of the Europeans' consciousness, i.e., their primitive, irrational "underworld" (1965:245).

13. The video *Gol-e Morad* was aired by *Jonbesh-e Iran* on 12/27/1988.

14. The music video *Mafia* was aired by *Iranian* in 1990.

15. Likewise, Sa'edi's play *Othello in the Land of Wonders*, written in exile, uses the famous play to savage the cultural politics of the Islamic Republic. For a fascinating analysis of this process of critiquing the self through an other, see Safa 1990.

16. One such example is Davud Behbudi's music video *Mimiram Barat* (I'll die for you), aired by various Iranian exile television programs in the 1990s.

17. Kambiz Gugush and Faramarz Asef are two male singers who have self-consciously attempted to model their act after the stage routines and the performance style of such American rock stars as Michael Jackson. In 1988, TV commercials for Gugush's first U.S. concert tour kept referring to him as the Iranian Michael Jackson and featured his break-dance style done to an Americanized Iranian pop tune.

18. On Iranian traditional theater, see Beeman 1982 and Gaffary 1984.

19. Women, too, had their own mimic theaters performed privately, in which women dressed up as men and imitated them (Shahriari 1986:83). It will be useful to read the "black" character through Janet Bergstrom's discourse on androids and androgyny in 1980s American cinema (1986).

20. As noted in chapter 2, the use of this figure in exile has been rather limited because it is so closely associated with a once-a-year affair and because in the context of the racist history of the host society, blackface can be construed to be racist.

21. For example, *Ebram dar Paris* (Ebram in Paris, 1964).

22. *Beyond Laughter* was aired by *Jam-e Jam* TV in 1985 and *Strangers* was aired by *Jom'eh* TV in 1986.

23. Perhaps one feature that endeared the Australian protagonist of the movie *Crocodile Dundee* to American audiences was his very large hunting knife which seemed very inappropriate—but at the same time very effective—in the streets of New York City.

24. The music video *Del Beh Del* was aired by *Jam-e Jam* on 3/21/1992.

25. This lack of fit is reminiscent of the petticoats that the nineteenth-century Iranian Qajar king, Nasereddin Shah, in imitation of tutus worn by European ballerinas, had his wives wear over their pants.

26. On a trip to the United States in the spring of 1992, Salman Rushdie expressed his worry that the protection he was receiving from the British security service might be waning. At the same time, the Bush administration, not wanting to further worsen its relations with Iran, refused to meet with him.

27. In the film *Crossing Borders: the Journey of Carlos Fuentes* (aired by PBS on 10/6/1989), Fuentes was accused of being a "chameleon" or a "guerrilla dandy." Likewise, Hamid Algar in his fascinating, if biased, analysis of Malkum Khan's life, critiqued him as advocating a "utilitarian concept of religion promoted in the absence of personal belief" (1973:ix). Rushdie's forced and prolonged isolation in British safe houses (to escape Khomeini-inspired assassins) is only the most celebrated and recent (if rather unusual) case of the type of state violence routinely waged against intellectuals in many countries.

28. See also Fanon 1961 and JanMohammed 1983.

# Bibliography

Aberle, David. 1965. "A Note on Relative Deprivation Theory as Applied to Millennarian and Other Cult Movements," in *Reader in Comparative Religion: An Anthropological Approach*. Second edition. William A. Lessa and Evon Z. Vogt, eds. New York: Harper & Row. 537–41.

Abrahamian, Ervand. 1989. *The Iranian Mojahedin*. New Haven: Yale University Press.

Adams, William. 1981. *Television Coverage of the Middle East*. Norwood, N.J.: Ablex.

Afkhami, Gholam Hosain. 1985. *Iranian Revolution: Thanatos on a National Scale*. Washington, D.C.: Middle East Institute.

Akrami, Jamsheed. 1991. "Cinema ii: Feature Films," in *Encyclopedia Iranica*. vol. 5, fascicle 6. Ehsan Yarshater, ed. Cost Mesa, Calif.: Mazda Publishers. 572–57.

Al-e Ahmad, Jalal. 1340/1961. *Gharbzadegi* [Westernstruckness]. Tehran. English translations: *Gharbzadegi (Westernstruckness)*. John Green and Ahmad Alizadeh, trans. Lexington, Ky.: Mazda Publishers, 1982. *Plagued by the West (Gharbzadegi)*. Paul Sprachman, trans. Delmar, N.Y.: Caravan Books, 1982. *Occidentosis: A Plague from the West*. Robert Campbell, trans., Hamid Algar, ed. Berkeley: Mizan Press, 1985.

Algar, Hamid. 1973. *Mirza Malkum Khan: A Study in the History of Iranian Modernism*. Berkeley: University of California Press.

Alexander, George. 1987. "Slipzones: Text and Art," *Art & Text* 26. 44–57.

Allen, Robert. 1985. *Speaking of Soaps*. Chapel Hill: University of North Carolina Press.

_____, ed. 1987. *Channels of Discourse: Television and Contemporary Criticism*. Chapel Hill: University of North Carolina Press.

Althusser, Louis. 1971. "Ideology and Ideological State Apparatuses (Notes Toward an Investigation)," in *Lenin and Philosophy and Other Essays*. Ben Brewster, trans. New York: Monthly Review Press. 127–89.

Altman, Rick. 1987. *The American Film Musical*. Bloomington: Indiana University Press.

Amanat, Abbas. 1989. "The Study of History in Post-Revolutionary Iran: Nostalgia, or Historical Awareness," *Iranian Studies* 22:4, 3–18.

Amin, Samir. 1974. *Accumulation on a World Scale: A Critique of the Theory of Under-development*. New York: Monthly Review Press.

Amirshahi, Mahshid. 1987. *Dar Hazar*. London: OrientScript.

———. 1988. "Dar Safar," *Asheghaneh* 44 [Houston, Tex.] (December 1). 44–45.

Anderson, Benedict. 1983. *Imagined Communities: Reflections on the Origin and Spread of Nationalism*. London: Verso.

Ansari, Abdolmaboud. 1988. *Iranian Immigrants in the United States: A Case Study of Dual Marginality*. New York: Associated Faculty Press.

Aoki, Guy. 1989a. "Video Fast-Forward Japan's TV Shows," *Los Angeles Times* (3/24). Part VI, 22.

———. 1989b. "Far Eastern Hits in Koreatown," *Los Angeles Times Sunday Calendar* (2/5). 5.

Arberry, A. J., ed. 1954. *Persian Poems: An Anthology of Verse Translation*. London: J. M. Dent & Son.

Ardalan, Nader, and Laleh Bakhtiar. 1973. *The Sense of Unity: The Sufi Tradition in Persian Architecture*. Chicago: University of Chicago Press.

Arlen, Michael J. 1981. *The Camera Age: Essays on Television*. New York: Penguin.

Ashcroft, Bill, Gareth Griffiths, and Helen Tiffin. 1989. *The Empire Writes Back: Theory and Practice in Post-Colonial Literature*. London: Routledge.

Atkinson, Terry, and Tammy Sims. 1989. "Middle Eastern Shop Gives Up," *Los Angeles Times Sunday Calendar* (2/5). 5.

Atkinson, Terry, and Paul Vargas. 1989. "Rimar International Stocks Films From the Philippines," *Los Angeles Times* (4/7). Part VI, 26.

Attar, Faridoddin. 1971. *The Conference of the Birds*. C. S. Nott, trans. Berkeley: Shambala.

Avini, Sayyed Mortaza. 1989. "Molahezati dar Bab-e Sinema," *Faslnameh-ye Sinema'i-ye Farabi* 1:2 (Spring), 106–80.

Bachelard, Gaston. 1969. *The Poetics of Space*. Maria Jolas, trans. Boston: Beacon Press.

Baiza'i, Bahram. 1344/1965. *Namayesh dar Iran*. Tehran: Kavian.

Bakhtin, Mikhail M. 1981. *The Dialogic Imagination: Four Essays*. Michael Holquist, ed. Caryl Emerson and Michael Holquist, trans. Austin: University of Texas Press.

Ball, George. 1982. *The Past Has Another Pattern*. New York: Norton.

Barnouw, Erik. 1978. *The Sponsor: Notes on a Modern Potentate*. New York: Oxford University Press.

Barrios, Gregg. 1989a. " 'Super' Videos with a Definite Spanish Flavor," *Los Angeles Times Sunday Calendar* (2/5). 4.

———. 1989b. "French Hits for *Le Cinema* Buffs," *Los Angeles Times Sunday Calendar* (2/5). 5.

Barth, Fredrick. 1969. *Ethnic Groups and Boundaries: The Social Organization of Culture Difference*. Boston: Little, Brown.

Barthes, Roland. 1974. *S/Z: An Essay*. Richard Miller, trans. New York: Hill & Wang.

———. 1975. *The Pleasure of the Text*. New York: Hill & Wang.

———. 1977. *Image, Music, Text*. Stephen Heath, trans. New York: Hill & Wang.

Bastide, Roger. 1979. "The Other Quilombo," in *Maroon Societies: Rebel Slaves Communities in the Americas*. Second edition. Richard Price, ed. Baltimore: Johns Hopkins University Press. 191–201.

———. 1985. "Problems of Religious Syncretism," in *The African Religions of Brazil: Toward a Sociology of the Interpretation of Civilizations*. Helen Sebba, trans. Baltimore: Johns Hopkins University Press. 261–84.

Bateson, Catherine. 1979. " 'This Figure of Tinsel': A Study of Themes of Hypocrisy and Pessimism in Iranian Culture," *Daedalus* (Summer). 125–34.

Bateson, Catherine, J. W. Clinton, J. B. M. Kassarjian, H. Safavi, and M. Soraya. 1977. "Safay-i Batin: A Study of the Interrelations of a Set of Iranian Ideal Character Types," in *Psychological Dimensions of Near Eastern Studies*. L. C. Brown and N. Itzkowitz, eds. Princeton: Darwin Press. 257–74.

Baudrillard, Jean. 1981. *For a Critique of the Political Economy of the Sign*. Charles Levin, trans. St. Louis, Mo.: Telos Press.

_____. 1983. *Simulations*. Paul Foss, Paul Patton, and Philip Beitchman, trans. New York: Semiotext(e).

_____. 1989. "After Utopia: The Primitive Society of the Future," *New Perspective Quarterly* (Summer). 52–54.

Baudry, Jean-Louis. 1970. "Ideological Effects of the Basic Cinematographic Apparatus," in *Movies and Methods Volume II*. Bill Nichols, ed. Berkeley: University of California Press. 531–42.

Bausani, Alessandro. 1975. "Muhammad or Darius? The Elements and Basis of Iranian Culture," in *Islam and Cultural Change in the Middle Ages*. Speros Vryonis, Jr., ed. Wiesbaden: Otto Harrassowitz. 43–57.

Baxter, John. 1976. *The Hollywood Exiles*. New York: Taplinger.

Beard, Michael. 1990. *Hedayat's* Blind Owl *as a Western Novel*. Princeton: Princeton University Press.

Beard, Michael, and Hasan Javadi. 1986. "Iranian Writers Abroad: Survey and Elegy," *World Literature Today* 60:2 (Spring). 257–61.

Beauchamp, Marc. 1988. "Welcome to Tehran, Calif.," *Forbes* (12/12). 60–66.

Becker, Ernest. 1969. *Angel in Armor: A Post-Freudian Perspective on the Nature of Man*. New York: George Braziller.

Beckland, Laurie. 1987. "Iranian Who Set Himself Afire Interred," *Los Angeles Times* (10/11). 27.

Beeman, William. 1982. *Culture, Performance and Communication in Iran*. Tokyo: Institute for the Study of Languages and Cultures of Asia & Africa.

_____. 1983. "Images of the Great Satan: Representations of the United States in the Iranian Revolution," in *Religion and Politics in Iran: Shi'ism from Quietism to Revolution*. Nikki R. Keddie, ed. New Haven: Yale University Press. 191–217.

_____. 1986. *Language, Status, and Power in Iran*. Bloomington: Indiana University Press.

Beer, Gillian. 1990. "The Island and the Aeroplane: The Case of Virginia Woolf," in *Nation and Narration*. Homi Bhabha, ed. London & New York: Routledge. 265–90.

Bellour, Raymond. 1986. "Segmenting/Analyzing," in *Narrative, Apparatus, Ideology: A Film Theory Reader*. Philip Rosen, ed. New York: Columbia University Press.

Benjamin, Walter. 1978. *Illuminations*. Hannah Arendt, ed. Harry Zohn, trans. New York: Schocken.

Bennett, Tony, Graham Martin, Colin Mercer, and Janet Woollacott, eds. 1985a. *Culture, Ideology and Social Process*. Milton Keynes, U.K.: Open University Press.

Bennett, Tony, Susan Boyd-Bowman, Colin Mercer, and Janet Woollacott, eds. 1985b. *Popular Television and Film*. London: BFI and Open University Press.

Bennett, Tony, Colin Mercer, and Janet Woollacott, eds. 1986. *Popular Culture and Social Relations*. Milton Keynes, U.K.: Open University Press.

Bergstrom, Janet. 1986. "Androids and Androgyny," *Camera Obscura* 15. 37–64.

Berko, Lili. 1989. "Video: In Search of a Discourse," *Quarterly Review of Film Studies* 10:4, 289–307.

Bernstein, Sharon. 1992. "Uncut British TV Shows Are Businessman's Cup of Tea," *Los Angeles Times* (7/27).F28.

Bhabha, Homi K. 1983. "The Other Question . . . The Stereotype and Colonial Discourse," *Screen* (November-December). 18–36.

———. 1985. "Of Mimicry and Man: The Ambivalence of Colonial Discourse," *October* (May). 125–33.

———. 1986. "Signs Taken for Wonders: Questions of Ambivalence and Authority Under a Tree Outside Delhi, May 1817," in *"Race," Writing, and Difference*. Henry Louis Gates, Jr., ed. Chicago: University of Chicago Press.

———. 1987. "Interrogating Identity," *ICA Documents* 6. 5–11.

———. 1989a. "The Commitment to Theory," in *Questions of Third Cinema*. Jim Pines and Paul Willemen, eds. London: BFI. 111–32.

———. 1989b. "Location, Intervention, Incommensurability: A Conversation," *Emergences* 1 (Fall). 63–88.

———. 1990. "DissemiNation: Time, Narrative, and the Margins of the Modern Nation," in *Nation and Narration*. Homi Bhabha, ed. London & New York: Routledge. 291–322.

Bhabha, Homi K., ed. 1990a. *Nation and Narration*. London: Routledge.

Blair, Betty A. 1991. "Personal Name Changes Among Immigrant Iranians in the USA," in *Iranian Refugees and Exiles Since Khomeini*. Asghar Fathi, ed. Costa Mesa, Calif.: Mazda Publishers. 145–60.

Blassingame, John W. 1972. *The Slave Community: Plantation Life in the Antebellum South*. New York: Oxford University Press.

Bloom, Peter. 1990. "Some Reflections on the Iranian Film Festival: 'A Decade of Iranian Cinema, 1980–1990,' " *Jusur* 6, 95–99.

Bordwell, David. 1985a. *Narration in the Fiction Film*. Madison: University of Wisconsin Press.

Bordwell, David, Janet Staiger, and Kristin Thompson. 1985b. *The Classical Hollywood Cinema: Film Style and Mode of Production to 1960*. New York: Columbia University Press.

Bourdieu, Pierre. 1977. *Outline of a Theory of Practice*. Richard Nice, trans. New York: Cambridge University Press.

———. 1984. *Distinction: A Social Critique of the Judgment of Taste*. Richard Nice, trans. Cambridge, Mass.: Harvard University Press.

Bozorgmehr, Mehdi. 1992. *Internal Ethnicity: Armenian, Bahai, Jewish, and Muslim Iranians in Los Angeles*. Ph.D. dissertation, sociology, UCLA.

Bozorgmehr, Mehdi, and Georges Sabagh. 1988. "High Status Immigrants: A Statistical Study of Iranians in the United States," *Iranian Studies* 21:3–4. 5–35.

Bozorgmehr, Mehdi, and Georges Sabagh. 1991. "Iranian Exiles and Immigrants in Los Angeles," in *Iranian Refugees and Exiles Since Khomeini*. Asghar Fathi, ed. Costa Mesa, Calif.: Mazda Publishers. 121–44.

Bozorgmehr, Mehdi, Georges Sabagh, and Claudia Der-Martirosian. 1991. *Religio-Ethnic Diversity Among Iranians in Los Angeles*. Los Angeles: UCLA Center for Near Eastern Studies Working Paper No. 6.

Branigan, Edward R. 1984. *Point of View in the Cinema: a Theory of Narration and Subjectivity in Classical Film*. New York: Mouton.

Brennan, Timothy. 1990. "The National Longing for Form," in *Nation and Narration*. Homi Bhabha, ed. London & New York: Routledge. 44–70.

Brooks, Peter. 1984. *Reading for the Plot: Design and Intention in Narrative*. New York: Random House.

Browne, Nick. 1975. "The Spectator-in-the-Text: The Rhetoric of *Stagecoach*," in *Movies and Methods Volume II*. Bill Nichols, ed. 1985. Berkeley: University of California Press. 458–75.

_____. 1984. "The Political Economy of the Television (Super) Text," in *Quarterly Review of Film Studies* 9:3 (Summer). 174–82.

Brunsdon, Charlotte, and David Morley. 1978. *Everyday Television: "Nationwide."* London: BFI.

Camus, Albert. 1972. *The Plague*. Stuart Gilbert, trans. New York: Vintage Books.

Carey, James W. 1989. *Communication as Culture: Essays on Media and Society*. Boston: Unwin Hyman.

Carpenter, Richard. 1973. "Ritual, Aesthetics, and TV," in *Mass Media and Mass Man*. Second edition. Alan Casty, ed. New York: Holt, Rinehart & Winston.

Castoriadis, Cornelius. 1987. *The Imaginary Institution of Society*. Kathleen Blamey, trans. Cambridge, Mass.: MIT Press.

Chanan, Michael. 1985. *The Cuban Image*. London: BFI Publishing.

Chelkowski, Peter, Jr., ed. 1979. *Ta'ziyeh: Ritual and Drama in Iran*. New York and Tehran: New York University Press and Soroush Press.

_____. 1985. "Shia Muslim Processional Performances," *The Drama Review* 29:3 (Fall). 18–30.

Cheng, Lucie, and Leslie Evans. 1988. "Brain Flow: The International Migration of the Highly Skilled—A Theoretical Introduction," unpublished manuscript delivered at the "Brainflow" conference held in August-September 1988 at the University of California, Los Angeles.

Clifford, James, and George E. Marcus, eds. 1986. *Writing Culture: The Poetics and Politics of Ethnography*. Berkeley: University of California Press.

Cohen, Anthony, P. 1985. *The Symbolic Construction of Community*. London and New York: Tavistock Publications.

Collins, Richard, James Curran, Nicholas Garnham, Paddy Scannell, Phillip Schlesinger, and Colin Spark, eds. 1986. *Media, Culture, and Society: A Critical Reader*. London: Sage.

Comolli, Jean-Louis. 1977. "Technique and Ideology: Camera, Perspective, Depth of Field," in *Movies and Methods Volume II*. Bill Nichols, ed. 1985. Berkeley: University of California Press. 40–57.

Cottam, Richard. 1979. *Nationalism in Iran*. Updated through 1978. Pittsburgh: University of Pittsburgh Press.

Cowley, Malcom. 1962. *Exile's Return: A Literary Odyssey of the 1920s*. [1934]. New York: Viking.

Curran, James, Michael Gurevitch, and Janet Woollacott. 1977. *Mass Communication and Society*. London: Open University Press.

Dadsetani-ye Enqelab-e Eslami-ye Tehran. 1363/1984. *Joz'iat-e Shekanje-ye Seh Pasdar-e Shahid-e Komiteh-ye Markazi-ye Enqelab-e Eslami Beh Dast-e Monafeqin*. Volume 1. Tehran.

Dallalfar, Arlene. 1989. *Iranian Immigrant Women in Los Angeles: The Reconstruction of Work, Ethnicity, and Community*. Ph.D. dissertation in sociology. University of California, Los Angeles.

Dasenbrock, Reed Way. 1985/86. "Creating a Past: Achebe, Naipaul, Soyinka, Farah," *Salmagundi* (Fall-Winter). 312–32.

Davis, Mike. 1990. *City of Quartz: Excavating the Future in Los Angeles*. London & New York: Verso.

Dayan, Daniel. 1974. "The Tutor-Code of Classical Cinema," in *Movies and Methods I*. Bill Nichols, ed. Berkeley: University of California Press. 438–50.

Debord, Guy. 1983. *Society of the Spectacle*. Detroit: Black & Red.

De Certeau, Michel. 1986. *Heterologies: Discourse on the Other*. Brian Massumi, trans. Minneapolis: University of Minnesota Press.

DeLauretis, Teresa. 1984. *Alice Doesn't: Feminism, Semiotics, Cinema*. Bloomington: Indiana University Press.

_____. 1987. *Technologies of Gender: Essays on Theory, Film, and Fiction*. Bloomington: Indiana University Press.

DeLauretis, Teresa, and Stephen Heath, eds. 1980. *The Cinematic Apparatus*. New York: St. Martin's Press.

Deleuze, Gilles, and Felix Guattari. 1983. *Anti-Oedipus: Capitalism and Schizophrenia*. Robert Hurley, Mark Seem, and Helen R. Lane, trans. Minneapolis: University of Minnesota Press.

_____. 1985. *Kafka: Toward a Minor Literature*. Dana Polan, trans. Minneapolis: University of Minnesota Press.

del Olmo, Frank. 1989. "TV Dispute Sheds Light on the 'Hispanic Myth,' " *Los Angeles Times* (5/29). Part II, 5.

Derrida, Jaques. 1978. *Writing and Difference*. Alan Bass, trans. Chicago: University of Chicago Press.

Devereux, George. 1975. "Ethnic Identity: Its Logical Foundations and Its Dysfunctions," in *Ethnic Identity: Cultural Continuities and Change*. George de Vos and Lola Romanucci-Ross, eds. Palo Alto: Mayfield. 42–70.

Devereux, George, and Edwin Loeb. 1943. "Antagonistic Acculturation," *American Sociological Review* 7. 143–47.

Dhareshwar, Vivek. 1989. "Self-Fashioning, Colonial Habitus, and Double Exclusion: V. S. Naipaul's *The Mimic Men*," *Criticism* 31:1. 75–102.

Doan, Mary Ann. 1987. *The Desire to Desire: the Woman's Film of the 1940s*. Bloomington: Indiana University Press.

Dogan, Mattei, and John Kasarda, eds. 1988. *The Metropolis Era: Mega-Cities*. Beverly Hills: Sage Publications.

Dolgin, Janet L., David S. Kemintzer, and David M. Scheider, eds. 1977. *Symbolic Anthropology: A Reader in the Study of Symbols and Meanings*. New York: Columbia University Press.

Dorman, William A., and Mansur Farhang. 1987. *The U.S. Press and Iran: Foreign Policy and the Journalism of Deference*. Berkeley: University of California Press.

Dowlatabadi, Zahra. 1989. "Goft va Shonudi ba Qasem Ebrahimian," *Par* 45. 28–32.

Downing, John D. H. 1987. *Film & Politics in the Third World*. New York: Praeger.

Eco, Umberto. 1979. *The Role of the Reader*. Bloomington: Indiana University Press.

_____. 1985. "Innovation and Repetition: Between Modern and Post-Modern Aesthetics," *Daedalus* (Fall).

Eisner, Lotte H. 1973. *The Haunted Screen*. Berkeley: University of California Press.

Ellis, John. 1985. *Visible Fictions: Cinema: Television: Video*. London: Routledge & Kegan Paul.

Elsaesser, Thomas. 1986. "Primary Identification and the Historical Subject: Fassbinder and Germany," in *Narrative, Apparatus, Ideology: a Film Theory Reader*. Philip Rosen, ed. New York: Columbia University Press.

Elsaesser, Thomas, ed. 1990. *Early Cinema: Space, Frame, Narrative*. London: BFI.

Elster, Jon, ed. 1987. *The Multiple Self*. Cambridge: Cambridge University Press.

Ettinghausen, Richard. 1979. "The Immanent Features of Persian Art," in *Highlights of Persian Art*. Richard Ettinghausen, ed. Boulder: Westview. xiii-xviii.

Ewen, Stuart. 1988. *All Consuming Images: the Politics of Style in Contemporary Culture*. New York: Basic Books.

Ewen, Stuart, and Elizabeth Ewen. 1982. *Channels of Desire: Mass Images and the Shaping of American Consciousness*. New York: McGraw-Hill Book Co.

Fanon, Frantz. 1961. *The Wretched of the Earth*. Constance Farrington, trans. New York: Grove Press. 1968.

Faruqi, Ahmad, and Jean Lerevellier. 1979. *Iran bar Zedd-e Shah*. Mehdi Naraqi, trans. Tehran: Amir Kabir.

Fassih, Esmail. 1985. *Sorraya in a Coma*. London: Zed Books.

Feuer, Jane. 1983. "The Concept of Live Television: Ontology as Ideology," in *Regarding Television: Critical Approaches—An Anthology*. E. Ann Kaplan, ed. Los Angeles: The American Film Institute. 13–22.

_____. 1987. "Genre Study and Television," in *Channels of Discourse: Television and Contemporary Criticism*. Robert C. Allen, ed. Chapel Hill: University of North Carolina Press. 113–33.

Fischer, Michael. 1980. *Iran: from Religious Dispute to Revolution*. Cambridge: Harvard University Press.

_____. 1984. "Towards a Third World Poetics: Seeing Through Short Stories and Films in the Iranian Culture Area," *Knowledge and Society: Studies in the Sociology of Culture Past and Present*. Vol. 5. 171–241.

_____. 1986. "Ethnicity and the Post-Modern Arts of Memory," in *Writing Culture: The Poetics and Politics of Ethnography*. James Clifford and George E. Marcus, eds. Berkeley: University of California Press. 194–233.

Fischer, Michael M. J., and Mehdi Abedi. 1990. *Debating Muslims: Cultural Dialogues in Postmodernity and Tradition*. Madison: University of Wisconsin Press.

Fiske, John. 1987a. "British Cultural Studies and Television," in Robert Allen, ed., *Channels of Discourse: Television and Contemporary Criticism*. Chapel Hill: University of North Carolina Press.

_____. 1987b. *Television Culture*. London: Methuen.

_____. 1989. *Understanding Popular Culture*. Boston: Unwin Hyman.

Fiske, John, and John Hartley. 1978. *Reading Television*. New York: Methuen.

FM-2030. 1989. *Are You a Transhuman?* New York: Warner Books.

Foster, Hal, ed. 1983. *The Anti-Aesthetic: Essays on Postmodern Culture*. Port Townsend, Washington: Bay Press.

_____, ed. 1985. *Recodings: Art, Spectacle, Cultural Politics*. Port Townsend, Washington: Bay Press.

Foucault, Michel. 1979. *Discipline and Punish: The Birth of the Prison*. Alan Sheridan, trans. New York: Vantage.

Frantz, Douglas, and Murray Waas. 1992. "Allies' Iraq Arms Sales Unopposed in '89," *Los Angeles Times* (6/11), A14.

Freud, Sigmund. 1961. *Beyond the Pleasure Principle*. London. Standard Edition 18.

_____. 1961b. "Fetishism," in *The Standard Edition of the Complete Psychological Works of Sigmund Freud*. Vol. 21. London: Hogarth Press. 152–57.

_____. 1969. *An Outline of Psycho-Analysis*. James Strachey, trans. and ed. New York: W. W. Norton.

_____. 1977. *Introductory Lectures on Psychoanalysis*. James Strachey, trans. and ed. New York: Norton.

Friedman, Lester D., ed. 1991. *Unspeakable Images: Ethnicity and the American Cinema*. Urbana: University of Illinois Press.

Friedmann, John, and Goetz Wolff. 1982. *World City Formation: An Agenda for Research and Action*. Unpublished manuscript. Graduate School of Architecture and Urban Planning, University of California, Los Angeles.

Furnham, Adrian and Stephen Bochner. 1986. *Culture Shock: Psychological Reactions to Unfamiliar Environments*. New York: Methuen.

Gabler, Neal. 1988. *An Empire of Their Own: How the Jews Invented Hollywood*. New York: Crown.

Gabriel, Teshome, H. 1988. "Thoughts on Nomadic Aesthetics and the Black Independent Cinema: Traces of a Journey," *Black Frames: Critical Perspectives on Black Independent Cinema*. Mbye B. Cham and Claire Andrade-Watkins, eds. Cambridge, Mass.: MIT Press. 62–79.

———. 1989a. "Third Cinema as Guardian of Popular Memory: Towards a Third Aesthetics," in *Questions of Third Cinema*. London: British Film Institute. 53–64.

———. 1989b. "Theses on Memory and Identity: In Search of the Origin of the River Nile," *Emergences* 1 (Fall). 131–37.

Gaffary, Farrokh. 1984. "Evolution of Rituals and Theater in Iran," *Iranian Studies* 17:4 (Autumn). 361–90.

———. 1991. "Cinema i: History of Cinema in Persia," in *Encyclopedia Iranica*. Vol 5, fascicle 6. Ehsan Yarshater, ed. Costa Mesa, Calif.: Mazda Publishers.

Gallagher, Dennis. 1986. "Introduction" to the special issue on Refugees, *International Migration Review* 20:2 (Summer). 141–47.

Gallop, Jane. 1985. *Reading Lacan*. Ithaca: Cornell University Press.

Gans, Herbert J. 1974. *Popular Culture and High Culture: An Analysis and Evaluation of Taste*. New York: Basic Books.

Gates, Henry Louis, Jr., ed. 1986. *"Race," Writing, and Difference*. Chicago: University of Chicago Press.

Geddes, Patrick. 1915. *Cities in Evolution*. London.

Geertz, Clifford. 1983. *Local Knowledge: Further Essays in Interpretive Anthropology*. New York: Basic Books.

———. 1988. *Works and Lives: the Anthropologist as Author*. Stanford: Stanford University Press.

Gellner, Ernest. 1983. *Nations and Nationalism*. London: Basil Blackwell.

———. 1987. *Culture, Identity, and Politics*. New York: Cambridge University Press.

Gibbs, Nancy. 1991. "Shades of Difference," *Time* (November 18). 66–70.

Giddens, Anthony. 1984. *The Constitution of Society*. Berkeley and Los Angeles: University of California Press.

Gilroy, Paul. 1987. *"There Ain't No Black in the Union Jack": The Cultural Politics of Race and Nation*. London: Hutchinson.

Gitlin, Todd. 1983. *Inside Prime Time*. New York: Pantheon.

———. 1989. "Post-Modernism: The Stenography of Surfaces," *New Perspectives Quarterly* (Spring). 56–59.

Glazer, Nathan, and Daniel P. Moynihan. 1970. *Beyond the Melting Pot: The Negroes, Puerto Ricans, Jews, Italians, and Irish of New York City*. Second edition. Cambridge, Mass.: MIT Press.

Golsorkhi, Khosrow. 1979?. "Farhang-e Puya va Farhang-e Mumia'i Shodeh," in *Yadnameh*. United States: Sazman-e Cherikha-ye Khalq-e Iran. 2–16.

———. 1980?. *Siasat-e Honar, Siasat-e She'r*. Tehran: Entesharat-e Morvarid.

Good, Byron J., Mary-Jo DelVecchio Good, and Robert Moradi. 1985. "The Interpretation of Iranian Depressive Illness and Dysphoric Affect," in *Culture and Depression: Studies in the Anthropology and Cross-Cultural Psychiatry of Affect and Disorder*. Arthur Kleinman and Byron Good, eds. Berkeley: University of California Press. 369–428.

Goodman, Dena. 1989. "Enlightenment Salons: The Convergence of Female and Philosophic Ambitions," *Eighteenth-Century Studies* 22:3 (Spring). 329–50.

Goodwin-Gill, G. 1983. *The Refugee in International Law*. Oxford: Clarendon Press.

Gordon, Milton. 1964. *Assimilation in American Life: The Role of Race, Religion, and National Origins*. New York: Oxford University Press.

Graham, Robert. 1979. *Iran: The Illusion of Power*. New York: St. Martin's Press.

Gramsci, Antonio. 1988. *An Antonio Gramsci Reader: Selected Writings, 1916–1935*. David Forgas, ed. New York: Schocken Books.

Gualtieri, Antonio R. 1984. *Christianity and Native Traditions: Indigenization and Syncretism Among the Inuit and Dene of the Western Arctic*. Notre Dame, Ind.: Cross Cultural Publications.

Guha, Ranajait, and Gayatri Chakravorty Spivak. 1988. *Selected Subaltern Studies*. New York: Oxford University Press.

Haery, Mohmood M. 1982. *Ru-Howzi: the Iranian Traditional Improvisation Theater*. Ph.D. dissertation. New York University.

Hall, Stuart. 1977. "Culture, the Media and the 'Ideological Effect,' " in *Mass Communication and Society*. James Curran, Michael Gurevitch, and Janet Woollacott, eds. London: Open University Press.

_____. 1980a. "Encoding/decoding," in *Culture, Media, Language*. Stuart Hall, Dorothy Hobson, Andrew Lowe, and Paul Willis, eds. London: Hutchinson.

_____. 1980b. "Recent Developments in the Theories of Language and Ideology: A Critical Note," in *Culture, Media, Language*. Stuart Hall, Dorothy Hobson, Andrew Lowe, and Paul Willis, eds. London: Hutchinson.

_____. 1982. "The Rediscovery of 'Ideology': Return of the Repressed in Media Studies," in *Culture, Society and the Media*. Michael Gurevitch, Tony Bennett, James Curran, and Janet Woollacott, eds. London: Methuen.

_____. 1986a. "The Problem of Ideology—Marxism Without Guarantees," *Journal of Communication Inquiry* 10:2 (Summer). 28–44.

_____. 1986b. "Gramsci's Relevance for the Study of Race and Ethnicity," *Journal of Communication Inquiry* 10:2 (Summer). 5:27.

_____. 1986c. "Popular Culture and the State," in *Popular Culture and Social Relations*. Tony Bennett, Colin Mercer, and Janet Woollacott, eds. Milton Keynes, U.K.: Open University Press. 22–49.

_____. 1988. "New Ethnicities," *ICA Documents* No. 7 [London]. 27–31.

_____. 1989. "Cultural Identity and Cinematic Representation," *Framework* No. 36. 68–81.

Hall, Stuart, Dorothy Hobson, Andrew Lowe, and Paul Willis, eds. 1980. *Culture, Media, Language*. London: Hutchinson.

Hammond, Charles Montgomery, Jr., 1981. *The Image Decade: Television Documentary 1965–1975*. New York: Hastings House.

Hansen, Mirian. 1991. *Babel and Babylon: Spectatorship in American Silent Film*. Cambridge, Mass.: Harvard University Press.

Hassan, Ihab. 1981. "The Question of Postmodernism," *Performance Arts Journal* 16. 30–37.

Heath, Stephen. 1977/78. "Notes on Suture," *Screen* 18:4, 48–76.

_____. 1981. "Narrative Space," in *Questions of Cinema*. Bloomington: Indiana University Press. 19–75.

Heath, Stephen, and Gillian Skirrow. 1977. "Television: A World in Action," *Screen* 18:2 (Summer), 7–59.

Hebdige, Dick. 1980. *Subculture: The Meaning of Style*. New York: Methuen.

Hedayat, Sadeq. 1957. *The Blind Owl*. D. P. Costello, trans. New York: Grove Press.

Heilbut, Anthony. 1983. *Exiled in Paradise: German Refugee Artists and Intellectuals in America, from the 1930s to the Present*. Boston: Beacon Press.

Helsey, D. Ray, and J. David Trebing. 1983. "A Comparison of the Rhetorical Visions and Strategies of the Shah's White Revolution and the Ayatollah's Islamic Revolution," *Communication Monographs*, vol. 50 (June). 158–74.

Hillman, Michael Craig. 1984. *Persian Carpets*. Austin: University of Texas Press.

Hoberman, J. 1991. *Bridge of Light: Yiddish Film Between Two World Wars*. New York: Museum of Modern Art.

Hobsbawm, E. J. 1991. *Nations and Nationalism Since 1780: Programme, Myth, Reality*. Cambridge: Cambridge University Press.

Hobsbawm, Eric, and Terence Ranger, eds. 1983. *The Invention of Tradition*. Cambridge: Cambridge University Press.

Hobson, Dorothy. 1982. *"Crossroads": the Drama of a Soap Opera*. London: Methuen.

Holley, David. 1986. "South Korean Ownership of TV Firm Admitted," *Los Angeles Times* (2/11). Part II, 1.

Holmlund, Christine Anne. 1991. "Displacing Limits of Difference: Gender, Race, and Colonialism in Edward Said and Homi Bhabha's Theoretical Models and Marguerite Duras's Experimental Film," *Quarterly Review of Film and Video* 13:1–2, 1–22.

Hondo, Abid Med. 1978. "The Cinema of Exile," in *Film & Politics in the Third World*. John D. H. Downing, ed. 1987. New York: Praeger. 69–76.

Horkheimer, Max, and Theodore Adorno. 1972. *Dialectic of Enlightenment*. John Cumming, trans. New York: Herder & Herder.

Houston, Beverle. 1984. "Viewing Television: The Metapsychology of Endless Consumption," *Quarterly Review of Film Studies* 9:3 (Summer), 183–95.

Huey, John. 1990. "America's Hottest Export: Pop Culture," *Fortune* (12/31). 50–60.

Huyssen, Andreas. 1986. *After the Great Divide: Modernism, Mass Culture, Postmodernism*. Bloomington: Indiana University Press.

*ICA Documents* no. 7, 1988, special issue, ed. Kobena Mercer, devoted to "Black Film, British Cinema."

Ilie, Paul. 1980. *Literature and Inner Exile: Authoritarian Spain, 1939–1975*. Baltimore: Johns Hopkins University Press.

Irigaray, Luce. 1985. *Speculum of the Other Woman*. Gillian C. Gill, trans. Ithaca: Cornell University Press.

Issari, Mohammad Ali. 1989. *Cinema in Iran 1900–1979*. Metuchen, N.Y.: Scarecrow Press.

Jackson, Robert L. 1992. "Rise in Immigrants, Drop in Car-Poolers," *Los Angeles Times* (5/30), A2.

Jaggi, Maya. 1988. "The Politics of Exile: Introduction," *Third World Affairs 1988*. 161–66.

Jameson, Fredric. 1981. *The Political Unconscious: Narrative as a Socially Symbolic Act*. Ithaca, N.Y.: Cornell University Press.

_____. 1983. "Postmodernism and Consumer Society," in *The Anti-Aesthetic: Essays on Postmodern Culture*. Hal Foster, ed. Port Townsend, Washington: Bay Press. 111–25.

_____. 1989. "Nostalgia for the Present," *The South Atlantic Quarterly* 88:2 (Spring). 517–37.

JanMohammed, Abdul R., 1983. *Manichean Aesthetics: The Politics of Literature in Colonial Africa*. Amherst: University of Massachusetts Press.

JanMohammed, Abdul R., and David Lloyd, eds. 1990. *The Nature and Context of Minority Discourse*. New York: Oxford University Press.

Johnson, Albert. 1990/91. "Moods Indigo: A Long View," *Film Quarterly* 44:2 (Winter), 13–27.

_____. 1991. "Moods Indigo: Part 2," *Film Quarterly* 44:3 (Spring), 15–29.

Jung, Carl G. 1958. *Psyche & Symbol: A Selection from the Writings of C. G. Jung*. New York: Anchor.

_____. 1965. *Memories, Dreams, Reflections*. Revised edition. Aniela Jaffe, ed., Richard and Clara Winston, trans. New York: Vantage Books.

Kaplan, E. Ann. 1983. *Women and Film: Both Sides of the Camera*. New York: Methuen. 23–35.

_____, ed. 1990. *Psychoanalysis and Cinema*. New York: Routledge.

Karimi-Hakkak, Ahmad. 1986. "The Literary Response to the Iranian Revolution," *World Literature Today* 60:2 (Spring). 251–56.

_____. 1991. "Up From Underground: The Meaning of Exile in Gholamhosayn Sa'edi's Last Short Stories," in *Iranian Refugees and Exiles Since Khomeini*. Asghar Fathi, ed. Costa Mesa, Calif.: Mazda Publishers. 257–79.

Katz, Elihu, and George Wedell. 1977. *Broadcasting and the Third World: Promise and Performance*. Cambridge, Mass.: Harvard University Press.

Katz, Jane. 1983. *Artists in Exile*. New York: Stein and Day.

Keller, Gary D. 1985. *Chicano Cinema: Research, Reviews, and Resources*. Binghamton, N.Y.: Bilingual Review/Press.

Kelly, Kevin. 1989. "Selling the World: Mouseketeers to Marketeers," *Whole Earth* no. 65 (Winter), 36–37.

Kelly, Ron. 1987. "The Death of Neusha Farrahi: An Immolation in Westwood," *L.A. Weekly* (October 23–29). 20–27.

Ketab Corp. 1989, 1991, 1992. *The Iranian Directory Yellow Pages*. Los Angeles: Ketab Corp.

Kho'i, Esma'il. 1987. "People in Between," in *Children from Refugee Communities: A Question of Identity: Uprooting, Integration or Dual Culture?* Oakwood, Derby (U.K.): Refugee Action (July). 5–13.

Khomaini, Ayatollah Ruhollah. 1981. *Islam and Revolution: Writings and Declarations of Imam Khomaini*. Hamid Algar, trans. Berkeley: Mizan Press.

_____. n.d. *Towzihol Masa'el* (ba Ezafat va Masa'el-e Jadid) [Clarification of problems]. No place of publication given.

_____. n.d. *Kashfol Asrar*. No place of publication given.

Kim, Ha-il. 1992. *Minority Media Access: Examination of Policies, Technologies, and Multi-Ethnic Television and a Proposal for an Alternative Approach to Media Access*. Ph.D. dissertation. UCLA Department of Film and Television.

Kipnis, Laura. 1986. "'Refunctioning' Reconsidered: Towards a Left Popular Culture," in *High Theory/Low Culture: Analyzing Popular Television and Film*. Colin MacCabe, ed. Manchester: Manchester University Press. 11–36.

Kirschenbaum, Grace. 1991. "The Persian Bookstore," *Publishers Weekly* (2/8), 28–30.

Kotkin, Joel. 1989. "Fear and Reality in the Los Angeles Melting Pot," *Los Angeles Times Magazine* (November 5). 6–19.

Kovacs, Katherine, S. 1991. "The Plain in Spain: Geography and National Identity in Spanish Cinema," *Quarterly Review of Film and Video* 13:4, 17–46.

Kroker, Arthur, and David Cook. 1986. *The Postmodern Scene: Excremental Culture and Hyper-Aesthetics*. New York: St. Martin's Press.

Kuhn, Thomas S. 1970. *The Structure of Scientific Revolutions*. Second edition. Chicago: University of Chicago Press.

Lacan, Jacques. 1977. *Ecrits: A Selection*. Alan Sheridan, trans. New York: Norton.

_____. 1981. *The Four Fundamental Concepts of Psycho-Analysis*. Jacques-Alain Miller, ed., Alan Sheridan, trans. New York: W. W. Norton.

Lamming, George. 1960. *The Pleasures of Exile*. London: Michael Joseph.

Lanternari, Vittorio. 1965. *The Religions of the Oppressed: A Study of Modern Messianic Cults*. Toronto: New American Library.

Laplanche, J., and J.-B. Pontalis. 1973. *The Language of Psycho-Analysis*. Donald Nicholson-Smith, trans. New York: Norton.

Leong, Russel. 1991. *Moving the Image: Independent Asian Pacific American Media Arts*. Los Angeles: UCLA Asian American Studies Center.

Lévi-Strauss, Claude. 1976. *Structural Anthropology Volume 2*. Monique Layton, trans. Chicago: University of Chicago Press.

Light, Ivan H. 1972. *Ethnic Business in America: Business and Welfare Among Chinese, Japanese, and Blacks*. Los Angeles: University of California Press.

_____. 1983. *Cities in World Perspective*. New York: Macmillan.

_____. 1988. "Los Angeles," in *The Metropolis Era: Mega-Cities*. Volume 2. Matteri Dogan and John Kasarda, eds. Beverly Hills: Sage Publications. 56–96.

Linton, Ralph. 1965. "Nativistic Movements," in *Reader in Comparative Religion: An Anthropological Approach*. Second edition. William A. Lessa and Evon Z. Vogt, eds. New York: Harper & Row. 499–506.

Lipsitz, George. 1990. *Time Passages: Collective Memory and American Popular Culture*. Minneapolis: University of Minnesota Press.

Lourdeaux, Lee, ed. 1990. *Italian and Irish Filmmakers in America: Ford, Capra, Coppola, and Scorsese*. Philadelphia: Temple University Press.

Lyotard, Jean-François. 1984. *The Postmodern Condition: A Report on Knowledge*. Geoff Bennington and Brian Massumi, trans. Minneapolis: University of Minnesota Press.

MacCabe, Colin. 1976. "Theory and Film: Principles of Realism and Pleasure," *Screen* 17:3 (Autumn), 7–27.

_____. 1986. *High Theory/Low Culture: Analyzing Popular Television and Film*. Manchester: Manchester University Press.

Mahmudi, Kambiz. 1992. "Chera az Hozur-e Rasanehha-ye Hamegani-ye Vabasteh beh Rezhim-e Tehran Vahshat Darid?" *Payam-e Ashena* (Farvardin 1371/March 1992), 9–10.

Mandel, Michael J., and Christopher Farrell. 1992. "The Immigrants: How They're Helping to Revitalize the U.S. Economy," *Business Weekly* (July 13), 114–22.

Marcus, George E. 1990. "The Modernist Sensibility in Recent Ethnographic Writing and the Cinematic Metaphor of Montage," *Society for Visual Anthropology Review* (Spring) 2–12, 21, 44.

Marcuse, Herbert. 1968. *Negations: Essays in Critical Theory*. Jeremy J. Shapiro, trans. Boston: Beacon Press.

Martinez, Ruben. 1991. "Nation of L.A.: A City at War With Itself," *L.A. Weekly* (January 3–January 9). 10–12.

Marx, Karl. 1967. *Capital: A Critique of Political Economy*. Volume 1. Samuel Moore and Edward Aveling, trans. New York: International Publishers.

Masson, J. M. 1980. *The Oceanic Feeling: The Origins of Religious Sentiment in Ancient India*. Dorrecht, Netherlands: D. Reidel.

Matin Asghari, Afshin. 1991. "The Iranian Student Movement Abroad: The Confederation of Iranian Students, National Union," in *Iranian Refugees and Exiles Since Khomeini*. Asghar Fathi, ed. Costa Mesa, Calif.: Mazda Publisher. 55–74.

Mattelart, Armand. 1979. *Multinational Corporations and the Control of Culture: The Ideological Apparatus of Imperialism*. Atlantic Highlands, N.J.: Humanities Press.

Matusow, Barbara. 1983. *The Evening Stars: The Making of the Evening News Anchor*. New York: Ballantine.

Mayne, Judith. 1990. *The Woman at the Keyhole: Feminism and Woman's Cinema*. Bloomington: Indiana University Press.

Mellencamp, Patricia, ed. 1990. *Logics of Television: Essays in Cultural Criticism*. Bloomington: University of Indiana Press.

Meskoob, Shahrokh. 1368/1989. *Melliat va Zaban*. Paris: Khavaran.

_____. 1991. "Goftogu dar Bagh," *Iran Nameh* 9:4, 533–40.

Metz, Christian. 1982. *The Imaginary Signifier: Psychoanalysis and the Cinema*. Celia Britton, Annwyl Williams, Ben Brewster, and Alfred Guzzetti, trans. Bloomington: Indiana University Press.

_____. 1976. "Story/Discourse: Notes on Two Kinds of Voyeurism," in *Movies and Methods II*. Bill Nichols, ed. Berkeley: University of California Press, 1985. 543–48.

_____. 1985. "Photography and Fetish," *October* 34 (Fall), 80–90.

Milani, Farzaneh. 1368/1989. "Zadgah," *Par* 43 [Washington, D.C.].

_____. 1992. *Veils and Words: The Emerging Voices of Iranian Women Writers*. Syracuse, N.Y.: Syracuse Union Press.

Miller, Jacques-Alain. 1977/78. "Suture," *Screen* 18:4.

Mindel, Charles H., and Robert W. Habenstein, eds. 1976. "Family Life Style of America's Ethnic Minorities: An Introduction," in *Ethnic Families in America: Patterns and Variations*. New York: Elsevier. 1–12.

Minh-ha, Trinh T. *Woman, Native, Other: Writing Postcoloniality and Feminism*. Bloomington: Indiana University Press.

Mirzadeh, Ne'mat. 1988. "Mas'aleh-ye Melli dar Iran Hal Shodeh Ast," *Par* 2:12 (January). 57–64.

Mitchell, John L. 1989. "A New Persian Empire," *Los Angles Times* (12/31). J1,2,4.

Mitchell, W. J. T. 1986. *Iconology: Image, Text, Ideology*. Chicago: University of Chicago Press.

Mofid, Ardavan. 1987. "Dar A'ineh-ye Ghorbat," *Iran News* (October 20). 15, 19, 56.

Mohaddesi, Javad. 1368/1989. *Honar-e Maktabi*. Tehran: Modiriat-e Farhangi-Honari-ye Mo'avant-e Farhangi.

Mojahedin-e Khalq-e Iran. 1364/1985. *Shohada-ye Javidan-e Azadi, Parchamdaran-e Enqelab-e Novin-e Khalq-e Qahreman-e Iran*. Supplement to Mojahed no. 261.

Moradi, Gilbert, Larry Peters, Marylie Karlovac, and David Meltzer. 1989. "A Cross-Cultural Study of Narcissism Among Iranians in Iran, Iranians in the U.S., and Americans." Unpublished manuscript.

Morgan, Anne. 1989. "Interview: Shirazeh Hushiari," *Art Papers* 13:6. 14–17.

Morley, David. 1980a. *The "Nationwide" Audience: Structure and Encoding*. London: BFI.

_____. 1980b. "Texts, Readers, Subjects," in *Culture, Media, Language*. Stuart Hall, Dorothy Hobson, Andrew Lowe, and Paul Willis, eds. London: Hutchinson.

_____. 1986. *Family Television: Cultural Power and Domestic Leisure*. London: Comedia.

Moslehi, Shahnaz. 1984. *Iranian-e Borunmarzi va Nemuneh-ye Los Anjelesi-ye an*. Encino, Calif.: Ketab Corp.

Mottahedeh, Roy. 1985. *The Mantle of the Prophet: Religion and Politics in Iran*. New York: Pantheon.

Mowlana, Hamid. 1979. "Technology Versus Tradition: Communication in the Iranian Revolution," *Journal of Communication* 29:3 (Summer). 107–12.

Moynihan, Elizabeth B. 1979. *Paradise as a Garden in Persia and Mughal India*. New York: George Braziller.

Mulvey, Laura. 1975. "Visual Pleasure and Narrative Cinema," in *Visual and Other Pleasure*. Bloomington: Indiana University Press. 1989. 14–26.

Myerhoff, Barbara. 1978. *Number Our Days*. New York: Touchstone Books.

_____. 1982. "Rites of Passage: Process and Paradox," in *Celebration: Studies in Festivity and Ritual*. Victor Turner, ed. Washington, D.C.: Smithsonian Institution Press. 109–35.

Nabokov, Vladimir. 1966. *Speak, Memory: An Autobiography Revisited*. New York: G. P. Putnam's Sons.

_____. 1990. *Ada, or Ardor: A Family Chronicle*. New York: Vintage.

Naderpour, Nader. 1365/1986. "Gorbat-e She'r va She'r-e Ghorbat," *Rahavard* [Los Angeles] 3:11–12 (Summer and Fall). 22–24.

Naficy, Hamid. 1979. "Iranian Feature Film: a Brief Critical History," *Quarterly Review of Film Studies* (Fall). 443–64.

_____. 1981. "Cinema as a Political Instrument," in *Modern Iran: The Dialectics of Continuity and Change*. Michael Bonine and Nikki Keddie, eds. Albany, N.Y.: SUNY Press. 341–59.

_____. 1984. *Iran Media Index*. Westport, Conn.: Greenwood Press.

_____. 1985. "Iranian Writers, the Iranian Cinema, and the Case of *Dash Akol*," *Iranian Studies* 18:2–4 (Spring-Autumn). 231–51.

_____. 1987. "The Development of an Islamic Cinema in Iran," *Third World Affairs 1987*. London: Third World Foundation. 447–63.

_____. 1989a. "Mediawork's Representation of the Other: The Case of Iran," in *Questions of Third Cinema*. Jim Pines and Paul Willemen, eds. London: BFI. 227–39.

_____. 1989b. "Television Intertextuality and the Discourse of the Nuclear Family," *Journal of Film and Video* 41:4 (Winter). 42–59.

_____. 1989c. "Autobiography, Film Spectatorship, and Cultural Negotiation," *Emergences* no. 1 (Fall). 29–54.

_____. 1990a. "Cinema Under the Islamic Republic," *Jusur* 6, 77–94.

_____. 1990b. *Exile Discourse and Television: A Study of Syncretic Cultures: Iranian Television in Los Angeles*. Ph.D. dissertation in theater arts, UCLA.

_____. 1990c. "The Aesthetics and Politics of Iranian Cinema in Exile," *Cinemaya* (Fall), 4–8.

_____. 1991a. "Women and the Semiotics of Veiling and Vision in Cinema," *American Journal of Semiotics* 8:1–2, 47–64.

_____. 1991b. "Televisual Fetishization in Exile," *Quarterly Review of Film and Video* 13:1–3, 85–116.

_____. 1991c. "From Liminality to Incorporation," in *Iranian Refugees and Exiles Since Khomeini*. Asghar Fathi, ed. Costa Mesa: Calif.: Mazda Publishers. 228–53.

_____. 1991d. "Cinema iii: Documentary Film," in *Encyclopedia Iranica*. vol. 5, fascicle 6. Ehsan Yarshater, ed. Costa Mesa, Calif.: Mazda Publishers, 579–585.

_____. 1992a. "Guneh-ye Film-e Jaheli dar Sinema-ye Iran: Barresi-ye Sakhtari-ye Film-e *Dash Akol*," *Iran Nameh* 10:3 (Summer).

_____. 1992b. "Islamizing Film Culture in Iran," in *Iran: Political Culture in the Islamic Republic*. Samih Farsoun and Mehrdad Mashayekhi, eds. London: Routledge.

_____. 1993a. "Diaspora Television: Middle Eastern Television in Los Angeles," *Afterimage* 20:7, 9–11.

_____. 1993b. "Popular Culture of Iranian Exiles in Los Angeles," in *Irangeles: Iranians in Los Angeles*. Ron Kelley and Jonathan Friedlander, eds. Berkeley: University of California Press.

Naficy, Hamid, and Teshome H. Gabriel, eds. 1993. *Otherness and the Media: The Ethnography of the Imagined and the Imaged*. New York: Harwood Academic Publishers.

Nairn, Tom. 1981. *The Break-up of Britain*. London: Verso.

Najmabadi, Afsaneh. 1987. "Iran's Turn to Islam: From Modernism to a Moral Order," *The Middle East Journal* 41:2 (Spring), 202–17.

Nandy, Ashis. 1983. *The Intimate Enemy: Loss and Recovery of Self Under Colonialism*. Delhi: Oxford University Press.

Naraqi, Ehasan. 1356/1977. *Ghorbat-e Gharb*. Tehran: Amir Kabir.

Neale, Stephen. 1983. *Genre*. London: BFI.

Nelson, Cary, and Lawrence Grossberg. 1988. *Marxism and the Interpretation of Culture.* Urbana: University of Illinois Press.

Newcomb, Horace M. 1988. "One Night of Prime Time: An Analysis of Television's Multiple Voices," in *Media, Myths, and Narratives: Television and the Press.* James W. Carey, ed. Beverly Hills: Sage. 88–112.

Newcomb, Horace M., and Paul M. Hirsch. 1983. "Television as a Cultural Forum: Implications for Research," *Quarterly Review of Film Studies* 8:3 (Summer), 45–55.

Nichols, Bill. 1981. *Ideology and the Image: Social Representation in the Cinema and Other Media.* Bloomington: Indiana University Press.

_____. 1991. *Representing Reality: Issues and Concepts in Documentary.* Bloomington: Indiana University Press.

Noriega, Chon A., ed. 1992. *Chicanos and Film: Essays on Chicano Representation and Resistance.* New York: Garland.

O'Sullivan, Tim, John Hartley, Danny Saunders, and John Fiske, eds. 1983. *Key Concepts in Communication.* New York: Methuen.

Oudart, Jean-Pierre. 1977–78. "Cinema and Suture," *Screen* 18:4, 35–47.

Park, Robert E. 1928. "Human Migration and the Marginal Man," *American Journal of Sociology* 33, 881–93.

_____. 1950. *Race and Culture: Essays in the Sociology and Culture.* London: Collier-Macmillan.

Park, Robert E., and Ernest W. Burgess. 1921. *Introduction to the Science of Sociology.* Chicago: University of Chicago Press.

Pearlstone, Zena. 1990. *Ethnic L.A.* Beverly Hills: Hillcrest.

Perry, Charles. 1992. "Nouruz: Have a Happy Equinox," *Los Angeles Times* (3/19). H15.

Petro, Patrice. 1989. *Joyless Streets: Women and Melodramatic Representation in Weimar Germany.* Princeton: Princeton University Press.

Pettys, Rebecca Ansary. 1982. *The Ta'ziyeh: Ritual of Renewal in Persia.* Ph.D. dissertation in theater and drama, Indiana University.

Pines, Jim, and Paul Willemen, eds. 1989. *Questions of Third Cinema.* London. BFI.

Portes, Alejandro. 1984. "The Rise of Ethnicity: Determinants of Ethnic Perceptions Among Cuban Exiles in Miami," *American Sociological Review* 49 (June). 383–97.

Portes, Alejandro, and Robert L. Bach. 1985. *Latin Journey: Cuban and Mexican-American Immigrants in the United States.* Berkeley and Los Angeles: University of California Press.

Price, Richard, ed. 1979. *Maroon Societies: Rebel Slaves Communities in the Americas.* Baltimore: Johns Hopkins University Press.

Puig, Claudia. 1992. "Univision President Bolts to Rival Telemundo," *Los Angeles Times* (5/27). D1,2.

*Quarterly Review of Film and Video.* 1991. Special triple issue: "Discourse of the Other: Postcoloniality, Positionality, Subjectivity," 13:1–3, Hamid Naficy and Teshome H. Gabriel, eds.

*Quarterly Review of Film and Video.* 1992. Special double issue: "New Directions in Television Studies," 14:1–2, Nick Browne, ed.

Rachlin, Nahid. 1978. *Foreigner.* New York: W.W. Norton.

Radhakrishnan, R. 1987. "Ethnic Identity and Post-Structuralist Differance," *Cultural Critique* 6. 199–220.

Rank, Otto. 1971. *The Double.* Harry Tucker, Jr., trans. and ed. Chapel Hill: University of North Carolina Press.

Rapp, Carl. 1987. "Coming Out Into the Corridor: Postmodernist Fantasies of Pluralism," *The Georgia Review* (Fall). 533–52.

Ray, Robert. 1985. *A Certain Tendency of the Hollywood Cinema, 1939–1980*. Princeton: Princeton University Press.

Redfield, Robert, Ralph Linton, and Melville Herskovits. 1936. "Outline for the Study of Acculturation," *American Anthropologist*. New Series 38. 149–52.

Riesman, David. 1951. "Some Observations Concerning Marginality," *Phylon* 12.

Ringgren, Helmer. 1969. "The Problems of Syncretism," in *Syncretism*. Sven S. Hartman, ed. Stockholm: Almqvist & Wiksell. 7–14.

Rose, Brian G. 1985. *TV Genres: A Handbook and Reference Guide*. Westport, Conn.: Greenwood Press.

Rosen, Phil. 1986. *Narrative, Apparatus, Ideology: A Film Theory Reader*. New York: Columbia University Press.

Rothman, William. 1976. "Against 'The System of Suture,' " in *Movies and Methods I*. Bill Nichols, ed. Berkeley: University of California Press. 451–68.

Roy, Asim. 1983. *The Islamic Syncretistic Tradition in Bengal*. Princeton: Princeton University Press.

Rushdie, Salman. 1985. "Introduction," in *On Writing and Politics: 1967–1983*. Gunther Grass. Ralph Manheim, trans. San Diego: Helen & Curt Wolff Books. ix-xv.

————. 1988. *The Satanic Verses*. New York: Viking.

————. 1990. "A Pen Against the Sword in Good Faith," *Newsweek* (2/12). 52–57.

————. 1991. " 'Free Speech is the Whole Ballgame,' " *Los Angeles Times* (December 13). B7.

Ruttenbeck, Jeffrey. 1991. "Toward a History of Ideology of Partisanship and Independence in American Journalism," *Journal of Communication Inquiry* 15:2 (Summer):126–37.

Sabagh, Georges, and Mehdi Bozorgmehr. 1987. "Are the Characteristics of Exiles Different from Immigrants? The Case of Iranians in Los Angeles," *Sociology and Social Research* 71:2 (January 2). 77–84.

————. 1991. "Secular Immigrants: Religiosity and Ethnicity Among Iranian Muslims in Los Angeles," manuscript. 1–36.

Sabagh, Georges, and Claudia Der-Martirosian. 1989. "Diversity Among Iranian Immigrants in Los Angeles," unpublished manuscript.

Sabagh, Georges, Ivan Light, and Mehdi Bozorgmehr. 1985. *Emergent Ethnicity: Iranian Immigrant Communities*. Proposal and Addendum to Proposal for National Science Foundation. Los Angeles: Department of Sociology, UCLA.

Sa'edi, Gholamhosain. 1983. "Degardishi va Raha'i-ye Avareh-ha," *Alefba* [Paris] 2. 1–5.

————. 1986. "Sharh-e Ahval," in *Alefba* [Paris] 7 (Fall). 3–6.

Safa, Kaveh. 1990. "Othello in the Islamic Republic," *Emergences* 2 (Spring). 131–63.

Safran, William. 1991. "Diasporas in Modern Societies: Myths of Homeland and Return," *Diaspora* (Spring) 1:1, 83–99.

Said, Edward. 1979. *Orientalism*. New York: Vintage.

————. 1983a. *The World, the Text, and the Critic*. Cambridge, Mass.: Harvard University Press.

————. 1983b. "Opponents, Audiences, Constituencies and Community," *Anti-Aesthetic: Essays on Postmodern Culture*. Hal Foster, ed. Port Townsend, Washington: Bay Press. 135–59.

————. 1984. "The Mind in Winter: Reflections on Life in Exile," *Harpers'* (September). 49–55.

————. 1986. *After the Last Sky: Palestinian Lives*. With photographs by Jean Mohr. New York: Pantheon.

Schatz, Thomas. 1981. *Hollywood Genres: Formulas, Filmmaking, and the Studio System*. Austin, Tex.: The University of Texas Press.

Schmidt, Hans-Peter. 1980. "The Senmurw: Of Birds and Dogs and Bats," *Persica* 9. 1–85.

Schoenberger, Karl. 1992. "Moving Between 2 Worlds," *Los Angeles Times* (7/12). A1.

Schramm, Wilbur. 1977. *Big Media, Little Media: Tools and Technologies for Instruction*. Beverly Hills: Sage.

*Screen*. 1983. Special issue, "Racism, Colonialism and the Cinema," 24:2, Robert Stam and Louise Spence, eds.

*Screen*. 1985. Special issue, "Other Cinemas, Other Criticism," 26:3–4.

*Screen*. 1988. Special issue, "The Last 'Special Issue' on Race?" 29:4, Isaac Julien and Kobena Mercers, eds.

Seither, Ellen, Hans Borchers, Gabriele Kreutzner, and Eva-Maria Warth, eds. 1989. *Remote Control: Television, Audiences and Cultural Power*. London: Routledge.

Shafa, Sa'id. 1989. "Sinemagaran-e Borunmarzi-ye Iran," *Simorgh* 6. 82–88.

Shahriari, Khosrow. 1365/1986. *Ketab-e Namayesh: Farhang-e Vazhehha, Estelahha va Sabkha-ye Namayeshi*. Volume 1. Tehran: Amir Kabir.

Shamlu, Ahmad. 1988. "Yadha va Yadegarha," *Par* 3:1 (February). 51.

Shari'ati, Ali. 1357/1978. *Bazgasht*. U.S./Europe: Daftar-e Tadvin va Enteshar.

Shayegan, Daryush. 1356/1977. *Asia dar Barabar-e Gharb*. Tehran: Amir Kabir.

Shohat, Ella. 1991. "Ethnicities-in-Relations: Toward a Multicultural Reading of American Cinema," in *Unspeakable Images: Ethnicity and the American Cinema*. Lester D. Friedman, ed. Urbana: University of Illinois Press.

Shorts, John Rennie. 1991. *Imagined Country: Society, Culture and Environment*. New York: Routledge.

Silverman, Kaja. 1983. *The Subject of Semiotics*. New York: Oxford University Press.

_____. 1986. "Suture" (excerpts) in *Narrative, Apparatus, Ideology: A Film Theory Reader*. Philip Rosen, ed. New York: Columbia University Press.

_____. 1988. *The Acoustic Mirror: The Female Voice in Psychoanalysis and Cinema*. Bloomington: Indiana University Press.

Simmel, Georg. 1950. *The Sociology of Georg Simmel*. K. Wolff, trans. Glencoe, Ill.: The Free Press.

_____. 1955. *Conflict and the Web of Group-Affiliations*. Kurt H. Wolff and Reinhard Bendix. New York: Free Press.

Singer, Ben. 1988. "Film, Photography, and Fetish: an Analysis of Christian Metz," *Cinema Journal* 27:4 (Summer). 4–22.

Siu, Paul C. P. 1952. "The Sojourner," *American Journal of Sociology* 56.

Sklar, Robert. 1975. *Movie-Made America: A Cultural History of American Movies*. New York: Vintage.

Smith, Mark Chalon. 1989. "Little Saigon's Video Kicks," *Los Angeles Times Sunday Calendar* (2/5). 5.

Smolowe, Jill. 1989. "Closing the Doors," *Time* (July 3). 24–26.

Sobchack, Vivian. 1984. "Inscribing Ethical Space: Ten Propositions on Death, Representation, and Documentary," *Quarterly Review of Film Studies* 9:4, 283–300.

_____. 1992. *The Address of the Eye: A Phenomenology of Film Experience*. Princeton: Princeton University Press.

Sollors, Werner. 1986. *Beyond Ethnicity: Consent and Descent in American Culture*. New York: Oxford University Press.

Soltanpur, Sa'id. 1349/1970. *No'i az Honar, No'i az Andisheh*. No publisher or place of publication noted.

Soruco, Gonzalo R. 1985. *Marketing Television Programs in the United States: The Case of the Hispanic Audience*. Ph.D. dissertation in mass communications, Indiana University, Bloomington.

Spicer, Edward H. 1968. "Acculturation," in *International Encyclopedia of the Social Sciences*. David L. Sills, ed. Volume 1. New York: Macmillan, Free Press. 21–26.

Spigel, Lynn. 1992. *Make Room for TV: Television and the Family Ideal in Postwar America*. Chicago: University of Chicago Press.

Spigel, Lynn, and Denise Mann, eds. 1992. *Private Screenings: Television and the Female Consumer*. Minneapolis: University of Minnesota Press.

Spivak, Gayatri Chakravorty. 1987. *In Other Worlds: Essays in Cultural Politics*. New York and London: Routledge.

Sreberny-Mohammadi, Annabelle. 1985. *The Power of Tradition: Communication and the Iranian Revolution*. Ph.D. dissertation, Columbia University.

Sreberny-Mohammadi, Annabelle, and Ali Mohammadi. 1991a. "Hegemony and Resistance: Media Politics in the Islamic Republic of Iran," *Quarterly Review of Film and Video* 12:4, 33–60.

———. 1991b. "Iranian Exiles as Opposition: Some Theses on the Dilemmas of Political Communication Inside and Outside Iran," in *Iranian Refugees and Exiles Since Khomeini*. Asghar Fathi, ed. Costa Mesa, Calif.: Mazda Publishers. 205–27.

Stam, Robert. 1989. *Subversive Pleasures: Bakhtin, Cultural Criticism, and Film*. Baltimore: Johns Hopkins University Press.

Steiner, George. 1971. *In Bluebeard's Castle: Some Notes Towards the Redefinition of Culture*. New Haven: Yale University Press.

Stevenson, Thomas. "Migration as Rite of Passage in a Highland Yemeni Town," in *Sojourners and Settlers: The Yemeni Immigrant Experience*. Jonathan Friedlander, ed. Salt Lake City: University of Utah Press. 33–47.

Stewart, Kathleen. 1988. "Nostalgia—A Polemic," *Cultural Anthropology* 3:3 (August). 227–41.

Stewart, Susan. 1984. *On Longing: Narratives of the Miniature, the Gigantic, the Souvenir, the Collection*. Baltimore: Johns Hopkins University Press.

Stonequist, E. V. 1937. *The Marginal Man*. New York: Scribners.

Studlar, Gaylyn. 1988. *In the Realm of Pleasure: Von Sternberg, Dietrich, and the Masochistic Aesthetics*. Urbana: University of Illinois Press.

Suhrawardi, Shihabuddin Yahya. 1982. "A Tale of Occidental Exile," in *The Mystical and Visionary Treatises of Shihabuddin Yahya Suhrawardi*. W. M. Thackston, Jr., trans. London: Octagon Press. 100–108.

Swallow, Norman. 1966. *Factual Television*. New York: Hastings House.

Swindler, Ann, Melissa Rapp, and Yasemin Soysal. 1986. "Format and Formula in Prime-Time TV," in *Media, Audience and Social Structure*. Sandra J. Ball-Rokeach and Muriel G. Cantor, eds. Beverly Hills: Sage. 324–37.

Tehranian, Majid. 1979. "Iran: Communication, Alienation, Revolution," *Intermedia* (March). 6–12.

———. 1982. "Communications Dependency and Dualism in Iran," *Intermedia* 10:3 (May), 40–45.

Thaiss, Gustav Edward. 1973. *Religious Symbolism and Social Change: The Drama of Hosain*. Unpublished Ph.D. dissertation in anthropology, Washington University.

Turner, Graeme. 1990. *British Cultural Studies: An Introduction*. Boston: Unwin Hyman.

Turner, Victor. 1967. *The Forest of Symbols: Aspects of Ndembu Ritual*. Ithaca: Cornell University Press.

———. 1969. *The Ritual Process: Structure and Anti-Structure*. Chicago: Aldine.

———. 1974. *Dramas, Fields, and Metaphors: Symbolic Action in Human Society*. Ithaca: Cornell University Press.

Valle, Victor. 1988. "Latino TV Re-Creates U.S. Images," *Los Angeles Times* (8/18). F1.

_____. 1989. "Chinese Videos Reinforce Culture," *Los Angeles Times* (6/2). Part VI, 23.

Van Gennep, Arnold. 1960. *The Rites of Passage*. London: Routledge & Kegan Paul [First published in 1908].

Vanderknyff, Rick. 1989. "India: Action, Song and Dance," *Los Angeles Times Sunday Calendar* (2/5). 5.

Wallace, Anthony, F. C. 1956. "Revitalization Movements," *American Anthropologist* 58. 264–81.

_____. 1965. *Culture and Personality*. New York: Random House.

_____. 1968. "Nativism and Revivalism," in *International Encyclopedia of the Social Sciences*. David L. Sills, ed. Volume 11. New York: Macmillan, Free Press. 75–80.

Waller, Gregory A. 1992. "Another Audience: Black Moviegoing, 1907–16," *Cinema Journal* 31:2 (Winter). 3–25.

Wallerstein, Immanuel. 1974. *The Modern World System*. New York: Academic Press.

Waltz, Susan E. 1990. "Another View of Feminine Networks: Tunisian Women and the Development of Political Efficacy," *International Journal of Middle East Studies* 22:1. 21–36.

Watanabe, Teresa. 1990. "Pulling the Plug on Pirate Videos," *Los Angeles Times* (1/8). D3.

White, Hayden. 1973. *Metahistory: The Historical Imagination in Nineteenth-Century Europe*. Baltimore: Johns Hopkins University Press.

White, Mimi. 1986. "Crossing Wavelengths: The Diegetic and Referential Imaginary of American Commercial Television," *Cinema Journal* 25:2, 51–64.

Whitehead, Margaret. 1981. *The Caribou Mission: A History of the Oblates*. Victoria, B.C.: Sono Nis Press.

*Wide Angle* 13:3–4 (July-October 1991), special issue on "Black Cinema," ed. Manthia Diawara.

Willemen, Paul. 1978. "Subjectivity Under Siege," *Screen* 19:1 (Spring).

Williams, Linda. 1989. "Fetishism and the Visual Pleasure of Hard Core: Marx, Freud, and the 'Money Shot,' " *Quarterly Review of Film and Video* 11:2. 23–42.

Williams, Raymond. 1975. *Television: Technology and Cultural Form*. New York: Schocken.

_____. 1977. *Marxism and Literature*. London: Oxford University Press.

Winick, Charles. 1956. *Dictionary of Anthropology*. New York: Philosophical Library.

Zavarzadeh, Mas'ud. 1991. *Seeing Films Politically*. New York: SUNY Press.

Zinder, Jac. 1991. "Other Musics: An Access Guide to the International Sounds of Los Angeles," *Los Angeles Reader* (6/14), 7–9.

_____. 1992. "The Eternal 6/8 Groove," *L.A. Weekly* (1/17). 45–49.

Zolberg, Aristide R., Astri Suhrke, and Sergio Aguayo. 1986. "International Factors in the Formation of Refugee Movements," *International Migration Review* 20:2 (Summer). 151–69.

Zonis, Marvin. 1971. *The Political Elite of Iran*. Princeton: Princeton University Press.

# Index

Hamid Naficy is the author of various publications on film and television and was also the managing editor of *Quarterly Review of Film and Video* from 1985 to 1988. He received both his MFA in theater arts and his doctorate in film and TV criticism from UCLA. His most recent book, co-edited with Teshome H. Gabriel, is *Otherness and the Media: The Ethnography of the Imagined and the Imaged*. He teaches media studies at Rice University in Houston and is working on a book on transnational independent cinema.